UNDERSTANDING AND PREVENTING VIOLENCE

The Psychology of Human Destructiveness

PACIFIC INSTITUTE SERIES ON FORENSIC PSYCHOLOGY
Edited by Harold Hall

With the support of Pacific Institute for the Study of Conflict and Aggression, Kamuela, Hawaii

Titles in this Series

Endangered Children: Neonaticide, Infanticide, and Filicide
Lita Linzer Schwartz and Natalie K. Isser

Detecting Malingering and Deception: Forensic Distortion Analysis (FEA), Second Edition
Harold Hall and Joseph Poirer

UNDERSTANDING AND PREVENTING VIOLENCE

The Psychology of Human Destructiveness

Leighton C. Whitaker

CRC Press
Boca Raton   London   New York   Washington, D.C.

Library of Congress Cataloging-in-Publication Data

Whitaker, Leighton C.
    Understanding and preventing violence : the psychology of human destructiveness /
Leighton C. Whitaker.
       p. cm. -- (Pacific Institute series on forensic psychology)
    Includes bibliographical references and index.
    ISBN 0-8493-2265-0 (alk. paper)
    1. Violence--Prevention.   2. Crime prevention.   3. Social psychology.   4. Psychology,
Forensic. I. Title II. Series.

HM886.W48 2000
303.6--dc21   00-037895

Preface

To choose to be constructive rather than destructive, we need to know the difference. Typically, however, only large or even extreme differences grab our attention in such a way that we are impelled to action. During the course of my writing this book in the 1990s, certain relatively subtle destructive influences damaging to human life, that were long in the simmering stages, finally began to grab attention in the U.S., particularly the surge in youth violence during the early and middle 1990s.

Overall, rates of lethal criminality in the U.S. lessened in the late 1990s, though not enough to remove the country from the list of the world's violent crime leaders. Meanwhile, certain more massively destructive events, such as the bombing of the World Trade Center in New York City and the Federal Center in Oklahoma City, were extraordinary; they were so different from "ordinary" violent crimes as to stir concern of a different kind and level. Those planned "sneak attacks" were utter surprises, the deadly results of conspiratorial planning by covertly organized groups. School violence in the late 1990s, including Colorado's Columbine High School lethal gun and bomb attack that resulted in 15 deaths, combined some of the ingredients of recent kinds of killing with other ingredients that brought terrorism even closer to home. The attacks featured both guns and bombs, youth violence, conspiratorial planning and execution, and a seemingly naive and unsuspecting citizenry ranging through parents, police, school officials, and students — all of them connected by partial, insufficient awareness of the student perpetrators' destructive mentality.

The Columbine tragedy resulted in a mix of reactions and responses. Many suspects were named: the personalities and the alienation of the perpetrating students, the easy availability of guns and bomb-making instructions, violence in the media and in entertainment of almost every sort, parental neglect, police underestimation of threatening behavior, inadequate school security systems, students who looked down on other less-popular students, and so on. As can be understood — but only when the true complexity of violence causation is understood — none of these suspected factors is singularly causative nor are any irrelevant. Not knowing how to understand, together with the wish to deny and not understand such tragic events, results in helpless, despairing conclusions such as, "We will never understand."

Hopefully, and for a change, certain somewhat more thought-out initiatives to prevent further violence have begun to be considered. For example, "the marketing of mayhem in movies, music, and video games," which became blatantly obvious in the 1990s, was finally getting more concentrated federal attention (Broder, 1999) and restrictions on gun availability became seriously considered. But attention peaks in the reactive period immediately after a sensationally destructive event and then fades.

We seem always to need more mayhem to provoke admission of the obvious. Following a further series of "madman shootings," a September 1999 editorial in the *New York Times* admitted that the "pathology" involved was not merely in the immediate perpetrators: "But there is only one overriding pathology, and it is guns" (Grasping the Obvious Pathology, 1999, page A22). Earlier that month, television's NBC News aired the Centers for Disease Control report that the U.S. has 250 million guns and nine times the rate of gun deaths than the average of the other industrialized nations. The data are available, but denial and deliberate obfuscation of the obvious retards understanding.

No initiatives will really succeed unless they are informed by sober realizations of the longer-term synergistic patterns of violence causation. These patterns must be understood by as many people as possible so that wise initiatives and constructive responses will have powerful grass roots support. We cannot merely depend on government leaders who, inevitably, must follow public opinion at least as much as they lead it.

Adequate understanding of how to counter the age-old problem of violence requires deeper and broader knowledge than we gather from current events at home in the U.S. We are rapidly becoming a world society affected by myriad cultures with deep historical roots. If we remain nearsighted and culture-bound, we will continue to be more reactive rather than knowledgeably initiating constructive changes.

Assuming that we want a long run for humanity on this Earth — a questionable assumption discussed early in this book — we need to discover the complex causation of both destructive and constructive behavior. In the process, we will have to unmask the denial and evasion of discovery that serve to perpetuate and escalate violence.

Why must we come to understand the subtleties of human mentality and relationships? After all, it's not rocket science. No, it's not. The art and science of constructive human relationships is far more difficult than rocket science! Even a glance at the 20th century shows that rockets with ever greater power, range, and precision are being developed at an accelerating rate while human destructiveness is also developing at an accelerating rate. We must dedicate ourselves to the demonstrably more difficult challenge. Humans have clearly demonstrated that rocket science is easy indeed compared to human relationships.

This book is meant to convey a deep and lasting explanation of destructive behavior and mentality to make possible constructive action by as many people as possible. We need everyone to become powerful enough to be a definite constructive influence.

References

Broder, J., Clinton orders study on selling of violence, *New York Times*, June 2, 1999, p. A20.

Grasping the obvious pathology, *New York Times*, September 17, 1999, p. A22.

National Broadcasting Co., 6:30 p.m. EDT News Report, September 8, 1999.

The Author

Leighton C. Whitaker, Ph.D., ABPP is in private practice, and is Adjunct Clinical Professor at Widener University's Institute for Graduate Clinical Psychology in Pennsylvania, Editor of the *Journal of College Student Psychotherapy*, and Consulting Editor for Mental Health of the *Journal of American College Health*. His 80 professional publications address both clinical and social subjects and include the *Whitaker Index of Schizophrenic Thinking* (Western Psychological Services, 1980) and *Schizophrenic Disorders* (Plenum Press, New York, 1992). He is a Fellow of the Society for Personality Assessment and the American College Health Association and is a past Chair of the Association's Mental Health Section. His previous positions include Associate Professor and Director of Adult Psychology for the University of Colorado Health Sciences Center, Professor and Director of the University of Massachusetts Mental Health Services, and Director of Swarthmore College Psychological Services. He has done forensic work for many years and has been a consultant to the U.S. Department of Labor's Job Corps Program.

Acknowledgments

The author thanks The Haworth Press of New York for permission to excerpt passages from three articles he wrote for the *Journal of College Student Psychotherapy*, all listed in the references, as follows: Macho and Morbidity: The Emotional Need vs. Fear Dilemma in Men; Myths and Heroes: Visions of the Future; and Violence is Golden: Commercially Motivated Training in Impulsive Cognitive Style and Mindless Violence. I also thank the publisher, Brassey, Inc. of Dulles, VA for permission to adapt for this book eulogisms peculiar to the Nazi regime in author George Victor's *Hitler: The Pathology of Evil*.

I also wish to thank Harold V. Hall, Ph.D., ABPP, Director of the Pacific Institute for the Study of Conflict and Aggression, who made suggestions for my earlier writing on violence prevention as well as for this book, and Barbara McPherson, Ph.D. for her contribution of source materials on the Central Intelligence Agency. During the past 30 years, Arthur J. Deikman, M.D. and Bertram P. Karon, Ph.D. have shared valuable ideas relevant to this work and I thank them. Additionally, I thank Corinne N.C. Whitaker, Ph.D. for discussions and suggestions regarding population issues.

Finally, I am indebted to hundreds of other authors whose works relevant to this book I have read over the years. I have selected 27 of their most valuable books for this book's annotated bibliography so as to introduce the reader to some of their works as well.

The manuscript was prepared in cooperation with the support of the Pacific Institute for the Study of Conflict and Aggression, Kamuela, Hawaii.

Dedication

To William Bowen,
African American Forensic Psychologist
whose courage, compassion, and competence
epitomized the constructive mentality and have
transcended his time on this Earth

Contents

Dilemmas for the 21st Century

1

This book is a search for answers to fundamental dilemmas that have been worsening over the millennia. Civilization purportedly serves to make human life safer and to enhance life by inhibiting the "animal instincts" to violence, selfish aggrandizement, and unrestricted sexual expression; yet the more we have become "civilized," the greater the rate at which humans have destroyed one another, whether for the sake of domination, material gain, notoriety, or to reduce population. Along the way, we humans have also been destroying the planet's resources needed to make our continuance as a species possible. Have we been merely substituting more humanly instigated destructiveness for nature's methods of population control? In effect, we are — by engaging ever more effectively in destroying human lives and the future of our own species as well as other forms of life.

What are the alternatives, if any? Can we find them and show how they can be used to our long-term and, perhaps, even short-term advantage? The latter is vitally important because it is difficult to persuade people to embrace behavior that is beneficial for them only in the long run. The search must elucidate not only the causes of direct lethal violence but also "paralethal violence," meaning activities that are not lethal themselves but are harmful and promote lethal violence.

Constructive and Destructive Mentalities

What are the differences between constructive and destructive mentalities? The word mentality has two meanings: first, mental power or capacity and therefore learning ability and intelligence; second, a mode or way of thought, a disposition, mental set, or outlook. As used in this book, mentality means both intelligence and mental set since both must be taken into account to predict and change behavior.

Intelligence by itself is not an effective predictor of constructive vs. destructive behavior. Unless we believe that the human species has become less intelligent over the centuries of recorded history, we cannot say that intelligence or learning ability, per se, are safeguards against destructive behavior.

Indisputably, highly intelligent human beings have invented and deployed ever more sophisticated weapons of destruction. And as our species has grown intellectually over the millennia, we have become more lethal overall.

If we compare ourselves as a species to our nearest though less intelligent relatives, the apes, clearly we are enormously more destructive. Our very nearest relatives, the Bonobo chimpanzees, are very similar genetically but not behaviorally in some important ways. Although long and closely studied, Bonobos have never been observed to kill others of their kind (Eisler, 1996, page 41); yet they possess 98% of the genetic structure of humans. Thus, merely fostering human intelligence and knowledge per se does not augur well for the survival of the human species, nor can we dismiss our destructiveness as the mere product of our genetics. Our highly developed human intelligence and knowledge can be used for constructive or destructive purposes.

Sometimes, failure to use our intelligence has destructive consequences, as we recognize when we remark, "That was a dumb thing to do" or, "So and so wasn't thinking or he wouldn't have done that." We judge that some destructive behavior shows a lapse in intelligence. Destructiveness may be an act of folly, a foolish failure to think ahead and realize consequences for oneself and others — the result of not using one's head, so to speak. Historian Barbara Tuchman's book *The March of Folly* (1984), discussed in Chapter 5 of this book, is a convincing account of how folly, defined as the pursuit of policy contrary to self-interest, has characterized a long series of mammoth debacles from the Trojan War to the euphemistically labeled "Vietnam Conflict." The leaders and followers of these follies were not without intelligence as it is usually defined. Some of the leaders were even called, justifiably according to the orthodox definition, "the best and the brightest."

Intelligence, the capacity to acquire and apply knowledge, is a neutral party that lends itself with equal facility to constructive or destructive behavior. People in the 20th century have used knowledge to perpetrate a quantity and rate of lethal violence that dwarfs that of the previous two centuries combined. The progressive acceleration of technological development, based as it is on intellectual achievement, has not only made possible but has been used to actuate massive human destructiveness in every realm, including the ecological as well as interpersonal. Yet, we cannot validly blame technology. The 20th century has also witnessed astounding improvements, largely ascribable to technology, in our capacity for healthy and humane living. Clearly, intelligence by itself does not guarantee constructive behavior.

Is our disposition, mental set, or outlook crucial to our behaving constructively? Not by itself. Kindly disposed people may not grasp the complexities of strategies needed to create constructive change. We have all heard concessions to this fact, such as "Well, his heart was in the right place" offered as an excuse for some negative outcome of well-intentioned behavior. The epigram, "The road to hell is paved with good intentions," speaks to this fact, as does Mark Twain's remark: "If a man came to my door to do me good, I would run for my life." Good intentions by themselves can have destructive consequences.

For example, in Calcutta, India 4 million cylinder-type wells were sunk as part of a safe-water program with the financial support of the Bangladesh government and charitable groups, principally UNICEF — all with constructive intent. But while the project saved many people from deadly bacteria in surface water, it poisoned others because, unwittingly, the cylinders had been sunk into an aquifer naturally tainted with harmful levels of arsenic (Bearak, 1998).

While neither intelligence nor intention by themselves are adequate to produce constructive behavior and outcomes, positive intentions paired with knowledge can be powerfully constructive while negative intentions paired with knowledge can be powerfully destructive. What do we mean, though, by good or bad intentions? And what do we mean by constructive and destructive behavior? People usually claim to be able to tell the difference between constructive and destructive behavior. But what is judged to be constructive or destructive depends largely on who is doing the judging. Virtually every individual murderer, to the extent that he admits to the act, defends it as constructive or at least necessary, and entire nations who are committing massive lethal violence against other nations or against their own citizens defend their actions as constructive. Such mentality is captured in the oxymoron "ethnic cleansing," which its advocates claim to be constructive.

To understand anything, we must contrast it with something else. Indeed, even to perceive anything at all, to simply recognize it or to give it a name, we must see it in contrast to something else. We cannot recognize day unless we experience night. The more stark the contrast, the more readily we see the difference and know, therefore, that something is present. Because our ability to perceive is dependent on experiencing contrast, to improve the balance between human destructiveness vs. constructiveness, we must clearly perceive and understand the differences even when they are subtle.

This task may seem easy. Doesn't everyone know the difference between constructive and destructive behavior and, for that matter, between constructive vs. destructive mentalities? The answer must be an emphatic NO! As will be illustrated in the early chapters of this book, much, perhaps most of our individual and collective or group behavior, is a complex mix of constructive and destructive behavior and mentality, and the differences are often subtle but important.

The easiest mistake to make in addressing human destructiveness, and probably the most frequent, is to limit causal explanation to one or even a few factors. Ron Rosenbaum's book *Explaining Hitler* (1998) shows how many even otherwise sophisticated attempts to explain Hitler's "demonic" behavior have lacked an adequate conception of causality. Too little credence has been given, in the vast majority of causal explanations of human destructiveness, to the dynamic interrelationship of the full array of historical and contemporaneous forces and circumstances influencing the mentality of personalities and groups. Even the most determined "evil" individual must be supported by circumstances and many other people in order to perpetrate genocide or other forms of mass killing that account for most of the immense 20th century-surge in lethal violence.

To avoid this mistake, particularly to avoid focusing excessively on the most proximate of causes, I shall emphasize the importance of paralethal causation: those indirect causative factors or influences that promote and facilitate lethal behavior.

Mapping the Journey of Discovery

To find answers means discovering various personal and institutional mentalities ranging from the conventionally acceptable to the controversial and on to those that are more blatantly destructive. Along the way we can become aware of commonalities in the destructive mentality, such as willingness to dehumanize vs. the insistence on respect which is characteristic of constructive mentality.

This chapter, Dilemmas for the 21st Century, introduces basic considerations and some working concepts. It begins to address fundamental threats to survival, including dehumanization, denial and distortion of truth, and population pressures. Chapters 2 through 5 depict a continuum of institutional destructiveness from the too-readily-acceptable to the most blatant forms.

Chapter 2 addresses social inducements to paralethal and lethal violence in our present Western civilization, with primary emphasis on the U.S. It shows how even relatively well-accepted institutions may be more destructive than we usually perceive. Although the U.S. may be the greatest nation on Earth, it is also a Western civilization leader in many kinds of destructiveness, as shown in rates of murder, violent crimes by and against youth, incarceration, weapons production and exportation, and illicit or morbid drug use. The causes of these behaviors are to be found mainly within rather than outside of our borders. It is largely a case of "We have met the enemy and it is us," wherein "us" stands for the U.S.

Nevertheless, insofar as the U.S. lives up to its democratic ideals, we are made far safer, along with other democracies, from the mass destructiveness of war and by death at the hands of our own government. Furthermore, our democratic society makes it possible to be watchful and constructively critical, as this book is intended to be. With all its flaws, which demand so much critical attention, we are extremely fortunate to be a democratic nation. As Winston Churchill said, "Democracy is the worst form of government except for all those other forms which have been tried from time to time" (as quoted in Humes, 1994).

Chapter 3, Inhibiting Fatal Group and Institutional Aggression, discusses clearly controversial institutions that emphasize secrecy and are not socially or legally accountable. They are exemplified by certain nongovernmental militia groups in the U.S. and by the Japan-based terrorist cult known as Aum. Each example illustrates the current trend toward terrorism by groups who feel disempowered. Within our nation, so-called militia groups comprise a mixture of legitimate concerns about individual rights together with concerns of a seemingly paranoid nature. Their more aggressive tendencies may become terroristic.

The second institutional example is of fairly recent origin in Japan. "Aum," as it is called, illustrates the deadly nature of terroristic cults which often tend to destroy themselves eventually as they seek to destroy "the enemy without." Aum also illustrates the increasing reliance of terrorist groups on chemical and biological means of destruction. Like so many institutions including our own government, these two antigovernment institutions, militia groups and Aum, readily lapse into being more sensitive to outsiders' faults than their own. They run the risk of self destruction as well as animosity from outsiders.

Chapter 4, The Central Intelligence Agency and Lethal Violence, is an historical account and commentary on a highly secretive organization, with its roots in World War II, that has extended its spying on and disruption of other nations to this day. It documents how institutions given governmental authorization to act in secrecy may destroy lives through their covert operations and undermine their own as well as other governments.

The CIA performed heroic duty as it responded to wartime exigencies, continued its seemingly needed covert work through the cold war, and now focuses largely on the considerable threat of international terrorism. But it also illustrates the dangers and damages wrought by compromising democracy, a compromise thought necessary to counter the destructiveness of more authoritarian nations, whether in hot or cold wars. Necessary or not, the CIA has engaged throughout the world in paralethal and sometimes virtually directly lethal activities, often with very limited accountability to even the U.S. government as well as to other nations. Thus, the CIA has sometimes exemplified the lawless, terroristic behavior it is supposed to counter.

The examples provided in Chapters 2, 3, and 4 suggest that both individual and institutional perpetrators of paralethal and outright lethal behavior believe in their own righteous cause. Thus, they would label their own behavior "constructive" though, or sometimes even because, they cause deaths.

Further along and reaching to the end of the continuum of institutionally based destructiveness are authoritarian governmental regimes, as illustrated in Chapter 5, Lethal Violence by Entire Governments. The most extreme governments are totalitarian, such as Hitler's Nazi regime which perpetrated vast numbers of atrocities against humanity. In these cases, power invested in the few is largely or entirely unchecked, unless by other nations. They not only thrive on secrecy and unaccountability, but have the added ominous advantage of extreme centralization of power enforced by the government itself. Unlike the institutions discussed in earlier chapters, their destructiveness is legally authorized and even mandated for nations as a whole. In these regimes, there is virtually no separation of powers to provide a balancing of powers and an opportunity for dissent. Dissent itself is considered destructive and readily ends in death for the dissenters.

Governments have been the perpetrators of the most massive lethal violence in human history, often killing their own subjects. Learning how such governments are formed, colluded in, and come to legalize and reward killing is essential to preventing the abject folly and madness of this most important form of human violence.

Chapter 6, Transcendence: Constructive vs. Destructive Mentalities, contrasts the paralethal and lethal mentalities, as already exemplified, with alternative or constructive mentalities as formed by individual and collective influences. How we treat the prevailing dilemmas of power, population, sexuality, and inequality in terms of appreciation vs. contempt for the diversity of life is shown to be crucial to the survival of the human race.

Staying Alive and Awake

On his retirement after a very long career, a wise, humorous, and esteemed psychiatrist remarked on what he felt were the two greatest challenges he had ever faced: staying alive and staying awake. His words stuck in my mind. The more I thought about them, the more meaning I attributed to them.

On the most superficial level, the speaker was simply being facetious. Instead of saying something learned, weighty, and profound, he was being flippant and perhaps even a little disrespectful to himself and perhaps to his own and kindred professions and the many practitioners who were celebrating him and his accomplishments. He was expected to say something deeply meaningful. Instead, he merely made a joke. And to assure listeners that it was just that, he explained that, because it was so difficult for him to stay awake, he used his many years of leadership status to take control of the coffee supply in his clinic, going so far as to brew the coffee himself and to make sure he and his colleagues would always have enough to stay awake.

I enjoyed the joke but was not satisfied with its surface meaning. The speaker had never been known to be disrespectful. He was known for his kindness, helpfulness, and wisdom. His remark grew in my mind, particularly as I was writing this book, and I made an interpretation.

Human beings have had, have now, and will always and everywhere have these two challenges: staying alive and staying awake. Superficially considered, these challenges may seem easy to meet, so much so that we tend on an everyday basis to take our survival for granted. "Of course," we say in agreement, "in order to function we have to be alive and awake but, if that is all we have to do, yes, of course, we can certainly stay alive and awake, granted that some people may need coffee to stay awake."

But these are difficult challenges for every person and for the entire human race. As will be documented later, when considered on a statistical probability basis the human race is going to lose the race sometime in the 21st century by destroying itself, given a continuance of the accelerating rate with which we have been and are continuing to perpetrate lethal violence. The only way that this statistical probability can be overcome so that we, or at least our successors, will stay alive, is for we humans to become more awake. Specifically, we will have to become more awake to be aware of the patterns of causation of human destructiveness and to become mindful of how we can be more constructive. We must become more aware of the differences: the contrast between constructive and destructive mentalities.

Awakening to the Subtleties of Dehumanization

"*The inevitable scare is the unfolding of the truth.*" Together with students in a class I was teaching, I heard this aphorism spoken by a young man being interviewed in a psychiatric hospital conference room, where he was presented as an example of "schizophrenia." As often happens during such demonstrations, the young man was making too much sense to fit snugly into his diagnosis, though the presiding psychiatrist said he did not need the psychologist's test evaluation report because he already knew this was a case of schizophrenia and knew what would be in the report.

The young man was going to be treated simply as another case of "schizophrenia," rather simply: a member of a category. His individuality and his particular characteristics and inclinations were deemed of no interest. This approach meant giving him major tranquilizing drugs to reduce his anxiety or, as he put it, his "scare." What the individual, the patient, had in mind when he spoke the aphorism about the scare would not be discussed, as it might have been in the interest of helping us and him to understand it. Perhaps doing so would have enabled him to take an active role in his treatment and not just be a passive object. Instead, the patient was quickly placed into a kind of "disease" category — schizophrenia — without reference to his individuality, and the same treatment ordered for him as any other "schizophrenic" would get. The patient's mentality was already quite sufficiently understood for purposes of treatment and disposition.

Having seen countless examples of the simply generic diagnosis and treatment approach, I was not surprised by the tenor of that conference. It was no different from a hundred other such conferences I had witnessed. But, next day, the students surprised me. Some of them approached me back on our college campus and said that all of the students needed to speak with me as soon as possible about yesterday's extremely upsetting experience. One of them pointed out that she had not been upset by the patient but by the way the patient was regarded by his psychiatrist and other mental health professionals during the demonstration. The students readily accepted the patient but not the way the interviewing psychiatrist had related, or failed to relate, to the young man who the students saw as a fellow human. They had been interested in everything the patient said, including his aphorism about "the inevitable scare." They considered him as not fundamentally different from themselves. So they were appalled at how dogmatically the interviewing psychiatrist insisted the patient was categorically schizophrenic and disregarded his individuality.

The students, it turned out, perceived a universality to the patient's fear of the future. His fear did not, in their eyes, make him so different from other people, even if his undiscussed fear was so extreme and yet vague as to be a nameless terror. The students could empathize with that young man. He didn't seem so different from themselves that they couldn't identify with him, although they had qualified as exceptionally high academic achievers, and felt he was stable and sane enough to be regarded by others as very far removed indeed from someone who spoke in a "strange" way of his fear. The students heard the young man speak of a universal kind of fear of the future, not unlike many existential philosophers, or of fear of the future as spoken less elegantly by countless other people. The students could readily admit that they, like the patient, feared the truths that would inevitably unfold in the future, including the inevitability of death.

What upset the students was seeing and hearing the patient seemingly dismissed as such a different entity from us and other humans. He was a case of "schizophrenia" or "a schizophrenic" rather than possibly schizophrenic. Labeling him with a noun rather than an adjective set him apart in a permanent-sounding way as a kind of object, rather than a human being who at the time might, or might not, be helpfully described as schizophrenic, implying a temporal state that might well change. The seeming segregation of the young man from other humans, however subtle, was appalling to the students, as were the segregators. The students sensed that the segregation might result in his being treated more like an object than as a fellow human being who, in reality, was more like his caregivers than not. They saw an ostensibly very mild, perhaps nonappreciable and certainly readily deniable, degree of dehumanization.

This degree of dehumanization would appear inconsequential in contrast to the regimes of Stalin and Hitler, although perhaps not at the outset of Hitler's regime; subtle, albeit cumulative and insidiously more dehumanizing legislative measures became laws that facilitated and justified progressively more segregation and persecution.

Eventually, being labeled a case of schizophrenia in the Nazi regime became a definite death sentence. In the regime's beginning stages, however, executions had to wait until the citizenry could become desensitized to what needed to be done to actuate the needed treatment. Like the Jews, Slavs, and French; the handicapped, homosexuals, political dissidents; and a growing number of other categories of the unfit, the schizophrenics first had to be deemed inferior, with supporting medical evidence, albeit of a pseudomedical and pseudoscientific kind that was inferior to real science. Then, Nazi legislation could be enacted to crack down on these deviants and undesirables for such periods of months or years as it took to proclaim that they were unfit to live.

Even Hitler, the world's most efficient destroyer of humanity, a dictator with seemingly absolute power, had to rely on medical doctors and scientists to provide dehumanizing diagnoses and treatments in order to effect an acceptable gradualism, thereby helping to avoid an excessive public outcry. The perceived differences could not be too great over a short period of time or they would grab attention. Thus, the world's all-time most efficient killing regime was limited to a gradual objectification of the victims that began by labeling them purportedly with genetic and disease-based diagnoses before they could be murdered. In essence, the "cases" first had to be "scientifically" diagnosed prior to being segregated, and then administered an "appropriate" or "needed" uniform type of treatment with the aim of dehumanizing them completely to the point of death.

In the United Soviet Socialist Republic (USSR), the label "schizophrenia" meant that such cases would be toxically treated with heavy doses of drugs that deprived them of liveliness and spontaneity and made them more zombie-like than human. Psychiatrists there invented "creeping schizophrenia," a diagnosis given to political dissidents whose deviant political ideology, the scientific medical specialists declared, was the disturbance of thinking, the irrational thinking that is the hallmark of schizophrenic disorders (Medvedev and Medvedev, 1979). In both Nazi Germany and in the USSR the already stigmatizing schizophrenia label lent itself, and was greatly needed, to dehumanize those stuck with it.

Typically, the process of dehumanization is very gradual, and must be aided and abetted by already existing bigotry and then be further supported and encouraged by prejudice. Such aid is highly effective, in both active and passive forms, when provided by a large portion of the people in a given group, institution, or country. A critical mass of support is needed, even by a ruler with "absolute" power.

If not caught early, the tendency to dehumanize people, whether they are called schizophrenic, mentally retarded, physically handicapped, homosexual, or listed as members of any of the seemingly innumerable "ethnic undesirables," readily leads to the destruction of ever larger numbers of people, including people in still other, additional, newly diagnosed and "treated" categories of undesirables. It is then that the inherently contradictory blaming of the victims becomes complete. The actual perpetrators of murder, of evil, proclaim that they have done humanity an enormously needed, though perhaps admittedly distasteful, service by "cleansing" the population of its contaminants.

Although dehumanization overall appears to happen less in democracies, at least in terms of lethal outcomes, it does happen, sometimes in extreme form. For example, Chapter 4, The Central Intelligence Agency and Lethal Violence, includes the story of how the U.S. and Canada supported psychiatric experimentation, under the guise of treatment, that severely and chronically disabled many unwitting citizens of these two democracies.

Denial in the 20th Century

To realize our essential likeness as human beings, we only have to admit the biological functions we have in common, our transience on this Earth, and the inevitability of our deaths. Reaching the point at which we can no longer be sustained biologically makes death the great equalizer. Certainly, we all know *about* the reality of death but we seldom sense how deeply we are affected by this ultimate universal reality. The inevitable scare is the unfolding of the truth that each and every one of us is going to die.

The Denial of Death, as Ernest Becker titled his 1975 book, is both a universal and complexly problematic defense against admitting the inevitability of death, including one's own. The "scare" makes everyone deny it, though perhaps to varying degrees. In this light, the possibly schizophrenic young man noted earlier may have sensed that he was in immediate danger of dying, at least psychologically, but failed to use one of the more acceptable denial mechanisms. In being blatantly afraid, he was showing himself unable to maintain the basic narcissism on which the denial of death and standard "sanity" is based.

> "This narcissism is what keeps men marching into point-blank fire in wars: at heart one doesn't feel that *he* will die, he only feels sorry for the man next to him" (Becker, 1975, page 2).

Coming to grips with "death anxiety" is a lifelong challenge for every individual and the entire human race. Will we address it so as to make the most of our own and others' lives, or short-circuit life? When we fail to reconcile ourselves to death in a constructive way, we cheapen life by passively going along with or actively perpetrating the lessening and destruction of life. Denying death and squandering life go hand in hand on the pretense that one's own life is not inherently limited. Acknowledging death makes recognizing the limitation and preciousness of life possible and makes the most constructive use of life.

The motivation behind the short-circuiting of life that is characteristic of destructive mentality is a temporarily gratifying lessening of anxiety.

> Destruction of one's own and others' lives provides a temporarily comforting reassurance: "I am dominant over death because I determine it. I am master over death, so death is not master over me."

Denial of death requires considerable effort to maintain. It is illustrated by the cartoon film in which the Road Runner races right off a cliff but does not fall until he looks down, i.e., faces reality. It is also demonstrated by the denial of a manic person who squanders money and energy in a desperate attempt to fend off depression, and who cannot tolerate others disagreeing, i.e., facing him with the reality of his own limitations. Such acting out of death anxiety is illustrated in more detail in the section on Hitler in Chapter 5.

Failing to have the courage to confront the realities of the passing of time and the inevitability of one's death may mean becoming destructive, even to the point we call evil.

> ...psychoanalysis revealed to us the complex penalties of denying the truth of man's condition, what we might call *the costs of pretending not to be mad.* If we had to offer the briefest explanation of all of the evil that men have wreaked upon themselves and upon their world since the beginnings of time right up until tomorrow, it would not be in terms of man's animal heredity, his instincts and his evolution; it would be simply in *the toll that his pretense of sanity takes,* as he tries to deny his real condition (Becker, 1975, page 30).

Language readily reflects our attempts to deny the reality of death. We create new desensitizing words and phrases, or attach new misleading meanings to old words and phrases; we talk and act as though death has not and will not occur by using language to create falsehoods about death and the "unpleasantness" of death. We can then feel less uncomfortable for the short term, but the price is high indeed. Death has reared its ugly head, at least by allusion, and the impression stays with us in the back of our own heads. The price goes up with time until the inevitable scare is upon us, albeit often in a disguised form so that we still cannot deal directly with death. The matter is rather like credit card debt on which the interest grows and compounds exorbitantly with each passing month.

We have all heard or used the most common denials such as "Oh, no!" as at least a first reaction to hearing that someone has died. And we are familiar with certain euphemisms used to soften the blow, for example, that someone has "passed away." Such terms can serve a temporarily constructive purpose by lessening the trauma and giving the bereaved person time to come to grips with the trauma. But if sustained beyond a quite temporary period, the denial mechanism itself takes a great and often ubiquitous toll by dulling, distorting, and disturbing our lives. If we persist in denying the reality of death, we become deadened mentally and emotionally.

What is needed to cope with the reality, the tragedy of death, is to have sober, sad realizations. At the extreme, grossly denying the reality of loss and death by not permitting ourselves to be sad — a much abhorred emotion typically confused with depression in much of the Western world — we become mad in the sense of that term's two most important meanings. As the *American Heritage Dictionary*, 3rd ed. (1992) puts it, mad means: "(1) angry; resentful, and (2) suffering from a disorder of the mind; insane." The expression "insane with grief" expresses the threat to sanity posed by acknowledging death. But the alternative to a failure to grieve is to sabotage life. Thus, the challenge is to become able to be sad, not to target sadness as a symptom to be eradicated.

The denial of death as expressed so pervasively in our language is frequently fortified by the further denial that our language is meaningful, as in the expression, "It's just semantics." But semantics is a matter of meaning, and we need to take meaning seriously, including when we are trying to discover the madness of the destructive mentality that is so strongly characterized by the denial of death. We need to mean what we say and say what we mean. To accept the use of a misleading term regarding violence, without objection, is to contribute to lying about it and densensitizing ourselves and others to it.

The list of examples in Table 1.1 is intended to provide some awareness of how destructive mentality is aided and abetted by euphemistic language. Chapter 5 lists additional euphemisms, with emphasis on those used in the Nazi regime.

Table 1.1   A Glossary of Modern Euphemisms: Definitions of Difficult or Specialized Words Used to Mask Violence

Every individual or national degeneration is immediately revealed by a directly proportional degradation in language (Joseph de Maistre).

Action picture: a movie designed to appeal to audiences by means of its depictions of violence

Bought it, or went for a Burton: World War II Allied fighter pilots crashing and being killed

Collateral damage: destruction brought about by misdirected bombs or missiles, sometimes resulting in the injuring and killing of civilians by the military

Defoliation: Vietnam War destruction of forests used by the enemy for cover

Guns: a term used to denote the number of soldiers or other military personnel equipped to kill other human beings, e.g., as used by Hitler in World War II

Ethnic cleansing: genocide; the systematic killing of people distinguished by their race, religion, nationality, linguistic or cultural heritage, e.g., as used by the Serbs in the killing of ethnic Albanians in the 1990s

Friendly fire: Gulf War killing of soldiers by their own comrades in arms

Hazing: training in cruelty, e.g., as practiced in the military or in college fraternities

Holy war: a war ostensibly declared and fought for a religious or high moral purpose, as to extend or defend a religion

Honor killing: justification of murder by attributing blame to the victim or the victim's associates

International conflict: war, as in "the Vietnam conflict"

Neutralize: to remove as a threat, usually by killing

Pacification: Vietnam War destruction of villages after evacuation of the inhabitants

Plausible deniabilty: a cover for lying, as in preparation for disavowing responsibility for committing or aiding and abetting criminal actions, including murder, e.g., as used by the Central Intelligence Agency (CIA)

Presidential finding: written executive authorization by the President of the U.S. to engage in harmful covert action such as espionage or aiding and abetting war

Recreational drugs: a term used generally to deny the harmful effects of drugs and to suggest only positive effects. A more accurate term would be "wreckreational drugs"

Recruitment of agents: inducing people to become traitors to their own nations, i.e., to persuade them to commit treason

Redact: make a document appear more innocuous before the public can gain access to and scrutinize it

Sex and violence: the contamination of sexuality by violence; an admixing of the two terms, sometimes with implied condemnation of both sexuality and violence as if both are bad, as in "sex and violence movies" and "sex and violence on television"

Target-rich areas: places where the most damage and destruction can be accomplished

Wet affairs: kidnappings and assasinations, e.g., page 85 in E. Thomas' *The Very Best Men* (1995)

Note: The use of euphemisms can be traced back to the Middle Ages, but the prevalence of such evasive and concealing (or fair-sounding) terminology has never been more marked than in the cruel social and political areas of life in the 20th century. *The New Fowler's Modern English Usage*, 3rd ed.

The Art and Science of Covert Destructive Persuasion

Theoretical and methodologic development of ways to fool people are as old as human history itself. But the art and science of covertly persuading people to harm themselves and others produced delusional depths of degradation in the 20th century. Such skillful falsification of reality has been used to sell people products harmful to their health and well-being and has contributed to the widespread morbidity in everyday life. It helps explain why so many people have become addicted to or dependent on tobacco, alcohol, and other drugs, violence "entertainment," processed and "fast foods," and other forms of self-abuse. A look at what is called "public relations" helps unmask this relatively subtle but sometimes massive form of destructiveness.

Typically, advertising is better understood than public relations because it is more direct; one is usually made aware of the product, even though the product may have no intrinsic relationship to what is associated with it in an ad. Good-looking women and celebrities, for example, provide absolutely no evidence of real merit for underwear, beer, or cars, but their images of beauty and prestige are associated with the product in the hope that such attractive images will make the product attractive. Some advertisers insist on a high standard for product quality itself, apart from creating interesting and attractive images to go with it, and advertising can lead people to buy truly helpful as well as harmful products. At least the potential buyer is made aware of the product itself.

In contrast with advertising, which is readily identifiable as such and clearly reveals to the potential buyer what it is that is being offered for sale, the indirectness of public relations is more capable of beguiling the buyer. While advertising's pitch reveals at least the product name and perhaps its appearance or other characteristics, public relations disassociates the product from the pitch used to sell it.

What Phillip Bernays did for 80 years, according to his autobiography (1965) and to Larry Tye's biography (1998), exemplifies the ways great masses of people were persuaded to buy products by buying into ideas and given no clue as to the product being pushed. Bernays, a nephew of Sigmund Freud, used his uncle's theories to fashion a powerful methodology. The bridge from theory to method came from a consultation with psychiatrist and psychoanalyst A. A. Brill, who advised:

> It is perfectly normal for women to want to smoke cigarettes.... The emancipation of women has suppressed many of their feminine desires. More women now do the same work as men do. Many women bear no children; those who do bear fewer children. Feminine traits are masked. Cigarettes, which are equated with men, have become torches of freedom (as quoted in Tye, 1998, page 28).

In essence, Brill advised Bernays to exploit what Brill saw as women's own deceptiveness in "masking" their "feminine traits," by suggesting to Bernays that he call cigarettes torches of freedom. One can wonder at Brill's professional integrity. He was apparently willing to do massive harm by exploiting what he saw as women's self-deception, whereas psychoanalysis as a form of psychotherapy aims at complete candor. And getting women addicted to cigarettes and thereby damaging them by their own hands, physically as well as mentally, is certainly antithetical to his avowed aims as a physician. Of course, the incentive for both Brill and Bernays was money, not women's liberation.

Bernays then sent a telegram signed by his secretary, a woman, to each of 30 New York City-area debutantes, maximizing the deception: "In the interests of equality of the sexes and to fight another sex taboo, I and other young women will light another torch of freedom by smoking cigarettes while strolling on Fifth Avenue Easter Sunday" (as cited in Tye, page 29). Similarly, an advertisement was run in New York newspapers, one such ad signed by a leading feminist.

This drug-pushing epic was so elaborately scripted, rehearsed, and executed that only Bernays' or Tye's detailed descriptions can begin to convey its insidious, conspiratorial success. The ever-so-carefully selected marchers were more than just marchers; they conscripted other women precisely as they came out of the best-known churches, providing them with Lucky Strike cigarettes (complete with a disavowel that they were advocating a particular brand) and helping them to light up their new found torches and join the march.

Protests from nonsmokers were countered immediately in the media, which itself mostly swallowed the propaganda, all the while not knowing the true source. The stratagems used in hiding the source were exhaustive, successfully obviating any and all attempts at discovery. Bernays' secretary, who was fully involved in the planning, execution, and follow-up, totally fabricated the nature of her involvement. Failing to mention her connection to Bernays, she told New York's *Evening World* that she first got the idea for this campaign when a man with her in the street asked her to extinguish her cigarette as it embarrassed him. "I talked it over with my friends, and we decided it was high time something was done about the situation..." A Shreveport, LA newspaper, meanwhile, wrote that, "Miss Hunt says she is not connected with any firm." ...And the communique she issued said pointedly that she and her comarchers had "no particular brand favored" (Tye, 1998, page 33).

Bernays special method was to research why the public preferred certain things, then to reengineer the public's preferences to meet his client's needs, all the while taking great care to deceive the public. Sometimes he clothed his client's interests in high causes such as health, even going so far as to suggest that cigarettes, when used as substitutes for sweets, promoted health. Meanwhile, the already negative effects of smoking on health, provided by bona fide scientific research, were downplayed.

Did Bernays believe, at least partially, in his own propaganda? According to his daughters, he tried hard though unsuccessfully to get his wife to stop her one-pack-a-day habit, including pulling out all her Parliaments from the pack, snapping them in half, and throwing them in the toilet (Tye, page 48). Bernays, a nonsmoker, admittedly preferred chocolates to cigarettes.

Despite his early awareness of the negative research literature, which he tried to counter, and his own dislike of cigarettes, Bernays denied for decades any knowledge of the damages to health until the U.S. Surgeon General and other medical authorities released incontrovertible evidence. Then, to his credit it would seem, he used his public relations talents to help undo the addictions he had been so successful at inculcating on a vulnerable public.

Bernays, like many other public relations and advertising professionals, also worked in behalf of "good causes" intended to benefit the public. But, whether public relations efforts are geared to constructive or clearly destructive purposes, we should be aware of the terrible price of such deception. *Even constructive purposes can be sullied when deception and manipulation are used successfully to persuade, because people are thereby estranged from the freedom and responsibility of critical thinking and genuine knowledge.*

The "spin" put on events by public relations, while often subtle and gradual, can turn the tide in human relations, even internationally. According to Tye, Bernays demonstrated that an ostensibly constructive enterprise could not only sully and set back, but actually destroy, the beginnings of democratic government in favor of dictatorship. Bernays gave a benign-sounding account in his autobiography (1965) of his nearly 20 years of public relations work for United Fruit Company beginning in the 1940s. In contrast, Tye (1998, page 156), who had access to 53 boxes of Bernays' papers concerning United Fruit, paints a picture of Bernays helping to unseat the elected leader of a nation who was fostering democracy. The propaganda campaign effected "...an undeclared war on behalf of United Fruit, one of America's richest companies — a war fought in quiet alliance with the U.S. government, on foreign soil, against the elected government of Guatemala.... The propaganda war Bernays waged in Guatemala set the pattern for future U.S.-led campaigns in Cuba and, much later, Vietnam." A military dictatorship ensued in the person of a Guatemalan man who, aided by the U.S. and its Central Intelligence Agency as well as the propaganda campaign, led an orchestrated military strike against the government.

Bernays did work on behalf of the "public good" in much of his career but he often put aside the truth and the public good in the interests of making money and creating a positive image of himself. Tye concludes: "Most of all, in his relentless bid to shape his own legacy, he offered a perfect portrayal of the full array of PR tactics and strategies, of manipulations and embellishments, and how they could be used to redefine reality" (Tye, 1998, pages 264 and 265).

Tye's biography and Bernays' autobiography ought to be carefully read, studied, and contrasted to fully grasp the enormous impact of public relations on molding minds. One can then see how pervasively we are covertly programmed so that we often rely more on spin than truth. Thus, individuals, groups, and governments can delude themselves and others.

Basic Considerations: A Dialogue with the Devil's Advocate

How can we explain why the "march of civilization" has brought with it an escalating rate of lethal behavior? Why are human beings more likely than ever before to die from the destructive behavior of other human beings? Is the killing serving a necessary or useful purpose in the great scheme of things?

As Harold Hall (1999) has summarized and R.J. Rummel (1997) has documented in great detail, the escalation of humanly perpetrated lethality over the past three centuries is striking. The 18th century's rate of 50 deaths per million population per year was superseded by the 19th century's 60 deaths per million population per year — a 20% increase. The 20th century's rate, calculated to 1988, was 460 deaths per million per year — 767% more than the 19th century and 920% more than the 18th century!

Rummel's analysis has shown that, on a worldwide basis, for every person killed in a war against external enemies, four to five are killed by their own government. He calls the latter "democide," meaning genocide and other forms of government-perpetrated murder of its own citizens and foreigners within its borders. Rates of both war against external foes and democide are overwhelmingly ascribable to a government's position on the continuum from democratic to authoritarian to totalitarian. Democratic governments virtually never massively kill their own citizens or wage war against other democratic governments, and they are less likely to wage war against authoritarian or totalitarian governments. The strongly implied lesson in these findings is that to prevent war and democide, we must promote democratic governments. But besides the extremely difficult challenge of promoting and maintaining democracy, there may be an even more basic dilemma.

Can promoting the democratic spirit and way of life largely solve the problem of lethal violence? Perhaps it can, but won't saving lives exacerbate the world population problem? If world population continues to boom, won't we be faced with food and other resource shortages that will result in oppressive crowding, conflict, hunger, and famine? Aren't we headed inevitably toward massively lethal disasters due to increasing overpopulation?

The world population was 1 billion in 1805, 2 billion in 1936, 3 billion in 1960, 4 billion in 1974, 5 billion in 1987 (Crystal, 1998), and it became 6 billion in 1999. Whereas it took 131 years, from 1805 to 1936, to increase from 1 to 2 billion people, it took one tenth that time (a mere 12 years, from 1987 to 1999) to add another billion people. World population growth is projected to slow, however, assuming increased contraceptive use in developing countries and aging of the world's population, so fertile adults will constitute a smaller percentage of the total world population. By this reckoning, the total will not reach 10 billion until the year 2070. Nevertheless, the question remains: can the planet sustain or tolerate so many people?

One answer comes in the form of projecting future lethal violence. Richardson (1960) studied the history of wars from 1820 to 1949. His Richardson Curve, which statistically plots the trend, extrapolates to predict wars of increasing magnitude occurring with greater frequency. Richardson predicts that, at some point in the future, even taking into account rapid growth in world population, human willingness — whether active or passive — to kill other humans will equal or exceed the world population.

The technological ability and resources capable of killing the world's entire human population were ample and rapidly growing by the year 2000. Specific methods of killing have proliferated in types, numbers, efficiency, and availability. In addition to nuclear weaponry being produced by more and more nations, other easier and less expensive mass extermination methods have proliferated. What used to be called "chemical and germ warfare," traditionally banned but sometimes actually used in war, has become so developed that not only many nations, but even relatively small groups of people, can kill huge populations. For example, the Japanese-based doomsday cult called Aum Supreme Truth, discussed in Chapter 3, has possessed and used saran gas and, although Aum's leader was imprisoned, Aum continued on its deadly mission.

Germ warfare was rapidly developed during the so-called Cold War by Soviet scientists in ways that could readily kill millions of people at a time (Alibek and Handelman, 1999). Both the Japanese cult and the Soviet government have been chillingly dedicated to their work of destruction. Theoretically, the Russian program was dismantled in the 1990s at the order of President Boris Yeltsin, but it would be naive to believe that the technology, once developed, cannot be used. Therefore, to prevent world destruction, we will have to become far more humane and respectful of life so that our technological advances do not continue to outrun our humanity.

The major definitions of the word "civilized" help to frame the dilemma inherent in the world's 20th century violence explosion. To be civilized means to have a highly developed society and culture — to have risen from barbarism to an enlightened stage of development. The civilized society shows evidence of moral and intellectual advancement; it is humane, ethical, and reasonable (*American Heritage Dictionary*, 1992). By this definition, we have not been more civilized in the 20th century than in previous centuries; we have had vastly more lethal violence. Our "intellectual advancement" has been skewed toward the technical, slighting the development and understanding of what is humane, ethical, and reasonable. In this light, *understanding human relations is a vastly more urgent and challenging subject than rocket science.*

We cannot take for granted that further "civilization," even including democratization, will mean a safer or more constructive world. If we project from the past, we would predict still higher rates of interpersonal destructiveness generally and lethal behavior in particular.

The "advance of civilization" has meant a disproportionate advance in technological means of killing one another relative to empathy, compassion, and forethought about human behavior. Will we, inexorably, keep on destroying one another at higher and higher rates? If not, what is needed for us to develop into more constructive human beings? What changes must we make in order to survive, and what can we do, beyond merely surviving, to enhance life experience? Or, must we reconcile ourselves to overpopulation or continued skewing of our intellectual development in terms of the usual narrow sense of the word, as exemplified by technological advancement, including extermination methodology?

As implied previously, a harsh answer to these questions is grounded in assessment of the realities of population growth. It is so objectionable that in 1898 when its progenitor, the Reverend Thomas Malthus, an economist and mathematician, published his essay predicting that the world's rapidly growing population would overwhelm the Earth's capacity to sustain it, he did so anonymously. Originally, Malthus' argument, condemned by many theorists, rested only on the fact that while global food supplies increase arithmetically, the world's human population increases exponentially, a vastly faster rate that would inexorably exhaust the availability of food. Bearing out Malthus' formulation, as noted previously the world's population in 1930 was about 2 billion and by the end of 1999 or early 2000 it reached 6 billion, with further growth predicted. Meanwhile, many areas of the world have continued to suffer mass starvation.

Today, there is little basic disagreement with Malthus' repugnant predictions. Malthus' scientific descendants have added to his argument, noting we are also threatened by "...the omnivorous consumption of nonrenewable resources, the irreversible destruction of habitats and species, the fouling of the air and seas, and consequent changes in climate, and many other effects of the growing human horde" (Browne, 1998, page F5). For example, in addition to the pressures exerted by the sheer facts of population growth, industrial technology and urbanization have resulted in people using 35 times as much water as they did 3 centuries ago and more than a billion people do not have access to clean drinking water (Stevens, 1998).

In *Beyond Malthus: Nineteen Dimensions of the Population Challenge*, Brown et al. (1999) analyzed, summarized, and predicted the consequences of overpopulation to the year 2050. Their 19 viewpoints, including grain production (Malthus' primary concern), fresh water, biodiversity, energy, fish catch, infectious disease, climate change, and urbanization all reveal severe problems in overrunning of the world's finite natural resources. In many cases, human per capita usage rates far exceed even the huge rates of population growth. For example, in the last half of the 20th century, global demand for energy multiplied more than five times — over twice as fast as population. The U.S., particularly, accounts for much of the increased per capita usage with "...nearly double that in other industrialized nations and over 13 times that in developing countries..." (page 47). Meanwhile: "Half the world's people are without access to sanitation and nearly this many — 2.7 billion — are without a reliable source of safe drinking water" (page 72).

Only 32 industrial countries have reached advanced or "stage three" development with population stabilization while in 160 "stage two" developing countries the birth rates remain high. But if world population continues its rapid growth, some relatively advanced countries will regress to "stage one" with accelerating death rates due to "demographic fatigue," the inability of their governments to deal effectively with the consequences of rapid population growth. Meanwhile, "...the resulting social stresses are likely to exacerbate conflicts among differing religious, ethnic, tribal, or geographic groups within societies" (page 124). Crowding, resource scarcity, and economic devastation readily promote scapegoating — the kind of destructive mentality that promotes deadly "ethnic cleansing."

Predictions of total world population by the year 2050 range from 7.3 to 10.7 billion, assuming that the decline in birth rates observed since the 1960s continues, with the lowest prediction predicated on couples having an average of only 1.6 children (Brown et al., 1999). Even the lowest prediction, considering the current level of resource destruction and deterioration and the accompanying effects on quality of life, gives a grim portrait. For example: "As developing countries prosper, they are also likely to use more materials just to provide basic services for their people. Nearly three fifths of the people in the developing world lack access to sanitation, a third do not have clean water, and a quarter live in inadequate housing" (Brown et al., 1999, page 78).

The harsh answer to this harsh assessment is that the ever-growing world population must be "trimmed" not only by the traditional means of war, famine, and disease (the only remedies Malthus first accepted in the original 1798 edition of his *An Essay on the Principle of Population*). According to this assessment, we need a yet greater rate of humanly instigated individually and group-perpetrated violence, including more wars and governments killing their own citizens. Accordingly, we are on the right path but moving too slowly; we would need to accelerate further the already accelerating rate of lethal violence.

While this assessment and answer to the population dilemma is based on what some might term "immutable realities" that govern human as well as animal populations, it can be argued that such a view takes inadequate account of our human capacity to change reality. The technological wizardry that has already produced astounding weapons of mass destruction has also conquered deadly diseases, provided better nutrition and shelter, and extended the human life span in much of the world.

Even so, the harsh realist can reassert the need for humanly instigated lethal violence. Conquering diseases and producing more food only means more people surviving and, on the average, surviving longer, thereby worsening the population problem. Therefore, according to the harsh realist or devil's advocate, our civilization needs to compensate for the escalating birth rate and the technological protections of life, including improved defenses against natural disasters. Taking this argument to its logical conclusion, we must further arm ourselves with the means of our own destruction and facilitate use of even more destructive weapons. Again, therefore, in this view our world civilization is proceeding in the right direction: we are not only presently continuing to escalate the rate at which humans kill humans, but by inventing and making available progressively more effective methods of individual and mass destruction we are contributing to the further critically needed increase in the human mortality rate.

The harsh view just outlined must be taken into account. It is factually based on objective studies of population expansion and control. Stated most simply, a population cannot long outgrow its food supply nor can it destroy the Earth's other myriad resources essential to sustaining human life for the more distant future. Competition for food is a law of nature governing all species, and humans, certainly more than other species, define their needs ever more grandly. Basic nutrition and shelter are not enough. With human power goes greater consumption of resources and products of all kinds. The human feeding frenzy extends the word "necessity" to a more and more luxurious lifestyle. Thus, in this view, what is commonly perceived as destructive may be regarded as constructive in the long run. International arms dealers, for example, who become wealthy by aiding and abetting needed reduction of the world's population and scaling back its standard of living, though seldom their own, are being constructive because they are performing a needed population control service. And the U.S. and France, as the world's leading exporters of weapons, deserve special credit as the most outstanding nations in supplying this method of population control.

But yet other considerations help to counter the harsh assessment. Let us assume that population control — perhaps achievable through what Malthus called in the 1803 second edition of his book "moral restaint" (see page 1675 of the *New Columbia Encyclopedia*) — is not only needed but feasible. Its feasibility is quite limited, however. In addition to general human disinclination to abstain from sexual intercourse and the attendant risk of conception, objections to any constriction on individual choice and freedom to procreate are abundant. For example, women's rights groups have objected and so has the Catholic church, albeit for rather different reasons.

But governments may accomplish by law what moral restraint cannot. In China, a couple is permitted only one child. In that case, however, human rights objections are clearly warranted because female newborns are often not only unwanted but "disposable," meaning poorly cared for, put up for adoption, or killed outright.

Probably the strongest and most feasible measure that preserves human rights is economic improvement of "underdeveloped countries." Such improvement tends to result in lower birth rates for reasons that are complex, including better health care and thus lower infant and child mortality. The explanation is linked to the tendency of a poor economy to be limited largely to simple forms of manual labor which often becomes the lot of children and women.

Where mass poverty persists, such as in undeveloped areas of Asia and Africa, high rates of procreation are "needed" to supply the labor force, especially when infant and child mortality is high, and women are seen almost exclusively in child-rearing and manual labor roles. In contrast, women in more advanced economies can be more financially productive, working in more sophisticated settings outside of the home. Ultimately, improving the status of women, including through enhancing their education and health, acts as a major factor in reducing population growth. "In every society for which data are available, the more education women have, the fewer children they have" (Brown et al., 1999, page 131).

Although economic development can greatly limit population growth, it must not be at the expense of overusing or wasting natural resources; otherwise, economic development will eventually make matters worse. More insidiously, while wars can be seen as effecting population control, both by directly killing people and causing famines such as those in Africa in recent decades, the "solution" they offer perpetuates a vicious cycle of destruction of resources, poverty, and higher rates of procreation.

Thus, *war and other forms of lethal violence contribute to, rather than solve, the dilemma of escalating overpopulation. The solution must include preventing lethal violence and sustaining life on Earth not only for humans but also for the immense but dangerously declining myriad other species of animals, vegetation, and other ecologically necessary supports.*

Clearly, the constructive mentality needed to solve the dilemma must be intelligent in the largest sense, by comprehending the past, calculating important trends, inferring the future, and discovering more about the Earth and forces outside the Earth than meets the unsophisticated eye. Just as clearly, constructive mentality requires good intentions. The same technologies that can preserve and enhance the Earth and life on it can be deliberately used constructively or destructively. Thus, intelligence and positive intent must be well integrated to guarantee constructive mentality.

Summary

Fundamental challenges for the 21st century are staying alive in the face of escalating lethal violence over the past three centuries, becoming awake to the subtleties of dehumanization, and finding solutions to the world population problem. Lethal violence in the 20th century dwarfs that of the two previous centuries. Our understanding of how to improve human relations has not kept up with our technologically advanced abilities to kill.

The motivation behind the short-circuiting of life, characteristic of destructive mentality, is a temporarily gratifying lessening of anxiety by providing an initially comforting reassurance: "I am dominant over death because I determine it. I am master over death, so death is not master over me." A glossary of modern euphemisms illustrates that denial of death is reflected and furthered in the burgeoning of euphemisms attending the marked cruelty of the 20th century. Covert destructive persuasion, crucial to effecting mass murder, is used by totalitarian regimes, but is also used in democracies as illustrated by the tobacco industry's public relations stategies.

Lethal behavior, including war, temporarily reduces the population but soon acts to increase population pressure by destroying the opportunity to advance to more prosperous economies with lower birth rates. Thus, lethal violence contributes to, rather than solves, the problem of escalating overpopulation. The solution to this urgent problem must include preventing lethal violence and sustaining life on Earth, not only for humans but also for the immense but dangerously declining myriad other species of animals, vegetation, and other ecologically necessary supports.

Bibliography

Brown, L.R., Gardner, G., and Halweil, B., *Beyond Malthus: Nineteen Dimensions of the Population Challenge,* New York: W.W. Norton, 1999, 168 pages.

A clear, concise account of the overriding dilemma of population growth and destruction of resources needed to sustain human life. The authors systematically relate population to grain production, fresh water, biodiversity, energy, oceanic fish catch, jobs, infectious disease, cropland, forests, housing, climate change, materials, urbanization, protected natural areas, education, waste, conflict, meat production, and income. They show how present and prospective runaway population growth, with attendant resource destruction, is killing and will increasingly kill humans as well as other animals and vital vegetation.

Becker, Ernest, *The Denial of Death,* New York: The Free Press, 1975, 315 pages.

Cultural anthropologist Becker's classic Pulitzer Prize-winning synthesis of thinking in many disciplines vital to understanding humanity's frightening confrontation with the mystery of life and death and the challenge of making the most of life, given that: "Creation is a nightmare spectacular taking place on a planet that has been soaked for hundreds of millions of years in the blood of all its creatures" (page 283). He suggested that humans will be less likely to poison the rest of creation if they live "in a condition of relative unrepression" (page 282) rather than trying to deny or forget.

Bernays, Edward L., *Biography of an Idea: Memoirs of Public Relations Counsel,* New York: Simon & Schuster, 1965, 849 pages.

A nephew of Sigmund Freud, Bernays applied his uncle's insights to selling products indirectly by assessing and changing public opinion. He used his talents in the service of a great variety of causes, including addicting people to cigarettes and, later, getting them to stop smoking, illustrating both destructive and constructive uses for his methods. Vigorous for most of his life, from 1891 to 1995, his autobiography spins a positive, industrious image of himself as the "father" of public relations, a nobler title than propagandist.

Tye, Larry, *The Father of Spin: Edward L. Bernays and the Birth of Public Relations,* New York: Crown Publishers, 1998, 306 pages.

This biography documents the destructive methods and effects of truth-bending and outright falsification as well as Bernay's constructive accomplishments. It is a well-documented depiction of mental manipulation methods Bernays applied variously to appeal to the best instincts of clients and consumers or "schemes he knew were wrong, and he willfully deceived the public" (page 53). Ironically, Nazi propaganda chief Joseph Goebbels read a Bernay's how-to book and used techniques nearly identical to Bernay's to make Jews the scapegoats and Hitler the embodiment of righteousness.

References

Alibek, K. and Handelman, S., *Biohazard: The Chilling True Story of the Largest Covert Biological Weapons Program in the World by the Man Who Ran it*, New York: Random House, 1999.

American Heritage Dictionary, 3rd ed., Boston: Houghton Mifflin, 1992.

Bearak, B., Sounding the alarm on deadly wells, *New York Times*, a special section, Faces, December 8, 1998, p. G9.

Becker, E., *The Denial of Death*, New York: The Free Press, 1973.

Bernays, E.L., *Biography of an Idea: Memoirs of Public Relations Counsel*, New York: Simon & Schuster, 1965.

Brown, L.R., Gardner, G., and Halweil, B., *Beyond Malthus: Nineteen Dimensions of the Population Challenge*, New York: W.W. Norton, 1999.

Browne, M., Will humans overwhelm the Earth? The debate continues, *New York Times*, December 8, 1998, p. F5.

Crystal, D., Ed., *The Cambridge Fact Finder*, 3rd ed., Cambridge: University of Cambridge Press, 1998.

Eisler, R., *Sacred Pleasure*, San Francisco: HarperCollins, 1996.

Hall, H., Collective violence: can we reframe our priorities in time? Introduction, in Hall, H. and Whitaker, L., Eds., *Collective Violence: Effective Strategies for Assessing and Intervening in Fatal Group and Institutional Aggression*, Boca Raton, FL, CRC Press, 1999, pp. xvii-xxiv.

Humes, J., *The Wit and Wisdom of Winston Churchill*, New York: HarperPerennial, 1994.

Medvedev, Z.A. and Medvedev, R.A., *A Question of Madness: Repression by Psychiatry in the Soviet Union*, New York: W.W. Norton, 1979.

Richardson, L., *Statistics of Deadly Quarrels*, Pacific Grove: CA: Boxwood Press, 1960.

Rosenbaum, R., *Explaining Hitler*, New York: Random House, 1998.

Rummel, R.J., *Death by Government*, New Brunswick, NJ: Transaction Publishers, 1997.

Stevens, W., Water: pushing the limits of an irreplaceable resource, *New York Times*, December 8, 1998, pp. G1, G7.

Thomas, E., *The Very Best Men*, New York: Simon & Schuster, 1995.

Tye, L., *The Father of Spin: Edward L. Bernays and the Birth of Public Relations*, New York: Crown Publishers, 1998.

Social Inducements to Paralethal and Lethal Violence

2

As long as people believe in absurdities they will continue to commit atrocities (Voltaire).

The purpose of this chapter is to develop understanding of social and interpersonal inducements to violence in the U.S. First, we must grasp the nature of the violence: what it consists of, what influences have formed it, how it is sustained, and where it is headed. Second, we have to motivate our society to stop denying the actual causal influences, by exposing the absurdities behind the denials and illusions. Third, we must counter and undermine the actual causal forces: the kinds of influences which, acting in concert with one another, conjointly result in various forms of morbidity capped by lethal violence. Fourth, we have to actively promote a societal orientation that is more nurturing, respectful, and life-enhancing.

The Violence Trend in the 20th Century

The fateful question for the human species seems to me to be whether and to what extent their cultural development will succeed in mastering the disturbance of their communal life by the human instinct of aggression and self-destruction (Sigmund Freud, 1856–1939).

By this criterion of cultural success, the U.S. has largely failed. We have become a world leader in both externalized and internalized forms of violence. Our externally directed violence leadership is epitomized by a higher murder rate than the vast majority of other Western or industrialized nations, and in our being the world's leading exporter of cigarettes, violence entertainment movies, and, together with France, weaponry. Our internally directed violence leadership is manifest in high rates of suicide, eating disorders, and drug dependencies. Our youth outdo the youth of most other nations in both externalized and internalized violence.

It may seem that not all of the phenomena just listed should appear in the category of violent behaviors, but violence perpetrators aid and abet one another by acting out and modeling morbidity. Accepting violence, however culturally acceptable the medium, means acceptance of violence simultaneously toward oneself and others. For example, "Although intense aggression toward others and suicide are often considered to represent very different problems, there is a surprisingly strong relationship between the two; violence-prone and assaultive adolescents are at much greater risk for suicidal behaviors" (Lore and Schultz, 1993, page 16). The two forms of violence — external and internal — are so closely intertwined that it is difficult to imagine how self-destructiveness cannot hurt others and vice versa. They must be considered together.

Though homicide rates in the U.S. have decreased somewhat in the '90s, they have been extremely high compared to other industrialized nations. Furthermore, the decrease has been accompanied by costly crime control measures, as will be discussed later.

In 1981, Isaac Asimov reported that "forty million Americans are murdered, maimed, raped, mugged, or robbed every year" (page 223). Our "civilized West" is the civilization in which a human being has been killed by others every 20 seconds in the half-century up to 1979, illegally or legally. This is three times the rate of the century preceding these 50 years (Asimov, page 222). The likelihood of being murdered in that part of the civilized West called the U.S. has been 7 to 10 times as high as in most European nations (Lore and Schultz, 1993). Lethal violence increased during the 1980s and early 1990s among youth as shown by the numbers of murderers and victims, according to the National Centers for Disease Control (Butterfield, 1994), whereas homicide arrest rates among males ages 15 to 19 went up 127% between 1985 and 1991, the rates for males ages 25 to 29 dropped 1%, and for ages 30 to 34 it dropped 13%. Consequently, males from ages 15 to 19 have became more likely than those in any other age group to be arrested for homicide. During the same period, 1985 to 1991, the annual rate at which 15- to 19-year-old males were being killed increased 154%, far exceeding the rate change for any other age group. Virtually all of this increase in youth homicide, 97%, has been directly associated with the use of guns.

Significantly, African American youths were more likely to be perpetrators and at least 10 times more likely to be victims, a fact the Centers for Disease Control hesitated to emphasize, perhaps to avoid fueling prejudicial interpretations. But, understanding causes requires disclosure of at least the major factors, of which racism is surely one.

Thus, the recent "violencing of America" is based largely on youth violence, most blatantly expressed in enormously increased youth homicide rates attributable to guns. In turn, this major increase in youth gun violence has been attributed to the coming of crack cocaine in the mid-1980s, when drug dealers put guns in the hands of teenagers assigned to enforce drug deals, especially in African American inner city ghettos characterized by poverty, poor education, and fatherlessness. But, as will be documented later in this chapter, our gun culture has been growing rapidly for many decades. Clearly, the gun culture has been appealing to our society overall, and is self-reinforcing as more guns are "needed" to protect us from "criminals with guns."

In addition, hate crimes, which include attacks on gays and various ethnic minorities, and often result in lethal violence, increased rapidly overall. A study by the New York City Gay and Lesbian Antiviolence Project showed an overall increase of 8% in reports of antigay attacks from 1993 to 1994, with 274 injured victims, including 9 homicides (Dunlap, 1995). In Pennsylvania, hate crimes increased by 130% from 1988 to 1993 (from 181 in 1988 to 1989 to 417 for 1992 to 1993) and preliminary data showed further escalation through 1994 (Moran, 1995). Youth were disproportionately represented, with 56% of the accused offenders and 37% of the victims being 11- to 20-year-olds. And though African Americans comprise only 9% of the state's population, they comprise 46% of the hate crime victims.

If American society at large is not suffering a greater homicide rate overall during the late 1990s, why is there such public concern? The concern is well founded. While the U.S. homicide rate fell in 1997 to its lowest rate in 30 years, gun killings by people 18 to 24 increased by 50% between 1980 and 1997 and people in that age group were also the most likely victims (Gun killings by young, 1999). Furthermore, the Justice Department figures omitted the even greater number of gun deaths through accidental shootings and suicides each year by people under 25 years old (Gun homicides by young people, 1999). Finally, youth violence has been reaching ever younger age groups. By 1988, 1 in 12 high school students had already attempted suicide and 1 in 4 had carried a weapon (Centers for Disease Control, 1992), and weapon carrying then increased further.

Because the future of any country is largely determined, sooner as well as later, by its youth, and the youth of our country are so inclined to violence, we can expect high rates of violence in our future. Violent youths tend to be violent adults and to raise violence-prone children.

Our society is not only affected by homicide, representing the most extreme morbidity, but by the vastly broader, more pervasive, and causally significant but less blatant phenomenon of "paralethal" violence: all those behaviors and influences, and their conjointly determined effects, that discourage the constructive, affirming, and nurturing orientations essential to a civilized society and to life itself. It represents the replacement of patient, hard-earned personal and social development, with facile destruction of our society for now, for the near future, and for generations to come.

Denials and Some "Solutions" that Contribute to Violence

Can't we safely avoid the admittedly arduous endeavor to understand the complexity of violence causation? Can't we react effectively by putting more money and effort into apparently simple "solutions" already at hand? No, because, as we shall see, the mentality behind the simple-minded solutions is too much like the fatally limited mentality of murderers themselves.

Let us consider, as examples, five reactive "solutions" to lethal violence: more and longer imprisonments; more death penalties; putting more police on the streets; allowing qualifying citizens to carry concealed weapons to protect themselves; and increasing use of corporal punishment, including as public spectacle.

More Prisoners

By 1995, we had already incarcerated nearly 1.5 million U.S. citizens, including over 1 million in prisons, and the others in jails and holding cells — a total of more than double the number of inmates just a decade before. While most inmates are males, female imprisonment rates rose 359% between 1974 and 1991 (Conn and Silverman, 1991). In contrast, Canada had only one fourth the U.S. imprisonment rate, while England and Wales had one fifth and Japan one fourteenth (Holmes, 1995). By 1991, the prison system had become the fastest growing sector of U.S. government employment and the cost of building a maximum security cell had risen to $50,000 — nearly the cost of the most expensive 4-year college education that year, and yet the chances that a murderer would never appear in a courtroom, let alone be imprisoned, were one in three (Conn and Silverman, 1991).

California provides an instructive example. In 1995, for the first time, our most populated state spent more on prisons than on its university systems which had been the pride of the state. Between 1980 and 1995 it built 17 new prisons and more than quintupled the number of prisoners from 23,511 to 126,140, and planned to build 15 more prisons by the year 2000. Between 1984 and 1999 California built 21 new penal institutions, a further acceleration compared to the 1980 to 1995 period (Egan, 1999).

By the year 2002, according to a Rand Corporation study (Butterfield, 1995b), if the "three strikes" law is implemented (mandating a prison sentence of 25 years to life for third-time offenders), the Department of Corrections will consume 18% of the California state budget, with only 1% left for the universities. At this rate, according to correction agency predictions, by the year 2027 California will have 401,000 convicts, more than the present convict population of all of Western Europe, Australia, Canada, Japan, and New Zealand combined. Now that the three-strikes law has been implemented, the cost of running the California system will soon be $4 billion a year (Egan, 1999).

Only lack of prison and jail space is preventing an even more rapid escalation of U.S. incarceration rates. What has been our society's response thus far? Arrest more criminals, build more prisons, hire more guards. In September 1994, President Clinton signed a $30 billion crime bill, including more than $10 billion to build new state and federal prisons. Has such a policy been effective in other countries? Russia, which has had a similar incarceration policy and the same incarceration trend and recent rate of incarceration failed to reduce its escalating crime. According to Vincent Schiraldi (1999), Director of the Justice Policy Institute in Washington, D.C., "The preponderance of research shows no connection between incarceration rates and crime rates" (*New York Times,* page A18).

By 1999, nearly 1 of every 150 people in the U.S. was in prison or jail, a figure much greater than for any other democracy. Soon, the number of U.S. prisoners will likely reach 2 million, almost double the number in 1990 and triple the number in 1980 (Egan, 1999). And, despite the fact that incarceration for drug crimes (often merely drug possession) has tripled in the past 15 years, drug use rates overall have not changed in the past 10 years but may have gone up among the young, including their use of heroin and methamphetamines. Meanwhile, it costs taxpayers at least $20,000 per year to feed and house each new inmate, not counting the cost of building new prisons and jails. Clearly, it would be far less expensive to pay for college educations than incarcerations but the "prison industrial complex" began to have a life of its own. Of course, prisons are educational institutions of a sort. Inmates are effectively trained in violent crime, including racist-motivated crime, as they learn from one another. We may be fostering more crime for the future, not only by present inmates but by their children.

As of 1999, 1.96 million children had a parent or other close relative incarcerated on any given day and another 5 million had parents who had been in jails or prisons or on probation or parole. Studies in the U.S. and England showed that about half of the incarcerated juveniles have a parent who has been incarcerated (Butterfield, 1999b). Thus, while the preponderance of research suggests that increasing incarceration rates does not reduce crime rates, the crime rate could eventually, in a generation or less, be increased by the influence of incarceration on children.

More Death Penalties

Advocates of the death penalty have managed to get legislatures to increase death penalty rates. Presumably, more applications of the death penalty will not only get rid of violent criminals but will make potential violent criminals think twice. But does the death penalty demonstrably reduce lethal violence? Not so far. Besides being enormously expensive, with an average of $20 million per case spent to kill the killer, the death penalty is hopelessly ineffective psychologically as a deterrent because those who commit lethal violence are almost never attuned to distant consequences. Even when perpetrators anticipate more immediate consequences, they may not feel they have anything to lose because the willingness to kill is often linked to suicide tendencies, shown most clearly in carefully planned terrorist-type "suicide attacks" with self-destruction built in, as well as when murderers take their own lives soon after murdering.

Furthermore, the death penalty is suspect in terms of fairness and justice as related to race. Though half of all citizens murdered each year in the U.S. are African American, an overwhelming 85% of convicted murderers executed since 1977 (the year of initiation of the modern era of capital punishment) had killed a White person, while only 11% had killed an African American (Eckholm, 1995). The General Accounting Office in Washington found in a 1990 review of 28 studies on race and the death penalty, that in 82% of the studies the race of the victim influenced the likelihood of the murderer being charged with capital murder or receiving the death penalty. "Other things being equal, the studies show, killers of white people are more likely to receive death sentences than killers of blacks." (Eckholm, 1995, page B4) Thus, we appear more ready to kill killers if they have killed White people than if they have killed African Americans. The resultant message is that White peoples' lives are more precious than the lives of African Americans.

Despite evidence that the death penalty is not a deterrent, more states have been enacting it into law. Governor Pataki, in March of 1995, made New York the 38th state with capital punishment. He declared in signing the death penalty bill, "It is a solemn moment because this is something aimed at preventing tragedy... And we've seen too many tragedies in the past" and added that the new law is "the most effective of its kind in the nation" (Dao, 1995, page A1). "The law took effect September 1, 1995 giving the state's district attorneys, most of whom had never handled death penalty prosecutions, 6 months to prepare for the enormous costs and technical problems of such cases" (Dao, 1995, page A1). The governor's claim that it will prevent tragedy may be politically expedient but oxymoronic: will it be the most effective of the ineffective measures? Even if it outstrips the other capital punishment laws by actually having at least some deterrent effect, can it possibly be cost effective?

Many death penalty supporters are not focusing on or claiming deterrence effectiveness. They talk "justice," meaning revenge. As one supporter said, "I'm a mother who's suffering every day. I have children at home who are suffering all the time for the loss of their brother. Number one, there has to be justice, and we talk about deterrence later" (as cited in Dao, 1995, page B5). While it is easy to empathize with this mother's feelings, when will our society, after such expense in time, money, and concern, get around to actual prevention instead of merely humoring a popular, but mistaken, opinion? As Winston Churchill put it, "Revenge is, of all satisfactions, the most costly and long drawn out; retroactive persecution is ... the most pernicious" (Humes, 1995, page 83).

On April 28, 1999 the United Nations Human Rights Commission (U.N. Panel Votes, 1999) voted heavily in favor of a worldwide moratorium on the death penalty. Twelve countries abstained. The U.S. and China, believed to be the most frequent users of capital punishment, voted no.

More Police

Surely, however, one can depend on the traditional tactic of "putting more cops on the street" to curtail crime. Police departments were established in this country more than 150 years ago. But no studies have shown convincingly that adding police officers lowers crime rates. Rather, the evidence from studies of this relationship in our cities show no effect, except perhaps to instill a false sense of security. A 1981 analysis of police beats in Newark, NJ, the most thorough study ever done, showed that foot patrols had virtually no effect on crime rates (Moran, 1995).

This is not to say that police forces do no good, but merely adding still more police may not help. We cannot expect the police, who are increasingly at risk as violence victims themselves, to solve a massive problem that cannot be attributed to them or their numbers. No matter how good a job they do, they cannot, by themselves, address the root causes of violence. They are kept mainly in reactive instead of preventive positions but are expected somehow to offset an ever-increasing supply of violent offenders who are obtaining more and more lethal weapons. But putting police into the community as part nurturers and part enforcers, rather like good parents, will probably help.

Our violence problem, however, is not really the fault of police who are increasingly being "out-weaponed." According to the Federal Bureau of Investigation (76 in Law Enforcement, 1995), 76 law enforcement officials were killed while on duty in 1994, 6 more than in 1993. All but one of the 1994 slayings was committed with a firearm, 6 officers were killed with their own weapon, and 33 of the officers were wearing body armor at the time they were slain.

Meanwhile, the attention of police has been aimed increasingly at "the War on Drugs," an essentially ineffective campaign in terms of drug use but one that has spawned even more arrests, incarcerations, and costs at the expense of education and other socially beneficial endeavors.

More Guns

By now, a large segment of our citizenry has concluded that police are not the answer, and has advocated not only arming themselves but also carrying concealed weapons. As Verhovek (1995, page A1) put it: "A powerful movement to allow ordinary citizens to obtain permits easily for carrying concealed weapons is taking hold across the country, a product of both the new Republican control of many state governments and of increasing fears that the police are incapable of protecting citizens from criminals." By 1995, 16 states had such legislation pending, and Texas, which already led the states in guns per capita, had passed such a bill. The U.S. has continued adding to its supply of 222 million guns already in circulation by 1994.

By December 1999, the last month of the 20th century, perhaps the most telling statistics of all about the mid-1990s gun craze came to more public attention. Wendy Cukier, a Toronto, Canada professor of justice studies noted "… that the U.S. had 3.5 times the number of firearms per capita as Canada and 3.6 times the number of deaths by firearms as Canada. The American rate for murder by firearms was 15 times higher than the Canadian rate." (Brooke, 1999) As Cukier concluded, it is extremely difficult to avoid the obvious; that these differences must be largely attributable to the greater availability of guns in the U.S. compared to Canada.

She concluded: "You are hard pressed to explain the difference in firearms deaths without touching on the availability of guns" (Brooke, 1999).

We know that the rapid rise of guns in circulation thus far is highly correlated with the rise of key forms of violence, especially youth violence and hate crimes, including murder and suicide. Just as the rise in murders among youth is highly correlated with gun availability, so is the rise of "successful " suicides in the young in contrast to the number of attempts, which is much more constant (Leary, 1995).

Furthermore, homicides have increased overall where concealed weapon restrictions have already been relaxed. Four out of five urban areas studied by the University of Maryland showed increases in killings by guns after laws were passed making it easier to carry concealed weapons (Killings said to rise, 1995). In Florida, after weapons laws were relaxed, the average monthly homicides committed with guns increased 3% in Miami, 22% in Tampa, and 74% in Jacksonville. Florida continued to have the highest crime rate in the nation and all of the cities studied in the state have shown higher rates of homicide with guns since the relaxed legislation took effect.

Of course, the theory is that only good citizens will be allowed to carry concealed weapons, but those weapons are likely to be as easily obtainable as a driver's license, which is obtainable by most violent and potentially violent persons, and the "good citizens" may include many who, having such a lethal weapon, will be more likely to react violently. If nothing else, this further arming of our citizenry may promote a despairing message, that all we can do as a society is to become armed and expect the worst from one another. Surely, that message will lead to an escalating war of nerves and greater societal distress.

That assumption — we can only rely on our own concealed weaponry — has already been popularized in our youth culture. High school students have experimented with weapon carrying, including for "self protection," and it doesn't work. According to the Centers for Disease Control (Newman, 1995), 1 in 10 high school students had carried a weapon to school and 1 in 14 had been threatened or injured in school. What is the mentality behind our persistent advocacy of freer access to weapons? Consider the following paragraph from reporter Maria Newman (1995): "At first, the two dozen or so students milling about outside Theodore Roosevelt High School in the Bronx agreed that schools need to be made safer. But in a few moments, swift as switchblades, the students produced a gleaming assortment of weapons" (page A1). Now envision the photograph that appeared beside it. Students are gathered around smiling and gleefully showing off their weapons which they easily smuggled into school. All of their weapons, they were proud to point out, were smuggled right through the school's metal detector. Isn't the message here that such expensive repressive measures will be met by successful undermining?

Now consider the above paragraph again, this time substituting adults for teenagers: "At first, the many legislators and the thousands of adult citizens lobbying in their legislatures agreed that society needs to be made safer. But in a few weeks, with hair-trigger swiftness, they produced a gleaming assortment of weapons." Now imagine a picture of a sample of such adults grinning with satisfaction as they display their vast assortment of guns for the camera, especially because they were able to smuggle them past the new weapon detectors developed by U.S. Justice Department grants from 1995 through 1997 (Butterfield, 1995a). Of course, the weapons in this case are not going to be mere switchblades, brass knuckles, or box cutters. They will be far more lethal and their carriers, licensed to conceal them on their persons or able to avoid surveillance, or both, will be far more numerous and mobile.

Meanwhile, inevitably, devices already invented during the Cold War with the USSR and now being adapted to surveillance uses in our own country have begun to be marketed. Pending permitting legislation, all concealed guns will be easily detectable using these devices. We have continued to produce an endless series of reactive countermeasures, all predicated on the despairing assumption that we cannot trust one another not to maim and kill. Thus have we become a nation at war with itself.

More Beatings

Sensing that present measures are not working, U.S. citizens and their legislators have mounted a growing movement, at both state and local levels, to institute beatings for convicted criminals, including making such corporal punishments into public spectacles (Copeland, 1995). By 1995, 23 states already allowed corporal punishment, and more severe versions were being suggested. Tennessee would command the county sheriff to administer floggings of from 1 to 15 strokes on the courthouse steps with a cane of a size and length determined by the state Supreme Court. Though such spectacles might entertain, much like public hangings used to and current television and movies do in growing abundance, and they might satisfy revenge thirst, there is no evidence that they would have a deterrent effect. Perhaps most importantly, society would be sending yet another message to the effect that, like the criminal, it does not wish to take real responsibility for thinking through the violence problem indigenous to its own influence, but instead will continue to act impulsively and to inflict violence much like ordinary violent criminals.

More imprisonments, death penalties, police, guns, and corporal punishment are measures sharing certain characteristics: they are emotionally appealing, simple-minded reactions already shown by studies to be far more likely to contribute to rather than resolve the violence problem. They mirror, mimic, and magnify, rather than counter, killers. If pursued further into our nation's future, they are likely to be ever more expensive financially, psychologically, and spiritually, and they will distract even more time, money, and energy which could be used constructively.

As distractions, the simple-minded reactive measures provide immediately gratifying diversions; they provide narcotic-like, illusory forms of relief from anxiety and anger that short-circuit needed understanding, planning, and truly helpful action. And, because they are so inadequate, expensive, and misleading, they result in more distress each year, adding to hopelessness and despair as we spend more, worry more, and perceive that our society has deteriorated.

Causal Influences

Why do we doggedly persist in devising and implementing measures that are disastrously counterproductive? What accounts for their immense popularity in the face of failures? The answer is not on the surface. We must look at these failures in terms of our deeper motivations. Do we design for failure? Psychiatrist Karl Menninger's (1968) words of wisdom from three decades ago still apply:

> The inescapable conclusion is that society secretly wants crime, needs crime and gains definite satisfactions from the present mishandling of it! We condemn crime; we punish offenders for it; but we need it. The crime and

punishment ritual is part of our lives. We need crimes to wonder at, to enjoy vicariously, to discuss and speculate about, and to publicly deplore. We need criminals to identify ourselves with, to secretly envy, and to strictly punish. Criminals represent our alter egos — our "bad" selves — rejected and projected. They do for us the forbidden, illegal things we wish to do and, like scapegoats of old, they bear the burdens of our displaced guilt and punishment" (*The Iniquities of Us All*, page 153).

Individuals who are guilty of outright criminal acts, but who deny that they have done wrong, are aided and abetted by a society which, neglectful of the nurturance needs of the young, is entertained by and often profits monetarily from murder and other crimes, but denies its facilitating role. Unless we cease *our* denial that disidentifies us with *our* criminals, we will surely never have enough jails, prisons, police, guards, security officers, locks, alarm systems, judges, lawyers, probation officers, emergency rooms, or as many or as destructive guns as we are told we need.

The O.J. Simpson Feeding Frenzy

The U.S. and much of the world was enthralled by the endless merchandising of the trial of athlete/actor/celebrity O.J. Simpson, who was accused of the brutal murders of his ex-wife and her male friend. Though such extreme attention was due, in part, to wanting to understand the law and how our courts work, the overwhelming interest has to be explained otherwise.

"The trial of the century," as it was touted, was immensely popular violence entertainment on television, in the press, and in books. Great amounts of money were being spent out of public coffers, and huge amounts have been garnered commercially. The trial and its offshoots became a vast public spectacle, a feeding frenzy for millions of spectators and at least thousands of entrepreneurs who cashed in by providing further titillation. The O.J. circus exceeded the wildest desires of a citizenry hungry for violence entertainment. As the Arts and Entertainment channel of cable television titled their special program about the O.J. case, the U.S. was "Merchandising Murder" (1995) with endless supplies of merchants and customers. A few other nations, at least, were reluctant to join in. Canada, which has only a fraction of our gun possession and murder rates, banned a popular tabloid-type television showing of "A Current Affair," which exploited the Simpson case. Perhaps we should have emulated our neighbor to the north! Apparently, our neighbor doesn't buy the standard tabloid mentality disclaimer: "We don't cause these things. We just reflect them." If the tabloid-type reporters were to view themselves in a mirror, they would see that their tabloid reflecting mirror is actually a magnifier of actual murder to the extent of at least 1 million portrayals to one actual murder, as is documented later in this chapter. Thus, as Menninger insisted, the causes of crime, lethal violence included, lie largely in our desire for it, our revelry in it, and our denial that we have anything to do with its causes.

Definitions and Denials of Responsibility

Lethal violence takes various forms, defined legally by the extent to which the form involves intent and justification. Vehicular homicide does not usually involve manifest intent to kill. War is usually justified as a societal decision and played out, rather like a game, within a certain set of rules. The forms are seldom pure, however. Sometimes, vehicular homicides or, more broadly, "accidental homicides," have conscious intent or at least an unwitting or unconscious motive. War typically is "justified" as a necessary expedient to avoid some greater destructiveness, but readily invites murder-minded participants motivated by egomania, greed, and destructiveness. As Voltaire said, "War is the greatest of all crimes; and yet there is no aggressor who does not color his crime with the pretext of justice" (from *The Ignorant Philosopher,* as cited in Seldes, 1978).

Generally, however, murder, without the cover of war is the paramount example of lethal violence because it is considered both clearly intentional and unjustified. Murder, defined legally as the unlawful killing of a human being by another with malice aforethought, is produced by an interplay of social, situational, and personal factors, none of which by themselves can explain it. Even a very defective or deranged person bent on murder must be aided and abetted by an opportune situation and a facilitating social context. Furthermore, the murderous tendency itself is the developmental culmination of paralethal interpersonal or social influences. Conversely, even an opportune situation and powerful social facilitation together do not guarantee a murderous act unless the would-be murderer has a personal proclivity to take another's life. For example, as discussed in Chapter 6, many courageous persons living under the Nazi regime risked their own lives to save Jews despite enormous social pressure and situational opportunity to kill Jews. *In essence, lethal violence is typically the end result of a momentous concerted coming together of destructive forces comprising social, situational, and personal influences, none of which by itself is adequate to cause it.*

But, both murderers and society at large almost always disavow responsibility. In my experience as a forensic psychologist interviewing and testing about 200 murderers, I have not seen any who really acknowledged responsibility or wrongdoing. (And Dr. Harold Hall, in a personal communication, has told me that none of the several thousand violent offenders he has evaluated thought he or she was "bad" because of their violence; most thought they did the right thing, or had no choice in the matter.)

In the vast majority of cases, the murderer talks about his or her crime in the third person as in, "I'm sorry *it* happened," rather than "I'm sorry *I* did it." Disavowal often goes even further, as in the case of the New York subway gunman who killed several people and injured many more but insisted at his trial in 1995 that he was "a humanitarian." (Perhaps this is the kind of person Mark Twain had in mind when he said that, if a man came to his door claiming he just wanted to do him good, he would run for his life.) Even when murderers acknowledge that they were actually agents in the murderous acts, they deny their real motivation and the actually destructive consequences in favor of attributing virtue to themselves. For example, hate crimes and even entire wars are usually buttressed with claims to save society, whether the agents are "Christian" skinheads saving us from the "Jewish menace" or an entire nation waging war to perform "ethnic cleansing."

At the very least, murderers do not acknowledge that they themselves did wrong. Even the murderer who expresses sorrow for *the* wrongdoing does not act as though it is *his* wrongdoing. For example, a young man called Adam, featured on a Sally Jesse Raphael (1995) television show, was quite clearly contrite about a brutal murder. But his attribution of causality in recalling his mental state at the time of the crime clears him of a mindful, intentional responsibility. Referring to his murderous beating of a man until his brains began to be disgorged from his skull, Adam said, "It just happened." This typical explanation or, more accurately, lack of explanation, expresses a deep-seated denial representative of the extremely passive, simple-minded, reactive mentality common to murderers and much of our societal propagation of violence. It represents our general agreement on a principle adhered to by those engaging in violent and paraviolent behaviors: lack of acknowledgment of causal responsibility coupled with simple-minded, not genuinely thinking responses of a reactive rather than reflective nature. And, as previously discussed, the denial is frequently topped off by rationalizations attributing virtue to the murderers. *The murderer and society aid and abet one another in this shared mentality of denial and pretentious claims to virtue.*

Legal Inducements to Violence

Contrary to popular perception, most inducements to violence are perpetrated legally. For example, pushers of legal drugs, including alcohol and tobacco, are responsible for vastly more deaths than crack cocaine pushers who are themselves notorious dealers in lethal drugs. Like the legal drug pushers, violence entertainment merchandisers disavow any harmful consequences of their actions. The following excerpt from Alexander Solzhenitsyn's 1978 Harvard University commencement speech has continued to be applicable:

Society has turned out to have scarce defense against the abyss of human decadence, for example against the misuse of liberty for moral violence against young people, such as motion pictures full of pornography, crime and horror. This is all considered to be part of freedom and to be counterbalanced, in theory, by young people's right not to look and not to accept. He concludes that we cannot rely on the legalistic organizations of life to defend against evil. (Solzhenitsyn, 1978).

It's the Rage: A Gun is Fun

In the U.S., gun promotion has proceeded at an ever more frenetic pace in recent decades, greatly outstripping gun possession rates in other nations. From 54 million guns in 1950, the number grew to 104 million in 1970 to 160 million in 1980 to 200 million by 1992 (Hollman and McCoy, 1992), and 222 million by 1994. We have come close to or may have passed the point of having at least one gun for every man, woman, and child in this country, and the guns have become more deadly. In the 1980s the gun industry introduced semiautomatic handguns, and in the late 1990s further increased the lethality of their weapons partly to offset the decline in hunting rifle sales, for example, marketing "pocket rockets" which are both more powerful and more easily concealed than older handguns (Butterfield, 1999a). Even in the face of increasing numbers of cities suing them, the gun industries are trying to increase their profits by enhancing lethality while disclaiming any responsibility for widespread criminal use.

Guns are widely and effectively advertised in direct fashion in regular advertising media, including magazines, and we see guns publicized by movies, television, newspapers, and novels. Even more strikingly, gun sales are also greatly stimulated by real-life news accounts of their destructive accomplishments. Such gun publicity spurs gun sales in a way that clearly shows the nature of their appeal. Violent entertainment models violent behaviors in fictional fashion while news accounts of actual, especially egregious, crimes provide real-life models. These real-life criminals who commit lethal violence quickly become heroes of a sort and the sales of whatever guns they used soar. Erik Larson (1993), noted that sales of the Mannlicker-Carcano rifle were undistinguished until Lee Harvey Oswald used it to assassinate President John F. Kennedy.

Even the murder of schoolchildren can increase sales. After Patrick Edward Purdy opened fire on a school yard in Stockton, California with an AK-47, sales of the gun and its knock-offs boomed. Prices quadrupled, to $1,500. Guns Unlimited felt the surge in demand. "I didn't sell an AK until Stockton in California; then everybody wanted one," James Dick said in a deposition (page 72).

> Our movies and TV shows do far more damage than simply enhancing the appeal of exotic weapons, however. They teach a uniquely American lesson: when a real man has a problem, he gets his gun. He slaps in a clip, he squints grimly into the hot noon sun, and then he does what he's gotta do (page 74).

Manufacturers, distributors, and sellers of guns have been supported enormously by money interests, including through the lobbying of legislators. Larson (1993) documented this collusion from his standpoint, that of a gun dealer. In showing how a gun became a murder weapon, he "provides a clear example of the culture of nonresponsibility prevailing in America's firearms industry; it is but one example of how their commercial ethos governed the gun's progress from conception to its use as a murder weapon in a Virginia Beach classroom" (Larson, page 50). The gun, the Cobray M-11/9 was advertised by its producer as "the gun that made the 80s roar."

During the 1990s the gun industry, together with the movie and television industries, made special efforts to put guns in the hands of women and children. The gun merchants massively produced, promoted, and marketed guns for women, including special guns designed to appeal especially to women (Herbert, 1994). Women have been especially active in lobbying for legislation permitting them to carry concealed weapons, and target ranges catering especially to women prospered, all with considerable support from the gun industry and violence entertainment. Though males were committing 88% of violent crimes in the U.S. (Miedzian, 1991), females have become more violent, a trend reflected by and seemingly endorsed by television. Women "in jeopardy" TV films and series are abetted by women who try to and do kill. According to CBS Vice President Peter Totorici, "…these programs were being produced in part because of success of reality-based shows coupled with the fact that women are the principal viewers of prime-time television" (Killer Women, 1992). The term "reality-based" is a euphemism for violence entertainment, similar to the euphemism "action picture." Meanwhile, gun merchants have seen a future in emphasizing the marketing of guns to youth, including through such public relations ploys as promoting target ranges especially targeted, as it were, at youth.

The Media and Violence Entertainment

Our society directly and indirectly fosters violence and helps develop violence-prone individuals in a great many direct (by commission) and indirect (by omission) ways that we deny. Most blatantly, our popular media culture spawns ubiquitous and innumerable sensational portrayals of violence which serve to train their audiences directly in paralethal and lethal violence. Television, movies, video games, sensationalistic magazines and newspapers, and many best-selling books sell themselves to consumers by appealing to violent proclivities. These wares are usually concocted to fit a well-known formula for commercial success: violence sells. The traditional tabloid newspapers follow the maxim, "if it bleeds it leads," meaning that gory violence is sure to be printed up in headline stories. In recent years, violence entertainment formulas have become more sophisticated, as will be discussed later.

But like murderers, the commercial violence pushers deny responsibility for contributing to violence, and often claim, much like the "humanist" New York mass murderer, that they are performing a socially valuable service. The industry's principal motivation by far is money. They know that "Violence is Golden" (Whitaker, 1993a).

Whereas television producers often claim that their shows merely reflect real-life violence and therefore are "reality-based," consider that the average 18-year-old has already seen 200,000 portrayals of murder as television entertainment but only about one in three 18-year-olds has witnessed an actual murder. Thus youths experience a ratio of 600,000:1 or a rate of 600,000 television show murders for every real-life murder directly experienced. Now add, to the left-hand side of this equation, television news of murders, news of homicides "justified" by war, movie murder portrayals, publications of newspaper and magazine accounts of murder, mystery and war stories, and, not least, the murders depicted in video games. Then the ratio is probably at least 1,000,000:1 or an average of 1 million portayals of murder for each murder experienced in real life by the age of 18. Yet, even this equation does not take into account the considerable trend toward more gruesome kinds of murder or include the far more numerous paralethal violence behaviors, short of murder, that are portrayed. These and many other considerations, to be discussed in this chapter, lead to the conclusion that popular culture, especially in the form of violence entertainment, also greatly fosters rather than merely reflects lethal violence.

We are confronted with violence portrayals nearly everywhere everyday. We see violence sensationalized and therefore promoted in most large- and small-screen presentations, throughout newspapers and magazines, on billboards, in a large percentage of best-selling books, and in the continuing proliferation of gun stores, and we hear it in the lyrics and strident beat of popular music. Meanwhile, the violence entertainment promoters deny any causal link between their commercial wares and our society's violence megatrend, just as the cigarette industry denied — still denies — any causal link between cigarettes and the diseases and early deaths with which they are so intrinsically associated. Their denial may or may not be witting, but that leaves only two possibilities. Either they know they are lying or they have deluded themselves. A previous spokesperson for the tobacco industry, who was dying of lung cancer and backing the nation's toughest antismoking bill

(Moss, 1995) asserted in a television interview that people in the tobacco industry actually do not believe in the vast aggregation of scientific evidence that cigarettes kill. In either case, it remains imperative to persist in disabusing as many people as possible of the insupportable claim that cigarettes are not addictive and lethal.

The combination of ubiquitous big- and little-screen violent entertainment heroes and publicity about actual murder heroes, all brandishing guns in macho exhibitionistic displays of power, trains especially impressionable young people to obtain and use guns, all the while telling them it's desirable behavior. Thus, our society supplies massive amounts of violent entertainment, drugs, guns, and various other methods for aggressing against others and oneself. These supplies must be in great demand by great masses of consumers, as illustrated in the next section of this chapter.

A Night at the Movies: Popcorn, Soda, and Splattered Brains

"Over 70 Critics Agree *Pulp Fiction* is the Best Film of the Year!" said a *New York Times* ad that I saw for many days (e.g., March 14, 1995). The ad boasted that this film has gotten seven academy award nominations, including one for best picture. Critic Janet Maslin called it "a stunning vision of destiny, choice and spiritual possibility!" and "a work of depth, wit and blazing originality." As a picture, it was nominated for the "comedy" category.

My wife and I went to a local showing of this "hilarious adventure" on a Saturday night in March, me with my clipboard and pad in an effort to experience the movie and audience reactions firsthand. Here's a condensed account of my experience.

Theater crowded but got good seats. Older woman by herself on my left. Each seat is equipped with a drink holder for sodas and most patrons have a soda and/or popcorn by now. The entertainment begins with a preview of *Tank Girl* consisting entirely of scenes of a woman who sadistically relishes perpetrating various sensational acts of violence. (I am reminded of the initiative taken by the television and movie industries in the summer of 1994 "to put more weapons in the hands of women.")

Pulp Fiction begins. Setting is Los Angeles (same as O.J. trial). Dictionary definition given on the screen: pulp fiction means it is lurid and the paper it is printed on is crude. Hatred of Jews, it's us or them, and readiness to risk others' lives and their own is the personal orientation of a man and a woman in early restaurant scene, where he talks about the anticipated ease of holding up people there in contrast to the difficulty of robbing banks.

Quickly, a shift to actors John Travolta and Samuel Jackson, the latter playing a bullying African American with a big gun. He casually kills one young man while questioning another (loud laughter response from many people in the audience) and further directly terrifies another man. Two other men are then killed. (Meanwhile, the older woman to my left says, in a voice loud and distinct enough to be heard by a dozen or so people around us, "Get a vocabulary!" which is her reaction to the preponderance of s... and f... words in the admittedly limited vocabulary of Travolta and Jackson.) My strong impulse 10 minutes into this movie is to leave with or without a refund. But I stay with this self-chosen assignment and continue writing in the dark.

Next, a boxer (played by Bruce Willis) near the end of a career in which he almost made it to the top of his brain-damaging "sport," is told threateningly that he must "go down in the fifth" so that bets can be rigged.

Next, we see a drug dealer and his girlfriend in residence; she is proud that her erogenous zones including lips, nipples, and clitoris are pierced to hold jewelry. Casual morbidity is clearly the sustaining theme by now, with no relief in sight. John Travolta (nominated for best actor in this role) is there to purchase "high quality" cocaine which he administers to himself right there. He leaves to keep an obligation to take care of a woman (played by Uma Thurman) at the request of her husband. At her suggestion, they go to dinner at a restaurant/club featuring personnel who impersonate entertainment celebrities. She uses cocaine in the ladies room and they then win a dance contest and go to her place. While Travolta is in the bathroom, she gives herself what she thinks is more cocaine, bleeds and is immediately near death. Travolta takes her, against the drug dealer's protests, to the latter's apartment where the dying woman is viewed with no caring whatever by two women there, but comes back to life when Travolta stabs her in the heart with adrenaline. Arriving back at her place, she is nonemotional except she does want to tell him a joke about a mama tomato who squeezes one of her little tomato children because the child is lagging behind, whereupon the child turns into ketchup — get it!

Butch the boxer lays bets that he will win, then beats his opponent who soon dies. He escapes in a cab driven by a pretty young woman from Columbia who repeatedly, sadistically, wants to hear how it *feels* to beat a man to death. On arriving at a motel to pick up his girlfriend, he learns that the watch handed down to him via his grandfather and father has been left behind. Butch goes to retrieve it, sees Vincent (Travolta) emerging from the bathroom and blows him away with Vincent's own huge gun.

Butch, still using his girlfriend's car, runs over the hit man who was looking for him, then totals the car, and goes into a firearms store emblazoned with a Confederate flag, and he is then caught prisoner, together with the injured hit man, by the owner who calls a police officer who turns out to be even more actively sadistic than the owner. The officer forcefully sodomizes the African American hit man who is then saved by the escaped Butch, who then collects his girlfriend, who can only have sex if the television is turned on loud to a war film.

For quite a while now the 20- or so year-old man sitting right behind me has been laughing uproariously at each sadistic event and pressing his knees spasmodically against the back of my seat. By this time he is joined in loud laughter by the young woman sitting next to him and many, but not a majority, of the audience. Lots of popcorn and sodas have been consumed throughout the theater. I try to take on a Zen-like orientation suited to observing without reacting to this provocation. I have given up hope that the movie will have any comic richness.

Hawkins is driving car with Travolta in front passenger seat holding his big gun casually pointed at a young African American man in back seat. Mistake. Gun goes off and the young man's head is blown apart, splattering his brains throughout the back-seat area. Travolta says that they may have hit a bump, causing gun to go off. They proceed anxiously to disengage themselves from possible detection, soon enlisting a man who specializes in getting rid of unwelcome bodies by using a car graveyard run by his woman friend. The man is very clever and efficient, thereby exciting admiration in Travolta and Hawkins despite their unpleasant cleanup work which he has them do. Hawkins discovers an injustice in that he, rather than Travolta, is cleaning up the brain-splattered back-seat area while Travolta only has to clean up other splatterings of blood and flesh in the front-seat area.

Finally, about two hours into this movie, we are back at the original restaurant scene with the young man and woman about to rob the customers and manager. It ends with an epiphany. Hawkins manages to use his gangster talents to abort the robbery and sends off the couple with $1500 of his own (illicitly gained) money; this after a personal, spiritual revelation of the true message contained in a Bible passage he has used many times previously to terrorize people. Thus we have a happy ending, complete with blazing message of free choice and redemption.

The theater lights go on. The popcorn and sodas have been consumed along with an orgy of violence entertainment made more innocent by a Hollywood-style saving grace. I do not have the impression that anything constructive has been learned by the audience though I am assured by critic Janet Maslin that "Quentin Tarrantino's film refutes the idea that drifting passively is a good way to fulfill one's destiny and to get through life" (frequently repeated ad in *New York Times* in 1995).

I am puzzled as to how Travolta, once killed, is alive and active at the end, but this is just a flashback. The woman on my left is also puzzled and she asks me how that can be. I tell her it is an earlier scene presented at the end. (I realize that this flashback gives the impression that Travolta is really alive despite having been killed. It reminds me of the childhood game: "Bang, you're dead. Now, get up." In other words, death is not for real and such violence is harmless.)

The woman on my left now says she is 67, the mother of five, and a grandmother. She looks much younger. She says she came to see this movie because she likes John Travolta and likes to go to the movies and had recently enjoyed the movie *Roommates* with Peter Falk. She found it "strange" that people laughed during the violent scenes in *Pulp Fiction* and says, "In my day people were taught to love, but it's different now." I replied, "Yes, it is."

On March 26, 1995 CNN television featured interviews with various people associated with *Pulp Fiction*. No one found anything objectionable about the film. After all, it won best picture at the Cannes Film Festival, and it was making enormous amounts of money for everyone associated with it. It is called "utterly original and humorous." Writer-director Tarrantino proudly talked of his ability to get the audience to like the male protagonists even though they are introduced right at the beginning of the film killing other men in cold blood — men "who weren't threatening them," Tarrantino emphasizes. Yet the audience likes these men; they even "love" them throughout the film. The artistic achievement, apparently, is to get people to like or even love evil people, and probably to model themselves after these ego ideals.

The newest movie genre fits a formula that studiously melds sex, violence, and "humor" so that one inevitably evokes the others. There is no sex without violence and no sex-violence without a pass at humor. It's sadomasochism presented "with a light side" and, often, no longer even with a claim to any saving grace, unless "artistic" cleverness qualifies as a compensating accomplishment. It's just for fun. *Naked Killer* is a recent example, incorporating women as the sadistic protagonists. A reviewer described this movie from Hong Kong as an amusing action-adventure spoof:

> ...sexy lesbian avengers executing quadruple leaping somersaults in a deadly assault against the opposite sex. Their campaign of assassination involves not only murder, but castration and genital mutilation as well. ...it must be counted as some sort of accomplishment that *Naked Killer* can treat its subject so lightly that the sex and violence seem as innocent and playful as an extended pillow fight (Holden, 1995, page C8).

Since when is it harmless to treat murder and genital mutilation as "an artistic triumph," as if these atrocities were nothing more than a pillow fight? What is being programmed into the minds of viewers? When does nothing but style matter? Isn't this the ancient art of sophistry, an argument that is correct in form and appearance but is actually invalid, an argument used for deception and the display of intellectual brilliance? Isn't this old-fashioned con artistry slickly done with modern means? And isn't the result much more insidious than if we were lied to less expertly?

I had written about the two movies, discussed above, just before going to bed for the night, wondering about what effects such material really has on peoples' psyches. Ostensibly, both movies are harmless spoofs. Maybe other people have very different deep affective consequences from mine. The following dream made mine clear.

I was on a crude field-like area. Long columns of men and women, two or three abreast, were walking like prisoners along the rim of a long ditch wide enough to hold their bodies should they fall or be pushed in. They appeared drab, resigned, and nearly lifeless, about 10 or 15 to a group, each group in a column like the people along the ditch. But, apart from these long columns, I saw small groups of men who were not yet fully arranged, as it were; they were merely sitting or standing idly instead of forming a long, trudging column like the men and women along the ditch. These men were talking casually among themselves, their ranks still askew in relation to the prisoners.

Then a lone, official-looking man appeared, prepared to shackle the men whose group I was closest to. I advised the men in this group that they were going to lose their freedom if they conformed to the demand made on them. I knew that, if they resisted, the official would summon his confederates who would try collectively to shackle one group at a time. But these men were apathetic and let themselves be shackled by the lone official. I now considered escaping from the field and finding allies to help me return to the field in a further effort to free the now newly shackled men. But then I saw that the men had no apparent desire to be free. I woke up with a sense of despair. I was reminded of an incident at a wedding I attended at the Congressional Country Club, where guests were invited to give advice to the bride and groom for their future together. A man stood up and, advising the entire group, as it were, said, "Be careful about what you put into your brains; be careful about watching television and movies."

But the question remains. Is our culture now really so pervaded with the lurid tabloid mentality that there are no safe havens? Two weeks after seeing *Pulp Fiction*, my wife and I searched hard and successfully for a film that was life-enhancing. We went to a select theater in Philadelphia and saw *The Secret of Roan Inish*, a film made in Ireland that features an orphaned 12-year-old-girl's experience as related to a Gaelic folk myth based on a children's' novel. It was really about love, that four-letter word which has a substance usually avoided now by Hollywood, though *Forrest Gump* did win the Oscar for best picture that year. When *The Secret of Roan Inish* "…was shown at the Philadelphia Festival of World Cinema last May, the children in the audience seemed to be mesmerized. Even the adults were quiet and well-behaved." (*Ritz Film Bill*, 1995, page 15).

The same Film Bill, however, gleefully announced the revival of *Faster, Pussycat! Kill! Kill!*, a 1966 "masterpiece" of "a Gothic melodrama centering around a gang of three psychotic go-go dancers and their thirst for violence…" and featuring their atrocities against "a young 'all American' couple who try to make friends." One of the lithesome threesome kills the young man after humiliating him. The threesome then go off, with his girlfriend as hostage, committing more atrocities featuring "a series of amazing scenes of seduction, scheming and action … culminating in a hellacious climax of catfights, rage and revenge, *and* one of the most entertaining B-movies ever made" (Schut, 1995, page 30). Thus, even the best of the movie houses merchandise morbidity.

Though this movie ran at only one theater, it was given a full newspaper review and a three-star rating (Rickey, 1995). "The virtue of the film is that … (it) … can be enjoyed either as the embodiments of male sexual fantasy (tough women built like marshmallow-soft centerfolds) or as female power made flesh. Or both" (page 5). "This movie leaves you so giddy it should be a controlled substance" (page 14). Yes, violence can become addictive.

Parties to the Sadomasochistic Violence-Addiction Contract

It should be no surprise that other countries are not only buying violence entertainment films from the U.S. but are making their own versions and selling them to the U.S. Thus, films like *Naked Killer*, made in Hong Kong, follows the Hollywood formula precisely. Nor is our dedicated, incessant cultivation of the violence mentality, now emphatic for women and children as well as men, limited to the tabloids, television, and movie making. What goes around does come around. We have made violence fashionable. As stated by Spindler (1995) in her Paris, March 15 column for an underground fashion newspaper distributed on the first day of the ready-to-wear shows for women, had as its opening piece a list of Paris' six most popular films:

> *Natural Born Killers, Pulp Fiction, Interview with the Vampire, True Romance, Serial Mom,* and *Reservoir Dogs.* Calling attention to their shared violence, the newspaper … asks: "New reality or fashionable attitude?" (page C13)

Like the columnist, Amy Spindler, I think both. The new Paris fashion designers for women propose tough, masculine, dangerous-looking clothes that are indistinguishable from men's to effect a camaraderie like that among gangsters. "...those sadomasochistic trappings have become such a common touchstone in fashion that they no longer shock" (Spindler, 1995, page 13). Meanwhile, what has happened to the Paris famous as a world center of high culture?

Product Formulation

How can our violence entertainment industries be so effective? How have we achieved leadership in drug use, violence entertainment, and lethal violence? What formulas, overt or covert, might there be for addicting people to sado-masochistic violence? The knowledge base for addicting people to violence is extensive and has proven formulas. Let's begin with a modern version that sells, "action movies."

As the U.S. simultaneously neglected its youth in recent decades and massively modeled violence and drug addictions for them, and complained of the results, we further increased our national debt and foreign trade deficit. Not coincidentally, as we became the world's greatest debtor nation we resorted to tactics well known to drug pushers. We strove hard to addict others as well as ourselves to whatever we could sell, with little or no thought about the moral and physical violence we have been and are continuing to perpetrate. The theme common to these phenomena is living impulsively in the present and thinking little about the future, particularly for our neglected youth who are becoming saddled with the national debt and adult-inculcated spiritual bankruptcy.

Anne Thompson (1988) noted the escalation of "action films," from strictly B-flick staples, that the "actioners" have been jazzed up by the studios for mass consumption. According to James Jacks, a Universal Studios acquisition executive, "Action pictures play perfectly to the TV generation" (as quoted by Thompson, page 1 F). These movies became hot exports as well as pleasers of the masses in this country, and were enormously profitable despite their extreme cost, exemplified by *Rambo III* costing nearly $60 million.

The close relationship between our violence culture and the drugging of America is evident in the fact that violence, like drugs, must be provided in ever larger doses to satisfy the consumer addict. In the words of James Glickenhaus (as quoted in Thompson, 1988), who directed *The Exterminator,* and *The Soldier,* he and other children played cops and robbers and cowboys and Indians, but in the modern action picture the viewer gets to

… wreck a lot of stuff and shoot people like you can't in real life. You have to end with a bang. If the beginning of a film is exciting, you have to top that. The more people get, the more they want (page 1F).

Serial killer Ted Bundy, who sadistically murdered more than 20 innocent women, gave eloquent testimony to the power of criminal training in the perverse monomaniacal contamination of sexuality with violence in our popular culture (Bundy Says, 1989). He noted that he gradually became addicted to

… pornography that deals on a violent level with sexuality … I would keep looking for more potent, more explicit, more graphic kinds of material … you begin to wonder if maybe actually doing it would give you that which is beyond just reading it or looking at it (page 4A).

Though Bundy's particular childhood experiences inevitably account for much of his adult personality, he said he found added inspiration from our culture's violence panderers. Most people exposed to pornography (the contamination of sex with violence) will not become killers, but they may tend to become more disrespectful and thus contribute to the mountain of paraviolence attitudes and behaviors that are capped by lethal violence.

Beguiling the Buyer

To take full effect, however, the sadomasochistic contract has to be agreed upon by all parties. The contract comes with a solid death-time guarantee: if fully executed according to instructions, the contract ensures destruction of all of the parties, whether they have been actively or passively agreeing. Those who do not die physically die spiritually.

Obtaining passive, nonthinking agreement is crucial for selling the contract. I thought about Erich Fromm's book *Escape from Freedom* (1969) which shows with deep insight how evil emanates from people's failure to accept responsibility for freedom. Fromm's initial purpose was to understand how the Nazis could tyrannize the world. The answer was that Hitler had not only powerful active help, but, just as importantly, deep-seated passive collusion from people everywhere, at least until they finally woke up many years after his tyranny became clear. Hitler appealed to the worst in people and there was plenty of that.

Hitler knew just what to do. His methods were based on an already sophisticated psychological science of propaganda, including what was known about hypnotism. He studied the tried and true propaganda methods to propagate his own credo. For example, he assembled great masses of people 'oward the end of the day, kept them standing when or until they were tired and ready to be passive, addressed them stridently while they were all facing him instead of one another, and then appealed to their weakness in the name of power, inducing and seducing them into manic idolatry: "Heil Hitler, Heil Hitler, Heil Hitler." His audiences grew, as even whole nations gave in and other nations wavered, tempted by the easy pleasures of scapegoating their "inferiors" so as to feel powerful and virtuous themselves. Yet, how could he have made so many intelligent people believe such great lies? Hitler knew his lies had to be huge and uncompromising, the opposite of the humble truths that the people did not want to believe. He declared, "The great masses of the people ... will more easily fall victims to a big lie than to a small one" (Kaplan, 1992, page 676).

Winston Churchill, that most indomitable enemy of tyranny in general and Hitler in particular, sized up his enemy well. Churchill understood that Hitler had not only to be produced by social and interpersonal influences but, to be successfully demonic on a large scale, had to fill a big power void. Churchill (as cited by Humes, 1995, page 154) stated:

Into that void strode a maniac of ferocious genius of the most virulent hatred that has ever corroded the human breast ... Corporal Hitler. This wicked man, the repository and embodiment of many forms of soul-destroying hatred, the monstrous product of former wrongs and shames.

The phenomenon of Hitler and the Nazis is discussed more fully in Chapter 5.

People who do not feel they are leading meaningful, empowered lives are ready to be drawn into cult forms of behavior that easily deteriorate into violence. As psychiatrist Arthur Deikman explained in his book *The Wrong Way Home* (1990), cults are not limited simply to what we are used to calling cults. They exist in often subtle group allegiances characterized by compliance with the group, dependence on a leader, devaluing the outsider, and avoiding dissent. Whether expressed as membership in the Nazi party, street gangs, the Ku Klux Klan, college fraternities, or even business and professional groups, members may be called upon to commit atrocities in the name of group allegiance, and for what the group calls virtue. Even more broadly, suggestible individuals do not even have to be members of an organization as such to be persuaded by group pressure to buy into clearly self-destructive and other-destructive practices in conformity with social myths, especially if the propaganda is expertly engineered by advertisers or public relations professionals.

Trickery, in one form or another, is a necessary method to employ at the very beginning to sell addictions, whether to cigarettes, alcohol or other drugs, memberships in gangs and other cults, or directly violent behaviors. For example, in March, 1995 the Japanese cult Aum Shinrikyo (Supreme

Truth), was found to possess vast supplies of death-dealing nerve gas ingredients, but denied responsibility for the mass nerve gas attack on Tokyo subway system. Then, Supreme Truth was found to advise supreme lying. The Japanese press reported an Aum secret recruitment handbook which instructs members in the ideal way to befriend an unwitting, potential recruit who doesn't know of the first person's Aum affiliation.

> ...and then a third person acting as an Aum representative invites them both to a sect program.
>   The covert Aum member responds enthusiastically, and the "friends" go together to a few Aum activities. All the time, the secret Aum member suggests that they both become more involved in the sect (Kristof, 1995).

Aum is discussed more fully in Chapter 3.

All addiction cultivation and the violence toward oneself and others that it inevitably brings, is predicated on lies. Atrocities do arise from absurdities as the French philosopher Voltaire insisted. Many perfectly legal, well-educated, "respectable" groups of people can and do play these cheap tricks. Such legal evil, expertly executed, and so incalculably insidious, is vastly profitable to the pushers who reap money, prestige, and power.

But how, exactly, do even "otherwise intelligent and thoughtful" people buy into addictions? The pushers do their best to get the buyer not to think, to try to ensure that actual active thinking will be preempted, much as it is in schizophrenic disorders (Whitaker, 1980, 1992). Schizophrenic thought disorder is simultaneously illogical, unwitting, and impaired. But, whereas false premises and illogicality may occur in schizophrenic persons without someone trying right then and there to induce it, the bypassing or short-circuiting of rational thinking is deliberately induced by pushers. The pusher's mission is to get the potential buyer's attention while making sure to short-circuit the buyer's tendency to think, especially to think critically. Usually, therefore, the buyer is approached on the simpler cognitive levels of sensation or perception; that is, below the level of thinking.

Thus, impulsive cognitive style represents the opposite of the responsible educational process which teaches the entire cognitive sequence that deserves the name "thinking," the active, critical process enabling both inhibiting unwarranted actions and taking *deliberate, actively wished-for actions*. As Shapiro noted, impulsive cognitive style is captured in the doer's nonexplanation: "I just *did* it — I don't know why" (Shapiro, 1965, page 135). In this style, thinking per se is short-circuited. The person really wasn't thinking. The common motto in impulsive cognitive style is simply accepting the impulse to "just do it!" In other words, "Don't think; just act!" The denial of the need to think is conveyed by the beer ad: "Why ask why?"

Social Structure and Dynamics of Paralethal Violence

Now, let us examine the social and dynamic structure of paralethal violence and then, within the causal paradigm, the nature of current youth culture and its determiners, with a view to how we as a society have produced and continue to produce it and — in the last section of this chapter — how we can counter lethal and paralethal violence.

Lethal Violence Causality and the Second Cybernetics

Lethal violence is the end result of many interacting, often synergistic, personal, social, and situational factors, each of which by itself is insufficient to produce lethal violence. Indeed, these factors, considered individually, are never enough to produce any form of violent behavior, let alone lethal violence. But, each by itself can be excused readily by its defenders, who serve to benefit at the expense of its victims.

For example, consider the situational factor defined as availability of a gun, which is necessary but not sufficient in murders committed with a gun; a gun cannot by itself explain any violent act, let alone lethal violence. But it is, of course, a powerful potentiating factor in violence, and a gun makes possible a lethal degree of violence. The well-known aphorism offered by people who would protect the right to bear arms, that "guns don't kill people, people do" recognizes that guns by themselves never have and never will kill anyone, while implicitly denying that guns are an extremely potentiating and enabling factor in the necessary mingling of paralethal influences.

Similarly, consider the factor of violence entertainment. Those who would deny its influence claim, with some evidence, that violence entertainment in movies, television, videos, magazines, books, and other communication media cannot (fully) explain why murders are committed. Yet, such a serial killer as Ted Bundy (Whitaker, 1990) has explained the important role violence depictions played in his increasingly murderous personal development. Thus, it is true, as its defenders claim, that violence entertainment definitely cannot (by itself) explain murder, that in fact only individuals who are already of a murderous personality proclivity would relate to violence depictions by behaving murderously. How can we conceptualize the causality of lethal violence in terms of this evident reality of mutually causative factors, in contrast to denying their causal influence by compartmentalizing them and taking them out of context?

We can consider any pattern of causally relevant factors as a gestalt: a structure or configuration of physical, biological, or psychological phenomena so integrated as to constitute a functional unit with properties not derivable from its parts in summation (*Webster's Third New International Dictionary*, 1966). A gestalt or functional unit may have, at any given time, equilibrating or deviation-enhancing causality. Such causality can be understood in terms of cybernetics: the well-established comparative study of the automatic control system formed by the nervous system and brain and by mechano-electrical communication systems and devices (as computing machines, thermostats, photoelectric sorters) (*Webster's Third New International Dictionary*, 1966).

We usually think of cybernetics as a science of self-regulating systems that are equilibrating, such as thermostats which maintain a constant temperature by registering and countering deviations from that temperature. But a particular gestalt or system of mutually causative factors may be deviation-amplifying, as in the processes loosely called "vicious circles" and "compound interests." Maruyama (1963) conceptualized these deviation-amplifying processes in terms of the "second cybernetics."

The first cybernetics helps to explain some phenomena pertinent to the causal structure and dynamics of paralethal and lethal violence, such as the maintenance of poverty, racism, poor education, and unemployment, because these four conditions tend to mutually maintain themselves and each other. The second cybernetics helps to explain the deviation-amplification that characterizes acceleration toward lethal violence. In these cases, an increase in factor A tends to increase factor B which, by being increased, increases factor A.

A simple exercise illustrates the difference between first vs. second cybernetics. Your task is to stand on one foot. First, try to maintain this position while fixing your gaze precisely on a nearby reference point, say, 5 feet away. If you carefully maintain your focus on this reference point, e.g., the exact corner of a table, you will probably find it relatively easy not to lose your balance. Now, standing on only one foot again, try to keep your balance while shifting your gaze about, e.g., from the table corner to an armchair, and then to the wall, so that your reference point varies in distance and location. You will probably find it much more difficult to keep your balance this time. Changing one factor induces change in a second which then induces further change in the first.

Deviation amplification (Figure 2.1) may be favorable or unfavorable in terms of violence. It may be favorable, e.g., when a positive father becomes involved in his family and in child-rearing. The more nurturing and dependable the father, the more inclined the child may be to pursue education. In turn, the father can now respond with further nurturance as he rewards the child's effort. Or, using this simple configuration again, a father's withdrawal may cause his child to lose interest in school, whereupon the father may retreat further, and so on.

The factors involved in lethal violence causation are usually more numerous. Consider the common gestalt of: fatherlessness; protest masculinity; drug use; violence entertainment; and gun availability. Applying the second

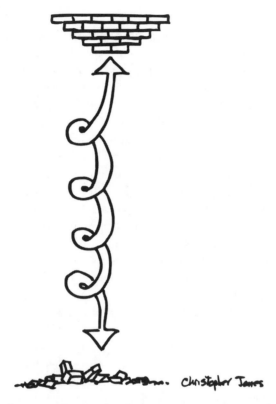

FIGURE 2.1 The Second Law of Cybernetics: Deviation amplification can be constructive or destructive.

cybernetics, we would envision a pattern of mutual reinforcement of deviation-amplification. Not only would fatherlessness tend to induce protest masculinity, which would tend to induce use of drugs, violence entertainment, and guns, but this causal "loop" would feed back on itself, further amplifying the lethal violence potential.

The second cybernetics model depicted here also lends itself to strategies to break out of the "vicious circle." One may see clearly where and how to intervene positively in such a gestalt of otherwise self-reinforcing causal paralethal violence factors. For example, providing positive role-model father figures and/or making guns and/or drugs, and/or violence entertainment unavailable can be effective means of incapacitating the vicious circle. Further, changing all of these influences together would have quite powerful effects even in the short run.

Institutional Factors in the Violence Culture

Consider the role alcohol plays in violence. While often associated with lethal violence via drunk driving and use of guns, alcohol is also a major co-determiner of violence even when cars and guns are not available. For example, guns are not allowed in institutions of higher education and, in contrast to many high schools, the no-gun rules at universities and colleges are generally effective, which probably helps to account for both lower suicide and homicide rates on college campuses (Schwartz, 1990; Schwartz and Whitaker, 1990; Whitaker and Pollard, 1993b). But college and university campuses have become much more dangerous in recent years. One causal factor, probably, is the influence of the increasingly violent surrounding culture's influence; as U.S. youth have become more violent, so have college students. Another contributor to violence on college and university campuses is that heavy underage consumption of alcohol is often tolerated on campus.

As many college personnel have observed, the much-publicized phenomenon of campus date rape rarely, if ever, occurs without use of alcohol by the rapist, or victim, or both; usually both have been drinking (Rivinus and Larimer, 1993). The attitudes of male students toward rape are predisposing or co-determining also: 35% have said they might commit rape if there was no chance of being caught, and 84% have said "some women look as though they're just asking to be raped" (Conn and Silverman, 1991, page 6).

While not receptive to the weapons industry, colleges and universities are very vulnerable to the alcohol industry and its oxymoronic pairings of alcohol and wholesome fun, even though most college students are under age 21 and their alcohol use violates state laws. Furthermore, colleges and universities usually receive some federal funding and are required thereby to assure the government that their campuses are kept drug free, but considerable illicit alcohol and other drug use continues on the vast majority of campuses. Thus, legal restrictions on alcohol and other drug use appear to have minimal effect at colleges and universities. College students are much less likely to use guns than their noncollege peers, but far more likely to drink alcohol, and are quite subject to alcohol-related violence.

Protest Masculinity

Many authors have elaborated on the close relationship between morbidity-infused images of masculinity and the much higher rates of homicide, suicide, and paraviolence behaviors in men (e.g., Cousy, 1975; Daniell, 1984; Gerzon, 1992; Mailer, 1984; Whitaker, 1987; and Whitaker, 1990). Real men, according to the popular mythology, show "strength" by dominating women and other men, and not showing their emotional needs except to act out anger. Their toughness is shown in being able to hold their tobacco, alcohol, and other drugs, and acting as though they are not afraid of killing or dying.

Rosemary Daniell (1984) coined the word "macha" to represent the female equivalent of the macho male. Like macho men, macha women are more prone to morbidity. Their numbers are increasing, as is especially evident in the acceleration of violent crimes committed by females and the greatly increased number of female prisoners. For example, the number of women prisoners increased 359% from 1974 to 1991 (Conn and Silverman, 1991).

Protest masculinity is a kind of false masculinity, an attempt at compensation for the lack of adequate fathers and father figures. This lack and the resultant internal void is illustrated by Mark Gerzon (1992) in his book *A Choice of Heroes*: "I recognized that what is missing in typical male macho behavior is not just the feminine but, even more important, the deep masculine" (page 272). Lacking genuine masculine role models, boys submit to the relentless barrage of false masculine images thrust at them by the vast popular media and advertisement industries, and become eager to emulate the powerful caricatures of men wielding huge guns positioned at crotch level. It is then but a short step to getting a gun or "hitting on a girl," or both. The script has no provision for fatherhood except the act of intercourse.

Large- and small-screen entertainment, video games, and much popular music present macho imagery every day and night as heroic. None of this macho heroism has value for would-be functional people unless they can join the presenters in making money from it. But the relentless, sensational role-modeling thus inculcated has far greater influence than the careful cultivation of respect for one's own and others' lives, because the latter is reliant on nonsensational personal examples in family, neighborhood, and school settings. After all, television is the prime baby and child sitter, and movies and television continue to play highly influential roles by programming behavior through all of the most formative years.

While an alarming number of high school graduates are illiterate on the whole, most prisoners in our society have not only failed to complete high school but have been infused with protest masculinity and thus lack both education and genuine masculine confidence. The lack of education and, thereby, job opportunities, tends to increase protest masculinity which, in turn, tends to make boys deride education.

The destructiveness inherent in protest masculinity has an especially strong appeal for spectators who, not measuring up to the real or fancied toughness of the gladiator-hero or his opponent, can feel superior to the opponent by identifying with the hero. Such was the pleasure in watching Roman gladiators. And such is the pleasure in boxing spectacles. Today's boxing spectator tries to deny his own fear and inadequacy by identifying with the "heroism" of the winning boxer-mutilator. The boxers themselves are typically minority males who can be more readily exploited and sacrificed in the ring, due to bigotry and their otherwise impoverished condition. "The Selling of Mike Tyson" is a newspaper article that captures the essence of the social, physical, and psychological morbidity inherent in machismo. Tyson's opponent, Mitch Green, brought to the ring an ominous reputation and the nickname "Blood" earned as a gang leader in Queens. However, Green's glowering facade quickly became an expression of real fear.

> Tyson smacked him in the mouth with such force in the second round that Green's mouthpiece flew out of the ring. In the third, the mouthpiece was sent flying again, along with a bridge and two teeth (Lyon, 1986, pages 1D and 4D).

When Green, in an attempt to survive, frantically clasped Tyson to his body, the crowd booed its displeasure. As the newspaper columnist observed, "People are anxious to worship a gladiator once more" (pages 1D and 4D). The fact that boxer-gladiators both cruelly inflict and are cruelly afflicted with brain damage was compensated for with enormous profits, in this case $2 million of television rights catering to many millions of sadistic viewers who thereby made the contracts possible. Tyson subsequently served a prison term for rape.

In contrast, consider a letter printed in the same newspaper on the same day, from a man who is extremely deviant but not morbid at all. He wrote Ann Landers, introducing himself as a 30-year-old man who has a steady girlfriend and a normal sex life. But when his girlfriend, Sara, is not with him overnight he sleeps with a Teddy bear she gave him, though he did not sleep with stuffed animals as a child. He began sleeping with his wonderful Teddy a year ago when his girlfriend gave it to him and now wonders if he should see a psychiatrist.

> ... I worry about this regression to childhood. Please give me your opinion — The Bear Facts in Bayside.
> **Dear Bay:** Not to worry. If the Teddy is a comfort to you, go ahead and sleep with it. Obviously, the symbolism is clear. Teddy is a substitute for Sara (Landers, 1986).

This apparently normal man, Bay, who is very "deviant" in terms of the prevailing macho culture, is reaching out for help, while truly morbid men who are not deviant are seldom motivated or able to do so, because of their macho orientation.

Fatherlessness, Poverty, and Race

As noted previously, fatherlessness, a rapidly escalating phenomenon in our society, tends to cause more protest masculinity. When nurturing and disciplining fathers are absent, male children are especially vulnerable to the endlessly persistent macho role modeling in violence entertainment. Furthermore, fatherless boys are increasingly surrounded in our society by other fatherless boys and are thus subject to a young peer culture that, on the whole, has little masculine guidance. Marshaling considerable evidence for this claim, David Blankenhorn (1995) asserted that "…if we want to learn the identity of the rapist, the hater of women, the occupant of jail cells, we do not look first to boys with traditionally masculine fathers. We look first to boys with no fathers" (page 31). From 1960 to 1990, the percentage of births outside marriage rose from 5.3 to 28.0 and the percentage of children living apart from their fathers rose from 17.5 to 36.3. This trend is probably having a cumulative detrimental effect, consistent with the continued increase from 1980 to 2000 of people generally, and males particularly, in jails and prisons and thus unavailable as parents.

A 1990 study commissioned by the Progressive Policy Institute showed that the "relationship between crime and one-parent families" is so strong that, when it is taken into account, the relationship between race and crime as well as between low income and crime is erased (Blankenhorn, 1995, page 31). However, it is important to understand the close relationships among fatherlessness, poverty, and race as a kind of causal gestalt of factors that is worsening. Fatherlessness typically results in the mother having to — not necessarily choosing to — leave her children in order to work outside of the home. Thus, the children are not only without their father, but their mother is less available. Furthermore, such fatherless families are usually much poorer than families with fathers, even when the mothers get outside jobs. Thus, the job of being a mother is neglected, often in favor of poor quality day care, the family is poorer economically, *and* the father is absent.

More, rather than fewer, U.S. citizens are becoming disadvantaged. Our poverty-fatherlessness-minority culture appears to be increasing. We have become the Western world nation with the greatest gap between the rich and the poor (Bradsher, 1995). Economic inequality has risen since the 1970s. By 1995, 1% of U.S. households — having a net worth of at least $2.3 million each — owned nearly 40% of the nation's wealth.

Noting that society is all too willing to rationalize the deterioration of the family, Blankenhorn (1995) posited that "a good society celebrates the ideal of the man who puts his family first" (page 5). Compare this ideal with that presented by the typical sensational "action movie" hero who represents protest masculinity at its worst.

Writing on the enormous rise in the U.S. of what has been diagnosed as "Attention-Deficit Hyperactivity Disorder" (ADHD), Peter and Ginger Breggin, in their book *The War Against Children* (1994), argued persuasively that chidren's "attention deficits" are better termed Dad Attention Deficit Disorder (DADD) or Teacher Attention Deficit Disorder (TADD). Whereas such children, mostly males, are seen as early delinquents who have a brain deficit and need psychiatric drug treatment, usually with Ritalin, neurologist Fred

Baughman, Jr. (1993) noted that studies have failed to confirm any definite improvement from drug treatment. However, such children often improve quickly if given more nurturing adult attention, including when discipline is nurturantly applied. Yet, the numbers of children and adolescents on Ritalin doubled from 1991 to 1995 (Breggin, 1995) and continued to increase.

The nurturing process we call education has also deteriorated in recent decades, especially in economically and socially disadvantaged inner-city schools where even high school graduates are often illiterate. Several indices reflect this decline. For example, between 1977 and 1991 the number of American children diagnosed as having learning disabilities increased 142%; between 1945 and 1991 the average number of words in the written vocabulary of a 6- to 14-year-old American child decreased from 25,000 to 10,000; in 1991, 36 million adult Americans read below the 8th grade level (Conn and Silverman, 1991). The vast majority of prisoners, not coincidentally, are especially poorly educated. The trend toward prison and away from education, and the value system behind it, are exemplified in California where spending on prisons grew 60% in the 1990s and where higher education saw virtually no growth. In 1999, a California prison guard made about $51,000 a year while first-year professors, who average several years more education than guards, are paid $41,000 (Egan, 1999). Thus, we have another good illustration of deviation amplification: the more rewarding it is to be a prison guard and the less to be a professor, the more impetus we have to place and keep people in prisons instead of schools.

Defenders of Paralethal Violence

Arguments by deniers of the destructive influence of various relevant factors including guns, violence entertainment, alcohol and other drugs, fatherlessness, poverty, racial prejudice, and early experiences of brutality, can successfully defend the factor of their choice on the limited basis of its being neither necessary nor sufficient to explain any violent act. (A common rationalization, for example, is "he didn't need a gun to do it; he would have found a way".) Yet, it is clear that all of these factors play roles in determining and facilitating outright lethal violence and paralethal violence. Thus, I call them paralethal factors.

The misleading nature of arguments by violence factor defenders is illustrated by a scene with Peter Sellers in a Pink Panther movie. Sellers is at a hotel desk where he sees a dog standing peacefully by the hotel clerk, and asks the clerk, "Does your dog bite?" The clerk says, "No." Then Sellers reaches out to pet the dog and is bitten. In shock, Sellers says, "I thought you said your dog doesn't bite?" The clerk answers, "But it's not my dog." In this instance, as in all instances when violence factor deniers help determine violent behavior, the abettor (the clerk) has misled his customer (Sellers).

He has contributed to the violence both by having the dog there and not advising of the danger, but he can facilely excuse himself. After all, he was not required by law to care about his fellow human being.

How We Can Counter and Replace Our Violence Culture?

Criticizing and understanding our society's innumerable inducements to violence implies innumerable ways to counter and replace such morbidity. Clearly, fostering nurturing, rather than abusive and neglectful, child-rearing practices, is key. By becoming a more nurturing society, we can hold youth and ourselves more accountable, just as constructive parents provide a foundation on which discipline can be based. We will then produce fewer people who, by neglect coupled with training to be violent, are disenfranchised and then express their anger, sense of entitlement, and power needs through violent behavior — people who act as though they have not been given much to begin with.

We need to redefine power as the ability to nurture, recognizing that, whereas anyone can destroy the fruits of nurturance, only genuinely powerful people can create meaningful lives. Whereas violence entertainment models and thereby programs and promotes destructive orientations, we need to nurture constructive orientations.

Beyond observing and promulgating these general truths, what can we do specifically to counter the presently violent culture we have given the youth of our country? The possibilities for practical, constructive programmatic actions are seemingly limitless, are usually much less expensive even in the short run than most current revenge measures, and are enormously preventive of future expense. A few are listed here.

Improve Parenting

Our most neglected but finest art is parenting. Our society has left far too much of it to people who are exploiting rather than nurturing. Encouraging men to be real fathers, rather than mere biological fathers, is probably our single greatest social challenge. But it can be performed by almost any man willing to try.

My own favorite example is The Bicycle Man from Belmont, North Carolina (Kuralt, 1985), who supplied and maintained youngsters with bikes they otherwise never would have had. This genuine hero, Jethro Mann, grew up without a bike and so he found special meaning and satisfaction in spending tremendous time and personal care, and his quite limited financial resources, teaching kids fun, caring, and responsibility. Mann fit stereotyped notions of being disadvantaged: he was Black, poor, and old. But he was really quite spiritually rich, living out his own powerful personal philosophy. Mann said, "I look at it this way. I have had a good life myself and I'm not apt to have much more. But whatever I do have, I hope it will contribute to someone else's welfare. And that is what I try to do" (Kuralt, 1985, page 13). Mann is a real man!

Blankenhorn (1995) offered 12 proposals for improving the fathering parental orientation, including grass roots neighborhood actions and government incentives to encourage active parenting. For example, he suggested forming fathers' clubs devoted to good fathering and cited already-active community groups.

Arthur Ashe (1993), the great athlete, scholar, and father emphasized the crucial importance his father had for his personal development, especially after the death of his mother. Ashe stated:

> My father was a strong, dutiful, providing man. He lived and died semi-literate, but he owned his own home and held jobs that were important to him and to people in the community where we lived. His love and caring were real to me from that Sunday morning in 1950 when he sat on the bottom bunk bed between my brother Johnnie and me and told us between wrenching sobs that our mother had died during the night. From that time on he was mother and father to us. And the lesson he taught us above all was about reputation (page 4).

James Michener (1992), bereft of both parents at birth, emphasized how father figures such as an "uncle" and other men in the community were essential in enabling him to avoid not only cigarettes and alcohol, but a criminal life style.

Any parent or parent figure, male or female, can perform an enormously helpful nurturing service to children by being affectionate and caring, reading to them, listening to and talking with them, and telling them stories. Reading to a child from the time they can begin to recognize words not only gives them a head start on becoming literate and invested in education, but can create an affectionate, mutually respectful bond between parent and child. Children are strengthened thereby both cognitively and socially and develop confidence in their own growing powers to understand themselves and the world around them. In the process, they develop a security base which will help them resist the omnipresent commercial inducements to disrespect and abuse themselves and others. The positive caring attention they get from being read to, listened to, and being told stories will very likely prevent the kinds of "attention disorders," hyperactivity, and delinquent behaviors increasingly targeted as symptomatic of "chemical imbalances" and needing drug treatment. Similarly, children taught to care for pets, to appreciate nature, and to learn about themselves and others without commercial pressures will become more independent and creative thinkers.

Recreational and sports activities can be enormously helpful also, depending on the spirit of engagement. Children can be taught to compete fairly, to be gracious winners and good losers, to take joy in the process, and to train to become more physically fit and respectful of their bodies.

Parents should be careful to keep harmful intruders out of the home, particularly in the form of violence entertainments emanating from television sets and VCRs, and now the Internet, when these electronic guests are busy inducing passive mindlessness, the better with which to inculcate destructive mentality. Screen, and screen out often, these otherwise ubiquitous babysitters. Make sure that children's (and adults') exposures are limited to constructive programming in the home and at movie theaters.

Teach Critical Thinking

Mindlessness is not a natural condition; it has to be learned through violent enforcement because all children, otherwise, are naturally endlessly curious until they are forced to stop being curious and to give up their capacity to be imaginative, thoughtful, and creative.

While impulsive cognitive style and its obliviousness to harmful consequences may characterize much of infantile behavior, children of even elementary school age show eagerness and ability to develop critical thinking. In fact, some of the most effective deterrents to cigarette smoking have been created by children. For example, Melissa Antonow of Our Lady of Hope School in Queens, NY produced the "Come to Where the Cancer Is" cartoon, a takeoff on the Marlboro Country cigarette ads. Her cartoon showed a skeleton of a man riding a horse alongside tombstones marked variously lung cancer, heart disease, and emphysema. Melissa's "ad" appeared in all New York City subway cars. Similarly, Caheim Drake of Public School 112 in the Bronx produced an antismoking ad showing a "Pack of Lies," a cigarette pack with each cigarette bearing a label such as Fun, Relaxation, Safe, Cool, Mature, and Popular (Howe, 1992).

If children, with the aid of their adult teachers, can cut through denial and engage in effective critical thinking which gets to the truth, formal education can serve to immunize children from the adult-instigated propaganda that exploits all consumers. This nurturing educational process requires that *we*, the adult teachers, engage in the critical thinking processes we have been trained to abnegate in our own commercialized upbringings. We will need to stop being so suggestible as to smoke cigarettes, to drink alcohol to the point of intoxication, and to participate actively *or* acquiesce passively in externally directed as well as internally directed mindless violence. We, as adults, will have to *actively criticize* all aspects of the cigarette, alcohol, weapons, and violence entertainment industries, instead of passively accepting them.

Some communities have demonstrated how adults can decrease the gross intrusion of destructiveness training. A largely Black community within the city of Philadelphia found itself targeted by an advertising campaign designed to addict Black people specifically to a new brand of cigarettes that was given a suave, cool image. Their protest resulted in the cigarette advertisers, i.e., drug pushers, calling off the campaign.

In Perth Amboy, NJ a neighborhood group sent its young people out on the streets to demonstrate how easy it *was* for persons under 18 to buy cigarettes (Teltsch, 1992). The underage young people were able to make cigarette purchases in 63 of the 94 stores they visited. The community of Perth Amboy was selected for such a drive against child and teenage smoking because it was saturated with billboards urging tobacco and alcohol use for Black and Hispanic residents. The advertisers know whom to prey on just as the regular, more obviously disrespectable street drug pushers do: target those with less power. But those with apparently less power, including minorities and the young, can protest effectively, as in these cases. And it so happens that Black youth are taking up cigarette smoking at far lower rates than their White peers.

More recently and comprehensively, Florida has shown how its statewide educational antitobacco campaign for teenagers has had impressive results in only 1 year, including a 19% decline in the number of sixth- to eighth-grade children who used cigarettes. Florida's "Truth" campaign's cornerstone features angry teenagers accusing tobacco companies of lying (Student Smoking Declines, 1999).

Counter Racism

Considered individually, fatherlessness, gun availability, commercial exploitation including violence entertainment, lack of education, and poverty obviously play enormous roles in violence propagation. So does racism. When Arthur Ashe (1993) was asked if AIDS was the heaviest burden he had ever had to bear, he replied, "Race has always been my biggest burden" (page 126). People of color are often held in lower esteem across innumerable situations in our society, ranging from country club membership exclusions to automatic assumptions of intellectual inferiority. Clearly, children should be taught to respect persons of all ethnic backgrounds and to resist absurd, oxymoronic pairings of race and religion with this or that supposed inferiority.

Racism and other ethnic prejudices also take the form of expecting less from minorities, in keeping with judgments of lower capacity. But, as many education experiments have shown, Hispanic children, given encouragement, may prove quite superior in calculus, Black children in chess, and so on. We do a disservice by expecting and encouraging less. Everyone needs nurturance and encouragement and everyone should be held accountable.

Probably, any field of endeavor made really open to minorities will lead to excellence by many. I have often thought, for example, about what would happen if Blacks were discouraged from entering any occupation but medicine. I predict that, within two generations, most of our best physicians would be Black just as most professional basketball players now are Black, because that occupation opened up wide during the past couple of decades.

Reform Education

As discussed earlier, our schools have been turning into armed camps where teachers are preoccupied with trying to establish a sufficiently secure environment for education to have a chance. Often, however, school is education in name only. Not only high school graduates but often college graduates are illiterate as well as undisciplined. Part of the problem, as exemplified in the California dilemma, is that schools have been stripped of adequate financing, largely because of astronomically increasing spending on more prisoners and punishments. Commercial enterprises are filling the void both outside and inside the classroom. For example, whereas commercial-free textbooks ordinarily would cost hundreds of dollars per student per year, in 1993 public school spending for textbooks, containing advertisements, averaged only $45.91 per student (Consumer Reports, 1995). What is happening to fill the great gap in ad-free education funding?

In addition to the 30,000 commercial messages sent to children every day by ads on TV, radio, billboards, and the like outside of schools, school properties themselves are now filled with commercials on radios, ads on walls, and even on school buses and, most importantly perhaps, in their study materials — according to an 18-month research project by Consumers Union's Education Services Department (Consumer Reports, 1995). Among the 160 examples of such ads were: "There are no endangered species, maintains the Council for Wildlife Conservation and Education, which turns out to be affiliated with the National Shooting Sports Foundation — an organization that has the same address as the National Rifle Association" (page 327). Actually, hundreds of species of life are already extinguished, and many more are endangered, one of which is the human being.

Despite such exposés of commercial invasion of public education, the trend continues. For example, a required textbook, *Mathematics: Applications and Connections*, published by McGraw-Hill and now used in 15 states, has a 1999 edition drenched with ads and even poses math problems in terms of the advertised products. For example, the following is a problem statement: "The best-selling packaged cookie in the world is the Oreo cookie... The diameter of the Oreo cookie is 1.75 inches. Express the diameter of an Oreo cookie as a fraction in simplest form" (as cited by Hays, 1999). Communities and their governments need to retake fiscal and programmatic responsibility for their school systems.

Fill the Spiritual Void

We have a compelling urge in our society to resort to legalistic solutions which are usually partial and temporary; they do not get at the heart of the matter, and they do not address the spiritual problem. Legalism cannot fill the void of disrespect.

Inherent in most, if not all, acts of violence, whether legal or not, is a failure of empathy. The only possible exception is when violence is truly needed to stop a greater violence, though this situation usually reflects earlier grave oversights. For example, the world stood by too long as the Nazis came to power (by filling a spiritual void in Germany) in large part because of lack of caring and empathy for Jewish people.

No list of ways to understand and counter social inducements to violence would be adequate without emphasizing the universal human need to find meaning in life. Of course, not just any meaning will do. The meaning has to be life-affirming and infused with respect for all human beings. Many supposed spiritual quests, often in the guise of a particular religion or cult, achieve the opposite. By positing the inferiority of outsiders, they become exclusive rather than embracing, threatening instead of comforting, and ultimately destructive instead of constructive. A truly spiritual orientation means that others' lives and one's own are sacred. In this sense, spiritual development means cultivation of a broad-mindedness that spans the universe of life rather than shrinks one's awareness. It means a sensitive awareness of oneself together with an empathic identification with others, rather than a blind, conformist following in the authoritarian tradition of mindlessness. Teaching and learning mindfulness, caring, and empathy are ways all of us can contribute every day to a better, nonviolent society. We can counter the current barrage of social inducements to violence by becoming a spiritually determined nation and world of mindful, wholesome "misfits."

Support but Do Not Rely upon Legal Solutions

Our legalistic culture relies too heavily on legislating for a better society, but legislative initiatives may serve to express and to demand more constructive mentalities and actions. Recent examples include legislation and lawsuits against the tobacco and weapons industries. One would hope that the consumer demand for these products would lessen through education and parenting. The current reality is that demand remains high although both cigarettes and guns have been losing favor. Because legal solutions are extremely costly and cannot supplant the other kinds of solutions discussed earlier, they demarcate failures to be active enough in taking other measures. Thus, the legally waged war on drugs has done little to deter people from abusing themselves and others with both legal and illegal drugs and a plethora of other toxic substances. We do need laws and law enforcement, but even more, we need such mentalities as this:

> I expect to pass through this life but once. If therefore there be any kindnesses I can show, or any good thing I can do to any fellow beings, let me do it now. Let me not defer or neglect it, for I shall not pass this way again.
> — A. B. Hegeman

Summary

This chapter outlines, analyses, and illustrates powerful social inducements to violence, particularly among youth in the U.S. whose internal and externalized violence rates increased markedly during the late decades of the 20th century. Causes were discussed in terms of neglect together with programming for violence addictions. Lethal violence was depicted as the capstone of a mountain of paralethal factors including the worsening of parenting, education, and poverty, and the growth of commercial violence cultivation and gun availability.

Denial of the nature of the inducements was linked with the popularity of expensive, reactive "solutions" that are generally ineffective: more prisoners, death penalties, police, guns, and corporal punishment. Criminals' disavowals of responsibility were likened to our society's disavowals of its contributions to violence in the media, entertainment, and weapons industries, and in the "pushing" of harmful legal as well as illegal drugs.

The role of the avid consumer of violence was illustrated by the "O.J. feeding frenzy," sensational television and movie portrayals inculcating sadomasochism, and in the readiness to join cults combining compliance with the group, dependence on a leader, devaluing the outsider, avoiding dissent, and consequent readiness to harm. Psychosocial methods for cultivating violence proclivities are analyzed and illustrated in terms of propaganda, public relations, and advertising methods, all of which rely on and cultivate passive cognitive style when trying to sell to violence addiction customers.

Suggestions for reversing violence proclivities include improving parenting and our educational systems, teaching critical thinking, and filling the spiritual void with dedication to the sacredness of one's own and others' lives. Illustrations depicting the nature of these needs and how to meet them are given.

We need greater awareness and acknowledgment of our shared denial and responsibility with increasing grass roots, spiritual, and governmental efforts to reverse the neglect and violencing of our society, with particular attention to nurturing and protecting our youth.

Bibliography

Blankenhorn, David, *Fatherless America: Confronting Our Most Urgent Social Problem,* New York: Basic Books, 1995.

Focusing on a crucial aspect of the psychosocial basis of the dissolution of the family and the accompanying youth violence megatrend, Blankenhorn posits a powerful argument. He integrates theory and considerable research evidence to show how the continuing demise of real fatherhood, as distinct from procreation, leaves boys, especially, with a great void in their identities, a void filled by a false "hypermasculinity" defining masculinity largely as abilities to dominate and destroy.

Fromm, Erich, *Escape from Freedom,* New York: Avon Books, 1969 (originally publ. 1941).

The author, a Ph.D. in sociology who became a psychoanalyst as well, escaped Nazi Germany and wrote this classic work on the appeal of totalitarianism. His thesis that people were eager to escape the freedom of their individuality by means of (temporarily) comfortable conformity to a dictatorial leader continues to explain myriad factors fostering violence. His many subsequent books, particularly *The Sane Society* (1955), further develop the thesis and suggest answers.

Gerzon, Mark, *A Choice of Heroes: The Changing Faces of American Manhood,* Boston: Houghton Mifflin, 1992.

An insightful perspective on the quick-to-violence hero images that have most influenced young men over the 20th century. Gerzon combines what he has learned in his own investigative travels with cultural history to explain how our youth adopt and are constricted by ill-fitting stereotypes. The frontiersman, soldier, and even the expert and the breadwinner are too often obsolete, so the author suggests new kinds of masculine heroes.

Miedzian, Myriam, *Boys Will Be Boys: Breaking the Link between Masculinity and Violence,* New York: Doubleday, 1991.

The author systematically relates the fact that most acts of violence are committed by males to how boys are relentlessly taught, through violent toys and games, television, music, participation in wars, and history lessons, to be violent. She also shows how females aid and abet this training by admiring male bravado. One might add that women are increasingly imitating violent male role models as well. Alternatives are suggested.

Whitaker, Leighton C. and Pollard, Jeffrey W., Eds., *Campus Violence: Kinds, Causes, and Cures,* New York: Haworth Press, 1993.

College students, who represent the future leadership of our society, have increasingly perpetrated and been victims of violence — phenomena that colleges and universities have tended to downplay. This volume frankly addresses the kinds and causes in terms of the surrounding culture, alcohol and other drugs, race relations, lesbian and gay students, and male role models. It gives special attention to actual lethal violence events on campuses and what to do to alleviate and prevent them.

References

76 in Law Enforcement Slain in '94 F.B.I. says, *New York Times,* April 3, 1995 p. A14.

Ashe, A. and Rampersad, A., *Days of Grace: A Memoir,* New York: Knopf, 1993.

Asimov, I., *Isaac Asimov's Book of Facts,* New York: Bell Publishing, 1981.

Baughman, F.A., Jr., Treatment of attention-deficit hyperactivity disorder, *J. Am. Med. Assoc.,* 269, 2368, 1993.

Blankenhorn, D., *Fatherless America: Confronting Our Most Urgent Social Problem,* New York: Basic Books, 1995.

Bradsher, K., Gap in wealth in U.S. called widest in west, *New York Times,* April 17, 1995, pp. A1, D4.

Breggin, P.R. and Breggin, G.R., *The War Against Children,* New York: St. Martins Press, 1994.

Breggin, P.R., Personal communication, April 13, 1995.

Brooke, J., Canada split as gun laws are tightened, *New York Times,* December 7, 1999, p. A9.

Bundy says porn fueled violent fantasies, *Philadelphia Inquirer,* January 25, 1989.

Butterfield, F., Teen-age homicide rate has soared, *New York Times,* October 14, 1994, p. A22.

Butterfield, F., Justice department awarding grants to develop gun detectors, *New York Times,* March 10, 1995a, p. A22.

Butterfield, F., New prisons cast shadow over higher education, *New York Times,* April 12, 1995b, p. A21.

Butterfield, F., To rejuvenate gun sales, critics say, industry started making more powerful pistols, *New York Times,* National Report, February 14, 1999a, p. 16.

Butterfield, F., As inmate population grows, so does a focus on children, *New York Times,* April 7, 1999b, pp. A1, A18.

Centers for Disease Control, Behaviors related to unintentional and intentional injuries among high school students — United States, 1991, *MMWR,* October 16; 41(41), 760-772, 1992.

Conn, C. and Silverman, I., Eds., *What Counts: The Complete Harper's Index,* New York: Henry Holt, 1991.

Consumer Reports, Selling to school kids, May, 1995, pp. 327-329.

Copeland, L., Caning criminals? It gains advocates, *Philadelphia Inquirer,* March 10, 1995, pp. A1, A20.

Cousy, R., *The Killer Instinct*, New York: Random House, 1975.

Daniell, R, *Sleeping with Soldiers*, New York: Holt, Reinhart, and Winston, 1984.

Dao, J., Death penalty in New York restored after 18 years; Pataki sees justice served, *New York Times*, March 8, 1995, pp. A1, B5.

Deikman, A. J, *The Wrong Way Home*, Boston: Beacon Press, 1990.

Dunlap, D. W., June '94 produced a record for antigay attacks, *New York Times*, March 8, 1995, p. B2.

Eckholm, E., Studies find death penalty tied to race of the victims, *New York Times*, February 24, 1995, pp. B1, B4.

Egan, T., Less crime, more criminals, *New York Times*, Section 4, Week in Review, March 7, 1999, pp. 1, 16.

Freud, S., From civilization and its discontents, in *The Freud Reader*, Gay, P., Ed., New York: W.W. Norton, 1995.

Fromm, E., *Escape From Freedom*, New York: Avon Books, 1969 (originally published in 1941).

Gerzon, M., *A Choice of Heroes: The Changing Faces of American Manhood*, Boston: Houghton Mifflin, 1992.

Gun homicides by young people, *New York Times*, Editorial, January 7, 1999, p. A30.

Gun killings by young defy drop in homicides, *New York Times*, January 4, 1999, p. A13.

Hays, C., Math book salted with brand names raises new alarm, *New York Times*, March 21, 1999, pp. A1, A28.

Holden, S., Mutilating, murderous lesbians, with a light side, *New York Times*, March 17, 1995, p. C8.

Hollman, L. and McCoy, C., The growing urban arsenal: are rising handgun sales only a reflection of the problem, or a cause too? *Philadelphia Inquirer*, August 2, 1992, pp. E1, E4.

Holmes, S.A., Ranks of inmates reach 1 million in a two-decade rise, *New York Times*, October 28, 1995, pp. A1, 25.

Howe, M., M.T.A. panel approves cut in cigarette advertisements, *New York Times*, Metro Edition, June 17, 1992, p. B3.

Humes, J.C., *The Wit and Wisdom of Winston Churchill*, New York: Harper Perennial, 1995.

Kaplan, J., Ed., Adolph Hitler. in *Familiar Quotations*, 16th ed., John Bartlett, Ed., Boston: Little, Brown, 1992, p. 676.

Killer women on TV, *New York Times*, October 12, 1992, p. C20.

Killings said to rise after gun laws are relaxed, *New York Times*, March 15, 1995, p. A23.

Kristof, N.D., With cult under cloud, its still his guiding star, *New York Times*, April 4, 1995, p. A4.

Kuralt, C., *On the Road with Charles Kuralt*, New York: Ballantine Books, 1985.

Landers, A., Letter from "The Bear Facts in Bayside," *Philadelphia Inquirer*, May 22, 1986.

Larson, E., The story of a gun, *Atlantic Monthly*, 271, 48-78, 1993.

Leary, W.E., Young people who try suicide may be succeeding more often, *New York Times*, April 21, 1995, p. A15.

Lore, R.K. and Schultz, L.A., Control of human aggression, *Am. Psychol.*, 48(1), 16-25, 1993.

Lyon, B., The selling of Mike Tyson, *Philadelphia Inquirer*, May 22, 1986, pp. 1D and 4D.

Mailer, N., *Tough Guys Don't Dance*, New York: Random House, 1984.

Maruyama, M., The second cybernetics: deviation-amplifying mutual causal processes, *Am. Sci.*, 51, 164-179, 1963.

Menninger, K., *The Crime of Punishment*, New York: Viking Press, 1968.

Merchandising Murder, Arts and Entertainment channel of cable television, March 31, 1995.

Michener, J., *The World Is My Home: A Memoir*, New York: Random House, 1992.

Miedzian, M., *Boys Will Be Boys: Breaking the Link between Masculinity and Violence*, New York: Doubleday, 1991.

Moran, R., Hate crimes increasing in PA, *New York Times*, February 24, 1995, p. B2.

Moss, D., MD snuffs out smoking in nearly every workplace, *USA Today*, March 3, 1995, p. 3A.

Newman, M., Weapons at school: box cutters escape detection, *New York Times*, March 10, 1995, pp. A1, B4.

Rickey, C., Once an adult movie, now a hoot, *Philadelphia Inquirer*, pp. 5, 14, April 2, 1995.

Ritz Film Bill, John Sayles changes course, Philadelphia: Entropy Design, March/April, 1995, pp. 15-17.

Rivinus, T.M. and Larimer, M.E., Violence, alcohol, other drugs, and the college student, in *Campus Violence: Kinds, Causes, and Cures*, Whitaker, L.C. and Pollard, J.W., Eds., New York: Haworth Press, 1993, chap. 4. (Published simultaneously in *J. Coll. Stud. Psychother.*, 8(1/2), 3, 1993.)

Sally Jesse Raphael, National Broadcasting Company, March 3, 1995.

Schiraldi, V., Crime rates and prisons, *New York Times*, letter to the Editor, January 4, 1999, p. A18.

Schneider, K., Hate groups use tools of the electronic trade, *New York Times*, March 13, 1995, p. A12.

Schut, E., Faster, Pussycat! Kill! Kill! *Ritz Film Bill*, Philadelphia: Entropy Design, March/April, 1995, p. 30.

Schwartz, A.J., The epidemiology of suicide among students at colleges and universities in the United States, in *College Student Suicide*, Whitaker, L. and Slimak, R., Eds., New York: Haworth Press, 1990, chap. 2. (Published simultaneously in *J. Coll. Stud. Psychother.*, 4, 3/4, 1990.)

Schwartz, A.J. and Whitaker, L.C, Suicide among college students: assessment, treatment, and intervention, *Suicide Across the Life Cycle: Risk Factors, Assessment, and Treatment of Suicidal Patients*, Blumenthal, S. and Kupfer, D., Eds., Washington, D.C.: American Psychiatric Press, 1990, chap. 12.

Seldes, G., Ed., *The Great Quotations*, Secaucas, NJ: Castle Books, 1978.

Shapiro, D., *Neurotic styles*. New York: Basic Books, Inc., 1965.

Solzhenitsyn, A.I., Solzhenitsyn on Western decline, Harvard University commencement address, June 8, 1978.

Spindler, A.M., In Paris, clothes that look tough, masculine and dangerous, *New York Times*, March 16, 1995, p. C13.

Student smoking declines amid a state campaign, *New York Times*, National Report, April 2, 1999, p. A14.

Teltsch, K., Keeping teenagers smokeless, *New York Times*, Metro Section, August 18, 1992, pp. B1,4.

Thompson, A., Action! The films that win audiences, *Philadelphia Inquirer*, May 1, 1988, p. 1F.

U.N. panel votes for ban on death penalty, *New York Times*, April 29, 1999, p. A4.

Verhovek, S.H., States seek to let citizens carry concealed weapons, *New York Times*, March 6, 1995, p. A1.

Whitaker, L.C., *Objective Measurement of Schizophrenic Thinking: A Practical and Theoretical Guide to the Whitaker Index of Schizophrenic Thinking*, Los Angeles: Western Psychological Services, 1980.

Whitaker, L.C., Macho and morbidity: the emotional need vs. fear dilemma in men, *J. Coll. Stud. Psychother.*, 1(4), 33-47, 1987.

Whitaker, L.C., Myths and heroes: visions of the future, *J. Coll. Stud. Psychother.*, 4(2), 13-33, 1990.

Whitaker, L.C, *Schizophrenic Disorders: Sense and Nonsense in Conceptualization, Assessment, and Treatment*, New York: Plenum Press, 1992.

Whitaker, L.C., Violence is golden: commercially motivated training in impulsive cognitive style and mindless violence, *J. Coll. Stud. Psychother.*, 8(1/2), 45-69, 1993a. (Published simultaneously in Whitaker, L.C. and Pollard, J.W., Eds., *Campus Violence: Kinds, Causes, and Cures*, New York: Haworth Press, 1993.)

Whitaker, L.C. and Pollard, J.W., Eds., *Campus Violence: Kinds, Causes, and Cures*, New York: Haworth Press, 1993b. (Published simultaneously in *J. Coll. Stud. Psychother.*, 8(1/2), 3, 1993.)

Inhibiting Fatal Group and Institutional Aggression   3

This chapter addresses group and institutional lethal aggression in terms of its dynamics and ways to inhibit it. Factors instrumental in facilitating or inhibiting this type of violence are elucidated from examples of both legal and illegal institutions, including professions, sports organizations, military institutions, deadly cults, and the militia movement.

The inhibition of group and institutional violence is a grave topic emotionally laden with ethical, political, social, psychological, and spiritual issues; it means inhibiting not just violent individuals but masses of individuals whose interaction can be synergistic and thus engender vastly more destructiveness than the sum of all of the individuals acting destructively on their own. Group violence is at the heart of the fundamental question of social as well as personal rights and responsibilities. Often, this topic is addressed with considerable heat but little light as possibilities for understanding are short-circuited by the heat of impassioned reactions, or it is reacted to with a sense of helplessness. We will do well, therefore, to strive for a thorough understanding rather than a rush to judgment or a facile giving up. Thus, we will have to guard against a blind righteousness on the one hand and an unseeing apathy on the other.

The term "institution" is defined broadly here as any organization of group effort to benefit itself, others, or both. The very term evokes the notion of inhibitions on the expression of individuals in favor of conformity to the group ethos. Membership in an institution does not necessarily, however, mean inhibitions against violence toward others outside of the group or even members within the group. In their pursuit of group conformity, institutions variously lure and pressure individual members to renounce certain personal behaviors and values for the sake of the group ethos. The members are trained, thereby, in the institution's particular ethnocentrism, a habitual disposition to judge foreign individuals or groups by the standards and practices of one's own culture or ethnic group. The tendency to become ingrown and intolerant of other people, therefore, is endemic to institutions as well as individuals.

The term "inhibition" is also defined broadly here. The most satisfactory definition I have found is from *Webster's Third New International Dictionary* (1966), wherein the primary meaning of the term is "an act or an instance of formally forbidding or barring something from being done," while an important extension of the term is "a desirable restraint or check upon the free or spontaneous instincts or impulses of an individual effected through the operation of the human will guided or directed by the social and cultural forces of the environment." The primary meaning relates to an agent or force external to the individual that represses the individual. The further meaning, which is not even mentioned in some dictionaries, includes restraining forces that are internal to or within the individual.

External restraints are usually obvious, whereas internal restraints tend to be subtle, though certainly not less important. The latter includes conscience, in both its prohibiting and idealistic forms; we may choose not to be violent in order to avoid consequent feelings of guilt or because we are empathic with and love the potential victims of our violent tendencies, or both. We may also be inhibited because we fear retaliation and loss. Often, there are admixtures of external and internal inhibitions in any given instance and, over time, what was an external inhibition can be transformed into an internal inhibition and vice versa.

The purpose of this chapter is to reach an understanding of how the violence potentials of institutions may be inhibited, including from the inside of institutions and from inside the individual members. A series of realizations must be developed to achieve this purpose:

1. That all institutions, by their inherent nature, may tend to commit violence toward both outsiders and their own members.
2. That this tendency to commit institutional violence toward both insiders and outsiders is greatest when "group centricity" is maximized so that there is little accountability to outsiders.
3. That in order to be constructive toward insiders as well as outsiders, an institution must deliberately build in safeguards and inhibitions against its own institutionally inherent destructive tendency.
4. That effective inhibitions against institutional violence can be incorporated in the design of new institutions, applied to the process of monitoring existing institutions, and used for intervention when egregious institutional violence is imminent or actual.
5. That the basis for any truly constructive society or group ethos must value nurturant partnerships more than violent dominator relationships.

Before suggesting specific ways to inhibit institutional violence, this chapter will emphasize developing a clear understanding of the context and workings of institutions in terms of their violence proclivities. Their structures and dynamics can be understood by explicating examples and deriving certain principles that, in combination, show us how institutional violence proclivities are facilitated or inhibited. We may learn, thereby, to effectively inhibit institutional violence in a variety of ways.

The Inherently Violent Tendency of Institutions

Many institutions have the potential for violence. In striving for group conformity, institutions require that their members make certain sacrifices "for the common good," ostensibly for the good of the membership as a whole. So, the members are at some risk according to the kinds of sacrifices they must make. Outsiders are at risk, too, because the goals of any given institution may be against outsiders' interests. It is not always true that "what is good for General Motors is good for the country" or the rest of the world. Thus, any institution may engender harm to both members and outsiders.

Because of their size and the synergy of interindividual relationships, institutions have greater violence potentials than an individual acting alone. As will be illustrated and explained, individuals may, as members of a group or institution, commit atrocities which they would never commit as an individual acting alone. Often, therefore, inhibitions against institutional violence, to be effective, must also be greater.

On close examination, no institution is totally free of harmful tendencies. Though most do not directly perpetrate lethal violence, it is evident that even the most respected institutions, when they pursue unenlightened group interests, may wittingly or unwittingly contribute to violence against outsiders. More subtly, the pursuit of "groupish self-interest" can readily damage the membership as well by requiring harmful self-sacrifices, as will be illustrated. Furthermore, externally directed violence begets internally directed violence by modeling uncaring, violent relationships or through resultant tendencies to harbor guilt which may be reacted to by means of denial, projection, or self-punishment — all in the service of trying to ward off or divest oneself of the guilt.

If an institution proceeds increasingly to demand conformity and to disdain nonconformists, the resulting "progressive group centrism" exerts more and more pressure on its members to deny individual and group responsibility except as it may serve what is perceived, expediently, as the group interest. But even this "benefit of group allegiance" lessens as the group becomes more centric and authoritarian until it is only the leader who is deemed important. When the group ethos becomes really only the ethos of an authoritarian leader, no behavior is considered acceptable except slavish devotion to the wishes of the leader. Yet, even such devotion carries no assurance of safety or even survival, as when the leader demands the deaths of loved ones or even the members themselves.

Most clearly, it is extremely authoritarian-led groups that fit this model of progressive group centrism leading to a kind of black hole destruction of its members. Vivid examples readily come to mind: the Nazi progression from dominating and destroying outsiders to more and more dissension within the party, albeit suppressed, attempts on Hitler's life by insiders, and to his eventual suicide; and the so-called Jonestown massacre in Guyana where the leader and his followers, abhorring outside influences, committed suicide together.

Arthur Deikman (1990) delineated the deadly course:

> The more authoritarian the human social system, the more likely a separatist world view will arise because any anger or resentment stimulated in the follower by his or her submission to the leader requires displacement onto other persons — the outsider, the infidel, the non-believer. Feelings of rebellion toward the leader, which are defined by the group as evil, make the cult member anxious, even ready to believe in Satanic possession, an apt metaphor to describe the sensation of being invaded by unwelcome feelings and images (page 104).

Most groups do not become so authoritarian as to actively and continually engage in progressive centrism or "black holeism" to the point of lethal violence. This fact holds out hope for efforts to check or ameliorate institutional violence. What happens within as well as outside of institutions to inhibit the blinding, destroying extremity of group centrism? Why do some institutions "hold the line" or even become more constructive toward their members and toward nonmembers? Some answers can be found in how many of our common, everyday institutions both engage in violence and check their own violence proclivities. While these organized group cultures do exact some destructiveness, they also manage to retain a modicum of general social approval as society actively evaluates whether they are beneficial overall or, at least, not harmful to an unacceptable degree.

Inhibitions against institutional violence include external surveillance and controls, the rules and ethos of the institution itself, and the personal internal inhibitions of the individual members. The risk of institutional violence is directly related to the presence or absence of three sources of inhibition: external, intra-institutional, and intra-individual, which dynamically affect one another. With this framework in mind, let us consider as examples some familiar institutions.

Examples of Mandated, Legally Limited, Institutional Aggression

The institutions to be reviewed illustrate the fact that *many, if not most, institutions require that their members be willing and able to materially damage — physically, financially, or psychologically — persons construed to be opponents.* An individual's failure to conform to this requirement will have certain negative consequences for the individual's standing in the institution, such as low ratings, exclusion, or death.

The Legal Profession

Traditionally conceived, the law serves the causes of fairness and justice. Like democratic government, which makes and enforces law, the law as a profession is designed to be an implementer of the principle of checks and balances, a principle intended to maximize fairness and justice. But, the lawful pursuit of justice is based on the adversary system which, inherently, guarantees deceit, and often more conflict and violence, adding to the conflict and violence which occurred originally to bring the matter to a court of justice. Attorney and ethicist Walt Bachman observed in *Law v. Life: What Lawyers are Afraid to Say About The Legal Profession* (1995):

> And behind it all, the cross-examining lawyer is motivated — indeed ethically driven — not by a sense of justice, not by a desire for truth, not by fairness or decency, but always by the interests of the client.
> Flowing from the overriding imperative of zealous advocacy is the duty to attack and, if possible, destroy a harmful witness by any means permitted by law. A trial lawyer, as the executioner of this obligation, wields a fearsome power (pages 34 and 35).

A trial lawyer admitted, after a long career in criminal law, that only one of the many defendants he saved from conviction was actually innocent. Not limiting himself to trial lawyers, Bachman asserted that "*law is the only learned profession in which one is ethically obligated to hurt people*" (page 36). "The lawyer's professional life is filled with aggressive, manipulative, half-truthful and other destructive behaviors" (page 107). For example, " When the principle of free religious expression is challenged, a lawyer will come forth not only in its defense, but also to profess the freedom of religious cults to brainwash converts" (page 89). Bachman emphasized that the harrowing pursuit of the ethical ideals of one's profession results not only in perpetrating violence on others, but violence on attorneys themselves, as the conflict between professional ethics and society-wide ethics takes its toll emotionally.

Like other socially accepted or at least tolerated institutions, the legal profession is systematically restricted externally by the extant body of law and other socially constructed inhibitions, and intra-institutionally by its own ethical standards. But intra-individual inhibitions are complicated by pressures on the lawyer to abide by the ethic of advocacy for his or her client, even at the expense of abusing others. This admixture of inhibitions means that no lawyer is permitted to commit murder as such, though a lawyer might substantially cause loss of life. For instance, a defendant or witness becomes so distressed by a trial lawyer's harrowing tactics in court as to commit suicide, but the suicide is not considered to be a murder. Thus, what observers might view as a "murderous attack" is legally not a murder and, like other legally accepted institutions, the law profession is not allowed to commit murder per se. And neither would the law profession itself, given its own institutional ethics, condone murder per se.

While Bachman made a compelling case for the destructiveness of the lawyering institution, other authors have made a case for including their own professional institutions as inherently destructive. They would not agree, apparently, that the law is the only learned profession in which one is ethically obligated to hurt people.

The Profession of Journalism

The journalist's profession has been likened by Janet Malcolm, in speaking of her own profession in *The Journalist and the Murderer* (1990), to that of the malevolent trial lawyer. She noted the "…ironic parallel between the methods of trial lawyers and of journalists" (page 45). "Evidently, to be a good trial lawyer you have to be a good hater. A lawsuit is to ordinary life what war is to peacetime. In a lawsuit, everybody on the other side is bad. A trial transcript is a discourse in malevolence" (page 63). But, she observed, unlike the trial lawyer whose adversary role is clear, the journalist must pose from the very outset as a kind of friend, even a psychotherapist, leaving the question of how to justify the "murderous" act.

> Every journalist who is not too stupid or too full of himself to notice what is going on knows that what he does is morally indefensible. He is a kind of confidence man, preying on peoples' vanity, ignorance, or loneliness, gaining their trust and betraying them without remorse. Journalists justify their treachery in various ways according to their temperaments. The more pompous talk about freedom of speech and the "public's right to know"; the least talented talk about Art; the seemliest talk about earning a living (page 3).

We are all familiar with myriad other institutions which even more clearly not only permit but have as their essential reason for existence the purposeful commission of violence, albeit violence shy of outright legally defined murder. Among such institutions, sports offer clear examples.

Sports

Sports may be defined generally as entertaining exercises in sublimated warfare that are characterized by competition and striving for dominance short of deliberate lethality. Deliberately lethal acts in sports are illegal.

Boxers are physically and mentally trained to hurt an opponent to the point that the opponent cannot continue. The preferred method is to induce a state of unconsciousness in the opponent, what is called a "knockout," a condition dependent on inducing insult to the brain, typically in amounts resulting in permanent brain damage. In the long and much revered tradition of the pugilistic arts, a boxer is rated not merely according to wins and losses but also by the number and proportion of knockouts, or brain-damaging results, he has achieved. To become a boxer-hero one has to have done considerable damage to one's opponents and, almost always, have tolerated considerable damage to one's own body and brain. None of the many boxing deaths in the history of boxing (an average of five per year in recent years) has ever resulted in a murder conviction though thousands of fans have knowingly and exultantly shouted "murder."

"Ultimate fighting," one of the names for a new sport, continues to raise strenuous objections but is now legal in many states including New York (Barry, 1997), where the state legislature was strongly supportive. Its supporters claim that it not as dangerous as boxing because there have been no reported deaths so far, and that it is better to legalize it in order to establish some control. *Esquire*, the magazine for men, devoted eight pages to an article on "ultimate fighting" (Kriegel, 1996), second only to a 10-page article entitled "In Praise of Dangerous Women," referring to women who ruin men's lives.

The object is to cause pain and submission. A fighter does whatever he can to cause his opponent so much pain and injury that the opponent is rendered unconscious or gives up but, hopefully, not before the typically vast audience has thoroughly enjoyed the brutality. Thus, a leading hero is "a purveyor of pain, he plays perfectly: his skill is nothing less than an American preoccupation. People just love to see the bad guy kick ass" (Kriegel, page 94). The hero is avidly followed by "the best-looking chicks." Except for eye-gouging, biting, and throat kicking, no moves are off limits. A fighter can kick his opponent in the groin, knock his teeth out, or rip his lips off. This ostensibly "new" sport, which is at least as old as Roman gladiators, is appealing to both the fighters and audiences because of its extreme sadomasochism. Like all sadomasochism, which ostensibly is highly sexual, it shows a preference for violence over sexuality, as made clear by a statement by its biggest "ultimate fighter" hero: "I'd rather fight than fuck" (Kriegel, page 98).

Football is a North American game that is inherently violent. While not explicitly designed to seriously injure or kill opponents, many of its heroes are the really "hard hitters" who down their opponents with a vengeance that has often resulted in crippling injury or even death, though not murder charges. A football player's much-valued toughness is associated with willing personal acceptance of punishment and injury. Special recognition is given for "playing injured," provided the player does not handicap his team thereby. Fans as well as players zealously endorse not only "beating" the opposing team but may be especially pleased at their team hitting opponents hard enough to force them out of the game.

A Special NFL Classic Edition of *Sports Illustrated* (1995) featured on the cover The Toughest Quarterback Ever and a section called "Tough as Nails" glorifies the most violent players. For example, a noted Hall of Famer, albeit not the very toughest or meanest, explained how only getting caught defined "dirty," outside-of-the-rules play. The player was quoted as saying:

> When we played … I was looking to head butt someone on every play. I'd set guys up by throwing a few cross body blocks, then throw a leg whip. And at 6'9", I could leg whip the crap out of you.

"This was a scary dude, on and off the field" (page 20).

All sports feature planned competition within the rules. But the rules may not be enforced. Just as football players can get away with dirty play when the rules are not rigorously enforced, so do other kinds of athletes exceed the official limitations on violence. Often, it is the beyond-the-rules activity that is most attractive to the fans.

Professional ice hockey players engage in a great many extracurricular battles on the ice which have nothing to do with the game of ice hockey. Their brawls, resembling a cross between wrestling and boxing, often persist for a minute or more as the referees stand by and fans are stirred to greater enthusiasm. A young superfan told me that he and his friends enjoy their season tickets primarily because they can see so many of these brutal, non-hockey, battles.

Baseball, the quintessential American game, involves a great many potentially injurious events over the course of even a single game played within the rules. Players may bend the rules and "accidentally" injure one another; for example, running to a base with spikes flying. And, though intimidation is part of the game, players are not killed. Players who are so skillful as to come close to physically harming opponents without actually harming them may get special recognition. For example, baseball pitchers make reputations on their abilities to intimidate but not physically harm opposing batters. "Sal the Barber" Maglie, pitcher for what was then known as the New York Giants, was less known for tonsorial skills as such than for his skill at "shaving" the faces of batters with his very close pitches. In *The Ultimate Baseball Book* (Okrent and Lewine, 1991), a famous Dodger pitcher defined his occupation, thereby explaining how he had opposing batters dodging his pitches and striking out instead of hitting. "Pitching", Sandy Koufax said, "is the art of instilling fear by making a man flinch." Yet his control was such that in 1966, Koufax set a National League record by pitching 323 innings without hitting a single batter (page 281).

Examples of Illegal Violence in Legal Institutions

Thus far we have examined only examples of institutions bound simultaneously by law, ethically defined limits, and careful supervision by a governing body. What happens when otherwise high-minded, legally constituted institutions are effectively exempt from the law and even their own institutional rules? This situation illustrates the principle that *exemption from the law, due to lack of enforcement or secrecy, serves to enhance violence proclivities.*

Colleges and Universities

Institutions of higher education have long failed, in relation to their students, to enforce laws, policies, and rules applicable to people outside of their campuses. They have been especially lax with regard to students' use of alcohol and other drugs and in relation to fraternities. For example, state laws against underage drinking have tended to be merely communicated to students rather than enforced. When these theoretical inhibitions are not really enforced, they are not real rules. Much of campus violence, including virtually all instances of date rape, occurs under the influence of alcohol (Rivinus and Larimer, 1993). In the absence of enforcement of the existing laws, policies, and rules by colleges and universities as institutions, or by local police, there is institutional sanction for, rather than against, this and other forms of campus violence.

As John Silber, the president of Boston University, observed in a *New York Times* op-ed piece entitled "Students Should Not Be Above the Law" (1996): "...today colleges and universities tend to circumvent the courts and bury serious criminal cases in their own judicial systems." What happens when effective exemption from the law is compounded by secrecy rather than openness? College fraternities, which by their nature are secretive, provide an example.

Anne Matthews (Crothers and Matthews, 1996) reported that "the fraternity initiation remains the most secret of campus rituals — and the most debauched" (page 50). She and photographer C. Taylor Crothers documented many hazing rituals at a conservative, selective, well-endowed East Coast university where students were joining one of the 10 largest North American fraternities. The fraternity's national headquarters said that the organization's purpose was to develop social responsibility and that hazing is officially condemned. Nevertheless, "new members of an all-fraternity drinking club entertain hundreds of students and alumni by drinking up to a case of beer apiece, chased by a fifth of vodka, tequila or 40-proof "Mad Dog" wine, followed by raw trout or Vienna sausage" (page 50). Of course, such practices result in serious injury and even death. Matthews quoted a fraternity rush chairman, "Hazing is very educational about human nature … the nicest, politest, most churchgoing people turn out to be so mean and angry. And cruel, if you give them a little power" (page 50).

By maintaining that its practices must be secret, an institution has free rein to engage in violent behavior. Then, even an institution supposedly governed by a superordinate institution, such as when a fraternity is governed both by its national organization and its college or university, can commit violence. The example of college fraternities illustrates that nonenforcement of the rules and secrecy allow and, thereby, foster institutional violence.

The Military

Military institutions in the U.S. as well as in many if not most other nations, clearly prepare for and engage in lethal aggression. Whereas sports may be thought of as sublimated warfare, the military is explicitly and usually legally devoted to actual warfare. Yet, most military institutions are mandated only to defend their countries and are restricted to "gentlemanly conduct," the rules of the Geneva Convention, and the like. They are not supposed to engage in exploitation and cruelty. Ostensibly, the military does not encourage cruelty, though some militaries, such as the Nazis, have been trained to be cruel in order to reduce resistance and to break the will of the enemy. In any case, the dangerous business of training people to be violent can readily lend itself to even blatant forms of cruelty, particularly if rules against cruelty are not enforced and practices are carried out secretly.

Critics complain about episodes of cruelty in the U.S. military as if cruelty is not integral to the legally and socially mandated mission of military institutions to train their members to injure and kill. Outrage ensues when it is discovered that a particular military training facility is a culture of abuse, though any military institution must have inherently destructive as well as defensive aims. Thus, a *New York Times* editorial (Citadel's Culture, 1997) said: "It is a sad commentary on campus morality that it took the presence of women to expose deviant conduct that victimizes male students as well. The Citadel's hazing tradition teaches young men that brutalizing others and denigrating women is what it takes to be a military officer." But this tradition is inherent to all institutions pledged to train its members in violence. "Hazing" is, of course, a euphemism; the practice is more accurately termed "training in cruelty."

Institutional inculcation of cruelty requires systematically training members to abide their own suffering as well as that of others. Riane Eisler (1996) noted, "It is instructive in this connection that the training of the Nazi SS officers who manned the mass extermination camps is said to have included the raising of puppies, which they were then ordered to feed, play with, and care for in every way — and then kill with no signs of emotion" (page 96). Whether called hazing or training in cruelty or simply obedience training, all institutions that have as at least one of their purposes the inflicting of pain engage systematically, officially or unofficially, in fostering callousness to their own and others' pain. As Eisler put it, "…once empathy and love are in any context habitually suppressed, this tends to result in what psychologists call blunted affect — a reduced and highly compartmentalized capacity to respond to feelings (affect) other than anger, contempt, and similar "hard" emotions" (page 96).

On Thursday, January 30, 1997 the television program "Headline News" showed a homemade videotape of 1991 and 1993 U.S. Marine Corps hazings marking the completion of paratrooper training. Officially, on completion of that training, Marines are awarded their "wings" in the form of a medal that is supposed to be pinned to the Marine's uniform. In the videotape, however, each of the many medal recipients wears only a T-shirt and stands still while another Marine pins the medal into his chest, making sure to maximize the pain by punching the medal in and rubbing the already inserted medal back and forth to further increase the wound and the pain. The recipients are shown grimacing and screaming in pain.

The Marine Corps officially proscribed this hazing practice of "blood winging" or "gold winging," which means smashing the medal into the chest, but recognizes that the hazing was going on in previous years and has continued. A quite similar hazing of a Navy submariner eventuated in a sailor's suicide after he was pressured to reveal the names of his tormentors or be court-martialed, as reported on the 6:30 p.m. news broadcast (National Broadcasting Company, February 12, 1997). Clearly, the official training in the military lends itself to such behavior which, therefore, must be vigilantly guarded against. In his comments on the hazing, Army General John Shalikashvili, chairman of the Joint Chiefs of Staff, said, "People get very charged up in this business. We demand people who are tough and who can stand up to adversity" (Ruane, 1997, page A10). But, of course, the legally authorized training itself is readily conducive to cruel behavior.

Psychologist Harold Hall has noted (personal communication, September 16, 1997) that in his own paratrooper training in 1966 the graduate was given special insignia that made him "airborne." These marks of distinction on one's cap and jump boots as well as badge, entitled the graduate to be sadistic to any lower or even equal ranking serviceman, especially in Vietnam.

Antigovernment Extremists, Terrorists, and Deadly Cults

There is no cruelty like the cruelty of the righteous — Arthur Deikman, in *The Wrong Way Home* (1990, page 106)

Having illustrated the propensities for and limitations against institutional violence in legally constituted and thus socially allowable institutions, let us examine institutions that simultaneously exempt themselves from the law, have no accountability whatsoever to anyone but themselves, are highly secretive, have as their purpose the commission of violence, demand that members commit even lethal violence to gain rank, and provide to members a sense of great entitlement and righteousness for doing so. Antigovernment extremists, terrorist groups, and deadly cults are three overlapping kinds of institutions that fit these criteria. It is important to understand their range of attributes, the differences among them, and their essential similarities.

This section will focus on two at least superficially quite dissimilar examples: the Patriot or militia movement in the U.S. and the Aum Doomsday Cult in Japan. The Patriots consist largely of economically and educationally poor White individuals while Aum draws considerable wealth and members who tend to be especially well-educated in the hard sciences.

In light of the principles previously articulated and the institutional characteristics of the Patriot and Aum groups, we will be able to grasp why they commit even lethal violence. But we will also ask why these groups are not more deadly than they are. What inhibits them in the absence of outside governance? Given that they require violent behavior, act as though exempt from the law, are secretive, and are motivated by "righteousness," what is to stop them? To answer this question, we must examine their natures closely, asking along the way what causes such violent institutions to form, how they maintain themselves, how they can resist the inhibitions that society promotes, and how their members can avoid becoming conscience-stricken. What already considered or new extragroup, intragroup, and intra-individual inhibitions are or can be effective?

The Antigovernment Extremist Patriots

This seemingly loosely organized collection of antigovernment extremists functions in an institutional manner that strongly encourages violence, albeit sometimes in the name of "protection" for themselves and perhaps others outside the group. The U.S. groups commonly label themselves Patriots (Southern Poverty Law Center, 1996). They are overwhelmingly White and Christian, and predominantly male, and they are "...a potpourri of the American right, from members of the Christian Coalition to the Ku Klux Klan — people united by their hatred of the federal government" (page 6).

Floyd Cochran (1996) is a former youth recruiter and national spokes-man for the virulent White supremacist movement, Aryan Nations. Since leaving the movement he has been making presentations, as "acts of atone-ment" designed to unseat the movement. He characterized its members as poor in education and literacy and stated that they spread their hate messages through the Internet, radio, and comic books. He gave talks and showed a videotape on November 6, 1996 at Delaware County Community College in Pennsylvania. He noted that 14- to 25-year-olds have been joining the move-ment in great numbers and that, as a young man, "I joined a hate group because it made me someone." He and other recruiters have used public relations techniques, such as friendly socialization, and they focused on rural, all-White areas where people are quite isolated. Cochran was able to use the media to propagandize: "My bigotry became palatable to the media who would just repeat what I said." He estimated that there are 3500 "skinheads" (young neo-Nazis) and 51 hate groups in Pennsylvania alone, but said the groups "do not mass in numbers because of their paranoia."

The movement's deadly aims are obfuscated by their methods for devel-oping a following. Members approach potential recruits with friendliness and recourse to the Bible. They proclaim that their racist orientation is called for in the Bible and that what they do is in the name of God and Christianity. These messages provide justification for hating and make the movement acceptable. The videotape shown by Cochran featured young male neo-Nazi members exulting in their strident messages such as: "God is hate," "I love my race to the point I kill," "Whatever is destroying our race must be elim-inated," and "The Bible says the Jews are descendants of Satan."

Having had ample time now for considerable thinking, the former evan-gelist for the Aryan Nations has said that ignoring the groups won't work and neither will combating them with violence because they truly are like the Hydra that grows two heads when one is cut off. He strongly recom-mended countering them with a vigorous multifaceted educational approach. Cochran has felt that such groups exist because of what is not taught in society, and that people are not sufficiently challenged to think. The clergy should emphasize correct quoting and interpretation of the Bible to counter the false versions. And stereotypes should be countered with the reality of human diversity. Cochran also suggested that Georgia's antimasking law (against wearing disguises) should be emulated by other states. In summary, he said that economic difficulties, poor education, and lack of information play key roles in recruitment susceptibility.

The Patriot movement followers may number as many as 5 million nationwide according to Morris Dees (1996). This figure may include any-body supportive of the Patriots. The hard core Patriots, however, who may number anywhere from 15,000 to 250,000, could be enough, given sufficient secrecy and the right equipment, to violently overthrow a nation, even the U.S.

The hard core Patriots appear to have a kind of group paranoia that stirs them to prepare to do what they fear the government is going to do to them. Helped by radical White supremacists, this antigovernment alliance proposes that extreme action is necessary and, because the government is armed they, too, must be armed. Accusing the government itself of unlawful activity destructive to its citizens and their rights, they react with unlawful activity themselves, including terrorist forms of violence. Though their tactics are disapproved by most citizens, in part they are able to gather sympathizers because not only they but many other people perceive the government as too restrictive of individual rights. The very notion of the government inhibiting them inspires more fear, hatred, and preparation because they are united by hatred of the government.

Morris Dees (1996), the chief trial counsel for the Southern Poverty Law Center and its Militia Task Force, has emphasized the relentlessness of the Patriots' loathing of the federal government. Inhibiting antigovernment extremists is especially difficult, in keeping with the Patriots' image of the Hydra which suggests that each act of inhibition or suppression may inspire a counterreaction more severe than anything that preceded it.

The Southern Poverty Law Center (1996) has made 14 recommendations for limiting the power and dangerousness of the Patriots. The first nine suggest legal and regulatory procedures. The next four suggest preventive actions by government employees, journalists, clergy, and schools. Recommendation 14 says that "charges of government misconduct must be investigated promptly and thoroughly" (page 45). This last recommendation raises the issue of how government can and does inspire aggression against it and the citizens it represents.

Government Facilitation of Antigovernment Extremists

No government can afford to be merely an inhibitor or repressor of its citizens. Its citizens must feel that they are nurtured and served in return for the self-sacrifices required in any organizational endeavor. Thus, highly repressive governments tend to be overthrown, though often in favor of equally or more repressive governments. For instance, the Russian revolution of 1917 seems inevitable in retrospect since czarist rule was blatantly out of touch with and negligent of its starving citizens who felt they had to revolt or die. Of course, czarist tyranny was immediately replaced by communist tyranny.

A wise government will ensure that its nurturance and sensitivity to its citizens' needs takes precedence over its inhibitory and regulatory actions, just as parents should make sure that the love of their children is paramount,

with discipline guiding rather than stifling them. The identifying characteristic of a totalitarian government is its intolerance of individual freedom.
Even a democratic government, however, can begin to behave in such an
inhibitory manner as to cause a loss of freedom indistinguishable from a
clearly authoritarian or totalitarian government. Such is the text of Philip
Howard's book *The Death of Common Sense* (1994).

Howard showed how the U.S., by wrapping itself in ever more laws and
regulations, has tended to strangle not only the actions of its citizens but
their ability to develop judgment and common sense. He noted the doubling
of federal agencies from 1960 to 1980; that by 1994 federal statutes and formal
rules totalled about 1 million words; that our tax law had 36,000 pages; that
the more the regulation, the more loopholes can be found by lawyers to
subvert their intent; and that, therefore, "a culture of resistance sets in"
(page 49). Citizens react negatively to the enmeshment of their bread and
butter institutions — schools, hospitals, and workplaces — in regulatory law.
For example, "hospitals now spend on the order of 25% of their budget on
administration, mainly to comply with these procedural requirements …
40% of all doctors say they would not choose the profession again, the main
reason being the hassle factor — the growing levels of paperwork" (pages 93
and 94). Of course, people with less income and less education than doctors
or lawyers are injured far more because they have fewer resources to cope
with.

The growing gap in income between richest and poorest (Holmes, 1996)
increases the aggravation. As of 1996, the U.S. had more children in poverty
than any other industrialized nation. A large portion of the most violence-
ready followers of the Patriot movement, such as the Aryan Nation, tend to
have low income and, therefore, are especially affected. They tend to blame
their troubles on cheap laborers from other countries and they are against
the United Nations as a symbol of a potential one-world government that
would threaten them because they have been left behind in our rapidly
escalating high-technology society.

As Howard observed, "The injuries are mounting, and Americans are
building up a reservoir of hatred. Just listen to the radio talk shows"
(page 154). Government is increasingly seen as the enemy, especially when
its protective functions are perceived as simultaneously restrictive of freedom
and wasteful of taxpayers' money. For example, in 1994, it was discovered
that the Defense Department was spending more on procedures for travel
reimbursement ($2.2 billion) than on travel ($2 billion) (Howard, 1994).
Quite significantly, as Morris Dees (1996) explained, the militia movement,
which crystallized in 1992, was formed by people who "felt frustrated by too
many regulations, threatened by a one-world economy, and frightened by a
government that had gotten too big and too powerful" (page 69).

Similarly, the National Broadcasting Company (NBC) in 1995 began a long series of programs called "The Fleecing of America" showing one government project after another that produced nothing or close to it, all at taxpayer expense. On June 4, 1996, NBC anchorman and narrator Tom Brokaw announced that, so far, their investigators reckoned that these projects had cost $58.2 billion. The "Fleecing of America" series about wasteful government spending has continued through 1999.

In light of these developments, such antigovernment institutions as the Patriots may be seen as representing merely an extreme version of disenchantment with the U.S. government, although a version that may readily lapse into paranoia and violence rather than nonviolent protest and reform. As in all cases of possible paranoid ideation and behavior, it is important to ferret out any basis in objective reality. Paranoid phenomena, which will be discussed more fully later in this chapter, often have some reality basis, albeit not nearly enough to fully explain the phenomena.

Like many other citizens, the Patriots resent being regulated minutely, taxed deeply, and subjected to wasteful spending of their hard-earned money. I make these observations not as excuses for their violence but as a basis for understanding and helping to redirect their efforts. Ironically, the paranoia of the bigoted Patriots is remarkably like that of the paranoia Black people were accused of in the 1960s (Whitaker, 1970; 1972a) when racial tensions erupted into violence as this disenfranchised population grew so frustrated with a government they saw, often correctly, as far more restrictive and unjust than nurturing (Higginbotham, 1996). Like the current Patriots, they did not trust the government, were prepared to be violent, and were determined to own rather than serve in others' institutions (Whitaker, 1972b).

Part of the solution is improving our government through democratic means, making it more sensitive and empathic, thereby lessening the motivation to violence and showing the viability of peaceful reform. Having less to rebel against in our society might lessen the rebellion, at least by reducing the reality basis for group paranoia. In order for people to trust institutions, the institutions, whatever their kind, must provide meaningful, empowered belonging (Deikman and Whitaker, 1979).

Dees (1996), the chief trial counsel for the Southern Poverty Law Center and its Militia Task Force, is widely known for his stand against the militia movement whose members have often made threats on his life. But, like all those who realize they have to understand "the enemy" to defeat or at least change him, he is also empathic. Having studied apparent militia events at Ruby Ridge (near Naples, ID) the Waco (Texas) Branch Davidian tragedy, and the Oklahoma City bombing, he has shown an understanding of where its members are coming from. He presented a hypothetical defense of Timothy McVeigh who was accused of the Oklahoma City bombing, presuming (correctly, it turns out) that McVeigh would likely be found guilty, but whose best chance to avoid the death penalty would be if the following were presented:

> The jury would learn about McVeigh's obsession with his hero in *The Turner Diaries* who blew up a federal building; his valiant service in the Desert Storm campaign; his anguish at seeing American soldiers serving under United Nations command in Somalia; his fears that his country's values will be lost to a godless one-world government; his outrage that FBI agents would murder innocent women and children; his anger at corrupt, overpaid politicians (page 167).

While empathy for murderous people might appear odious indeed, it provides both a realistic understanding of motivation and practical ways of inhibiting them. For one thing, it leads to a clear realization that *military training, i.e., training to harm and destroy as well as to protect, can readily be transferred to causes unintended by the trainers.* Historically, civil wars and overthrows of governments have usually involved people using government training and tactics, designed originally to defend the government, to war against the government. The old adage seems to hold: those who live by the sword die by the sword. Our government ought to emphasize nurturance and negotiation more than training in destruction.

Institutional training in paralethal and lethal violence is dangerous for all concerned, including the government or other institutions that conduct such training. All that need happen is that the trainees become disenchanted with their trainers, such as the government, and ache to use that training against the trainers. Currently, as Dees (1996) has noted, a clandestine group called the Special Forces Underground, formed in 1992, has as its goal forcing the federal government "back into its constitutional prison" (page 213). This group relies mostly on active duty military personnel and ex-service members who have had covert operations training. Furthermore, there are periodic reports of active duty soldiers linked to White supremacist groups killing Black citizens. For example, a paratrooper was charged with shooting and killing a Black couple in Fayetteville, NC in December 1996 (Soldier, 1997).

The Aum Doomsday Cult

Aum Shinrikyo, a cult originating in Japan, is in many ways the opposite of the Patriot movement. Whereas the Patriots are loosely configured to the point of apparent leaderlessness, Aum is tightly organized and clearly headed by an absolute leader. The Patriots are virtually all White, Aum virtually all Asian. The Patriots are poor in formal education and financial resources while Aum members tend to be very highly educated in the natural sciences and have immense financial resources. Aum's five "commandos," who led the massive nerve gas (sarin) strike in the Tokyo subway system on March 20, 1995 were a cardiovascular surgeon, a graduate student in particle physics, an applied physics graduate, an applied physicist who graduated at the top of his class, and an electronics engineer. Aum "…is the story of the ultimate cult: a wired, high-tech, designer-drug, billion-dollar army of New Age zealots, under the leadership of a blind and bearded madman, armed with weapons of mass destruction" (Kaplan and Marshall, 1996, pages 2 and 3).

Aum has continued to use sophisticated methods for infiltrating communities, continuing to attract converts, and marshaling legal support for its imprisoned leaders, many of whom were released in 1999. The vast majority of Japanese citizens, remembering that Aum killed 12 people and made 6000 others ill in their 1995 saran gas attack in the Tokyo subway system, have resorted to harsh but generally ineffective methods to get rid of their approximately 5000 members (Sims, 1999). In addition to finally acknowledging their actions in the 1995 Tokyo subway attack, on December 2, 1999 Aum took "…responsibility for other attacks and promised compensation, but victims' relatives dismissed the move as self-serving" (Cult, 1999, page A8).

The apparently gross differences between the Patriots and Aum are rather superficial compared to the similarities in their core identities and ideology. Though the Patriots say they are leaderless and they realize that fostering antigovernment sentiments is more acceptable in public than preaching racism and Ayran superiority, some of the most violently inclined have been known admirers of Adolf Hitler (Cochran, 1996; Dees, 1996), including Timothy McVeigh (Dees, 1996, page 52). Thus, it is highly probable that the Patriot movement, including the Aryan Nation particularly, is more identified ideologically with Hitler than would appear from what they offer for public consumption. Some members who resemble Hitler in stridency, righteousness, and bigotry have been ideologic leaders of the movement. But knowing that blatant bigotry turns most people off, and not wishing to lose potential recruits, even these leaders often downplay their bigotry in public in favor of culling animosity toward the government. Both the Patriots and Aum are authoritarian to the core.

Furthermore, both institutions preach impending doom. Aum's leader, Shoko Asahara, linked his authority to Lord Shiva the Destroyer, who reigns over the Hindu pantheon of gods. Thus, Aum is like the Patriots who predict a doom they themselves appear to be implementing. Aum, too, has engaged avidly in actions that would wreak havoc even on ordinary citizens, all in the name of what Aum calls the supreme authority or the supreme truth.

Both institutions maintain that they are serving a spiritual good, a cleansing action that would make a holy recreation possible. The idea is that first we must destroy, and that the process will require supreme sacrifices. The holy figures in these cases are Hitler and Asahara who himself has venerated Hitler. This observation leads to yet another similarity.

Both institutions carry out deceitful recruitment, and the training mandates sacrifices by inculcating bold lies. In accord with Hitler's claim that "the great masses of the people ... will more easily fall victims to a big lie than a small one" (Kaplan, 1992, page 676), Asahara has engaged in big lies. He pretended he could levitate, read minds, see the future, hear the voice of God, and more. Asahara even repackaged his dirty bath water as "miracle Pond" and sold it for nearly $800 per quart" (Kaplan and Marshall, 1996, page 18). "Believers who donated over $2000 to the Shambalization Plan Fund received the best prize, two gallons of Asahara's dirty bath water" (page 19). But the leaders of deadly cults are not perceived by genuine devotees as dirty or dishonest.

As documented in Chapter 2, Aum's recruitment tactics involved Aum members pretending to have no affiliation, but then leading on potential recruits. Like most duplicitous cults, Aum also convinced members to give up large amounts of money to the cult as protection from doom. The message common to the Patriots and Aum, and myriad other deadly cults, has been that only devout members would survive the certain advent of doomsday. Both of these institutions are totally devoid of humor about themselves; they are deadly serious. As will be discussed later, people who are severely paranoid are strikingly devoid of a sense of humor. We might say that they take themselves far too seriously.

The natural progression of such a cult follows the same general pattern regardless of its initial constitution. The differences in the initial characteristics of cult members and the society in which they emerge, e.g., the differences between the Patriots and Aum, recede in significance. Their progressively greater secrecy, lying, unaccountability, repression of dissent, and urging of violent behavior in the name of religion result in their having to exert more and more force against (1) the threat that members will begin to question and think for themselves, and (2) attempts by those external to the cult to redress its wrongs. Such a cult, therefore, engages more and more in paralethal and lethal practices against both members and outsiders. As the practices of high-pressure indoctrinations become inadequate in the face of growing skepticism, both inside and outside of the cult, outright punishments must be introduced. And when even harsh punishments are not enough to suppress dissent, then atrocities, including murders, must be committed.

In the case of Aum, successful recruiting appeals to alienated youth were followed by stripping them of their possessions, isolating them from their families and outside society, and other methods of divesting them as much as possible from their identities as individuals. Members were made to endure extreme hardships in hypnotic-inducing circumstances featuring extreme isolation, sleep and food deprivation, and ceaselessly strident propagandizing. Later, members were made to submit to what was acknowledged as "brainwashing," by means of drugs and cranial electrical shocking devices. Members were told that their paths to higher spiritual enlightenment would be facilitated by these devices which would reduce brain activity, as measured by electroencephalography, to the almost nonexistent level of their supreme master himself. Asahara claimed it, but had no such low level himself. If a member was still questioning and wanting to leave the cult, that member had to be murdered without a trace of the body left for would-be investigators to discover. At the insistence of their leader, Aum members also murdered an attorney who was investigating them, together with the attorney's wife and children.

The Art and Science of Inducing Violent Behavior

Violent behavior can be induced quickly and fairly readily in most people who are subjected to strong, uniformly authoritarian pressure that suggests they would be right in submitting. The social psychologist Solomon Asch (1952) demonstrated in a classic series of experiments that even the pressure of a group of six students (who were Asch's confederates) could induce a given individual to override his or her own visual perception of lengths of lines in favor of conforming to the group's clearly incorrect judgment. As Riane Eisler (1996) has pointed out, "What has not received even a fraction of the attention paid to that finding is what Asch's experiments demonstrated about dissent: that when just *one* of Asch's six confederates disagreed with the answers of the majority, the rate of conformity declined to a mere 5 percent!" (page 388). Clearly, an individual would-be dissenter can be greatly encouraged to dissent if supported by even one other individual in an otherwise unified group pressure situation. But when there is no one supporting the would-be dissenter in such a situation, even quite "normal" people may perform egregious forms of aggression.

Studies by Stanley Milgram (1974) strongly suggested that most apparently normal people could be influenced to administer what they believed to be severe shock to an apparently hapless experimental "subject," as instructed by a white-coated experimenter and his assistant. Ninety percent of the real subjects, who thought they were teaching memory tasks to the "subject," actually pressed the switches that indicated the most extreme pain, despite hearing the subject screaming in apparent pain, if they were at a physical distance from the subject. As one of Milgram's subjects said, "You really begin to forget that there's a guy out there, even though you can hear him. For a long time I just concentrated on pressing the switches and reading the words" (page 38). Thus, the combination of an authoritarian leader and distance from the victim, which serves to dehumanize the victim, can induce ordinary people to inflict pain and suffering on innocent persons.

Like all deadly cults, the Aryan Nation and Aum rely on these two techniques — authoritarian leadership and distance from the victims — and on certain additional conditions and techniques because highly reliable training in violent behavior is not sufficiently based on inducements of a temporary sort. Thorough inculcation is effected by frequent repetitions and admonitions which can be optimally influential with especially vulnerable subjects. Thus, among the conditions needed are voids in the nurturance and education of young potential recruits, and the leader's ability to structure the environment in ways favorable to hypnotic forms of transformation.

The Aryan Nation or, more broadly, the Patriots have tended to especially recruit poorly educated youths whose ignorance greatly facilitates bigotry and suggestibility. Though Aum recruited many youths who were exceptionally well-educated in the physical sciences, like others in Japan's school systems they lacked much schooling in anything else. Other conditions were also important. Kaplan and Marshall (1996) put the matter succinctly, "It would be easy to dismiss Aum as a peculiarly Japanese case, and indeed there are conditions in Japan that shaped the cult's unique character. The straitjacket schools and workplaces, the absentee fathers and alienated youth no doubt helped fuel Shoko Asahara's rise to power. But ... ineffective and bungling police, fanatic sects, and disaffected scientists are hardly limited to the Japanese" (page 289).

Like other youths lured into cults, once recruited, Aum inculcated them in a "religion" that promised to fill their spiritual voids with supreme truth while requiring they submit to an absolutely authoritarian leader who was to be their god. Their old straitjackets were replaced by even more constricting garments. Asahara declared himself to be the divine leader of a completely nonviolent religion. As stated by Kaplan and Marshall (1996):

> Inside the growing communes, though, Asahara or his disciples would beat followers for the smallest act of disobediance. This was termed "karma disposal," the dumping of spiritual baggage that holds one back in this life or the next. "I often pick on my disciples," Asahara freely admitted. "It's not because I am a sadist. It is because I have to rid them of negative karma." Asahara's theory of karma was simple: pleasure bad, pain good (page 23).

A similar progression characterized the Nazi movement as it was largely freed from societal inhibitions, thanks to enabling by economic distress together with widespread bigotry, not only in Germany but in other countries where there were ample sympathizers. In contrast, the Patriots in the U.S. are aware that their bigotry is relatively unpopular in the larger society so they must be careful to emphasize only the government as the enemy of the people. But, with fewer inhibitions emanating from society, the Patriot movement, like the Nazi movement which has served as a model, could quickly become more openly bigoted and destructive.

Reality vs. Paranoia

Frequently, various cults, hate groups, terrorists and the like are dismissed simply as "paranoid" or, in less restrained terminology, they are called "crazies." But we have seen that the matter is far more complex. A considerable foundation of pervasive social and personal conditions underlies and supports lethal group and institutional aggression. We must take into account the supportive structure for lethal institutional aggression, which is schematized in Table 3.1, if we are to understand and effectively inhibit it. The apparent paranoia of these groups is largely shared and supported in various forms by a vast number of other individuals and groups.

Were Asahara's claim that Aum's development of weaponry was only for purposes of self-defense, or the Patriots claim that they must arm for self-defense merely the propaganda of con artists, or are such claims believed by the "liars" themselves? The answer depends on understanding all of the contributions to these claims. As we have seen, sometimes there is a partial reality base to claims of persecution. And sometimes leaders knowingly lie while members are instilled to believe. Typically, however, both the leaders and members of deadly cults share at least some genuinely paranoid proclivities, albeit proclivities shared to a lesser degree by a vast, less radical supportive structure in the larger society. To survive, massive myths must have massive support.

While the paranoia of the militia, terrorist, and deadly cult institutions has some grounding in truly oppressive conditions, such as difficult economic straits in Hitler's pre-Nazi Germany and in a large segment of today's U.S.,

Table 3.1   The Supportive Structure for Lethal Institutional Aggression

Terrorists
Hate Groups
Authoritarian Institutions
Excessively Regulating Government
Societally Pervasive Dominator Mentality
Failure to Educate for Partnership Relationships

and in the alienation of Japanese youth, as examples, the paranoia also has a genuinely morbid or irrational aspect. When such institutions portray certain outsiders as the *sole* cause of their difficulties, their claims are at most grounded in only partial truths. Their slogans falsely suggest that they would be fine "if only we could get rid of the Xs or the Ys or the Zs!" (fill in Jews, or Blacks, or Catholics, or homosexuals, the mentally ill, or any nonbelievers, people with genetic defects, or the federal government). Ultimately, this kind of *failure to admit or to discover factual truth leads to trying to exterminate anyone who is different. Inevitably, the success of such movements would result in a biological genetic disaster as well as a psychogenetic disaster because extreme inbreeding weakens and eventually destroys the hereditary line, both physically and psychologically. In reality, it is not the destruction of variety among or within species but the natural diversity of humankind as well as all animal and plant life which gives the greatest promise of survival. If this natural law is disobeyed, if diversity is destroyed, then the "in-group" will be destroyed also.*

What is the individual personality basis for developing a paranoid condition? As noted in a previous work (Whitaker, 1992):

> Common to schizophrenic, bigoted, and paranoid conditions are extreme problems with self-esteem or self-worth. Paranoid and bigoted orientations are ways to raise oneself, no matter how irrationally, from a condition of devastatingly low self-esteem. Schizophrenic persons differ from groups of bigoted people in that they have not established a consensus or communion with others with whom they can share their beliefs; they are unable to convince others of the correctness of their beliefs. Schizophrenic persons are exceedingly individual, or idiosyncratic (page 7).

The paranoid form of morbidity manifest in scapegoating would be called a paranoid psychosis were it not so fully shared in common with other scapegoaters. Clinical psychology and psychiatry have no adequate clinical terms for group paranoid disorders with the small exception of *folie a deux* (literally "madness of two"), which means that two people may share the same delusional beliefs. But, as Erich Fromm noted in *The Sane Society* (1955), "just as there is a *folie a deux* there is a *folie a* millions" (page 15).

How can we further distinguish, for the practical purpose of knowing whether or what kind of intervention is advisable, genuinely morbid paranoid group phenomena from other group movements that are more rationally grounded? What is the difference, if any, between the current Patriot movement and the American Revolution, for example? A key difference is that between autonomy and domination strivings.

The revolutionaries who created the U.S. aimed to be free of English domination but had no evident aim to conquer England or to cleanse the world, as it were, of English citizens. They were content to gain their freedom from what they perceived as English oppression. In sharp contrast, the Nazi movement aimed not simply to establish or fortify German independence or autonomy but to conquer the world and to cleanse the world of its seemingly innumerable "inferior peoples." Insofar as the current Patriot, Aum, or other aggressive group movements strive not merely to establish their own independence but to dominate and destroy others to assert their superiority and to eradicate the "inferiors," they are acting out a form of paranoid ideology: "if it were not for the inferiors, whom we must dominate and destroy, we would be recognized as the superiors;" for example, as racially superior.

Even people who would individually be perceived as quite normal may become very destructive if they are subjected sufficiently to the conditions and training that make for blind obedience. Because a vast number of individuals have the rather common tendency to engage in unwarranted blaming of others for their problems, it is not difficult to understand the making of deadly cults. While paranoid proclivities make vulnerable recruits, being schizophrenic does not.

Paranoid schizophrenic persons show greater idiosyncrasy than can be tolerated in group paranoia. Persons who are schizophrenic are so idiosyncratic or distinctively different from others, including other schizophrenic persons, that idiosyncrasy is a hallmark of schizophrenic disorders (Whitaker, 1992). Thus, if a schizophrenic patient is confronted with another person who has the same delusion, something gives. For example, in the case of two women who each thought she was the Virgin Mary, one concluded that she was not the Virgin Mary but must be Mary Magdalene, thus preserving each woman's claim to individual distinction. Group identity and cohesion are not staples with persons who are schizophrenic. But individuals who are paranoid, though not paranoid schizophrenic, are more likely to band together, provided they can agree on a common enemy.

The extreme cohesiveness of Aum, whose members shared patently absurd beliefs inculcated by their leader, surely suggests a highly consensual "folie a groupe" to use Fromm's concept. Members of the militia and Patriot groups appear to be a strongly united force only in terms of having the government as their common enemy, but many are united also in their belief that minorities, homosexuals, Whites who like Black music, etc. are also enemies in common. Similarly, but in their more advanced phase, Aum members believed that they had to rid the world of all outsiders in order to cleanse it — to make a clean start in preparation for a new world order. Given this kind of thinking, but not a pervasive kind of thought disorder, nor quite idiosyncratic beliefs, these extremists would not be called schizophrenic, but they might meet the criteria for a paranoid disorder if we had such a designation for a group.

The structure of the militia movement does allow and even promotes extreme individuation within the bounds of the single-faceted scapegoating group identity. *The Seditionist* (Beam, 1992) is the title of the most popular militia operations manual other than *The Turner Diaries* (Pierce, 1978). Leaderlessness serves the strategic purpose of making it difficult, if not impossible, for the government to focus its detection, surveillance, and antiterrorist work on any overall organization. Instead, there is a movement consisting mostly of "cells" as small as a few members each. Members of a cell can claim, with some evidence, that they are basically unrelated to any other group or cell that the government challenges. This strategy happens also to lend itself to a kind of paranoid freedom of ideation and expression that suits more idiosyncratic individuals who detest authority of any kind, whether it be irrational (authoritarian) or rationally authoritative and democratically determined. But this apparent leaderlessness could quickly give way to clearer centralization of authority.

Given the strategic and psychological characteristics of leaderless cells, what would it take to unite such groups into an even more destructive, massively united movement? One decisive condition would be many, if not most or all, cells perceiving a new "clear" and massive injustice on the part of the government. Ruby Ridge and Waco have provided considerable grist for the milling of a united movement, because many people besides militia members could question the need for the harsh government tactics that were employed. In the case of the Oklahoma City bombing, the worst terroristic attack in the history of our country, the bombing has been touted by extreme members as a government plot.

A second decisive condition is that militia members' insistence on individualism, or resistance to becoming more massively united, is lessened if they find other scapegoats in common. Dees (1996) noted that "of the 441 militia and 368 Patriot groups that existed between 1994 and 1996, 137 had ties to the racist right — to groups like the Aryan Nations and the Ku Klux Klan. Of all the militias, these groups and the types of members they attract are the most dangerous" (page 200).

Both the Aryan Nations and Aum fit the paranoid pattern comprising two synergistically interacting dynamics captured in the assertions: "I would be very great if I were not so very persecuted," and, "I am persecuted because of my great qualities." Grandiose and persecutory delusions go hand in hand to form an explanation which simultaneously serves to boost self-esteem, albeit precariously, and to vent hostility. As exemplified by *The Turner Diaries*, the paranoid process engenders a grand pseudocommunity where everything that exists fits into the underlying delusional system.

Youths who become alienated through lack of nurturance and social success must somehow raise their self-esteem and avoid feeling inferior. It is then but an easy step to feeling oppressed and seeking redress in a "family" that elevates their self-esteem by identifying them with supremacist groups like the Aryan Nations and Aum, or a hate-mongering street gang.

Having become members, they are then strongly bonded with supposedly only superior people. The group's unifying mission — to cleanse their neighborhood or their nation, and eventually dominate their world — satisfies a powerful need to turn the tables on the innumerable "inferior" beings who have contaminated or would contaminate them. If fully adopted, this mindset fits the paranoid pattern: the now denied sense of inferiority, unworthiness, and vengeance is projected onto other people. When acted out, this mindset means behaving in the oppressive, hostile manner they attribute to their "persecutors." If the available supply of persecutors dwindles and resentment toward the leader and other members increases, intragroup violence will increase as members doubt one another. To paraphrase an old saying, "Sometimes I think only me and thee are acceptable and sometimes I doubt thee." Ultimately, paranoid group movements tend to evolve into a "black hole" mentality wherein the members find each other unacceptable and may kill one another or commit suicide together.

Blueprint for Inhibiting Institutional Violence

Many methods can be effective for inhibiting group and institutional lethal aggression. No one method is likely to be very effective by itself but certain combinations may be very effective. As noted previously, we can categorize inhibitions as coming from three sources: extra-institutional, intra-institutional, and intra-individual. Table 3.2 shows examples of inhibitions that can be effected within each of these categories.

The following blueprint suggests both potentially effective inhibitions and their limitations, beginning with the most simply reactive and, therefore, probably the least effective, and progressing to the level of potentially more effective solutions. The less-effective solutions are included here because they may be partially effective in some circumstances where harm is imminent, and they are sure to be included in any politically acceptable program of intervention and, thus, are important to take into account.

Repression

The most common governmental reactions to unlawful violent behavior are repressive. Essentially, repression means trying to identify and deactivate those suspected of wrongdoing. In the case of antigovernment militants, the federal government, and the state governments, although under federal control, would be authorized to undertake surveillance methods that may be

Table 3.2   Sources and Examples of Inhibitions against Institutional Violence

Extra-Institutional

Enacting Laws against the forming of militias whose intent is the violent overthow of the U.S. and wearing masks in public, or using telephones, the mails, or Internet for hate messages. (Banning masks or clothing used to disguise may be unconstitutional.)

Conducting Surveillance, such as by electronic devices to monitor telephone calls, meetings, and other communications initiated by or among suspects.

Conducting Searches, in conformity with search and seizure laws; for example, having police look for materials and resources that could be used to commit violent acts.

Educating for Democratic Living, such as teaching empathy, tolerance, compassion, and personal responsibility at home, in schools, and in society generally.

Intra-Institutional

Developing Democratic Processes, such as free and open elections, allowing dissent, and actively reviewing complaints and suggestions.

Encouraging Extra-Institutional Relationships; for example, involvement with family, friends, and other groups in the broader community.

Actively Cultivating Diversity to enrich the institution ethnically, by encouraging a broad variety of personal viewpoints and opinions.

Taking Stands Against Bigotry both within and outside of the institution through education, formal protests, and reaching out to help oppressed people.

Intra-Individual

Examining one's own tendencies to project and displace hostility vs. accepting personal responsibility and contributing to democracy.

Checking with Others Outside to see what they would think of the workings of one's institution or group, and what changes they suggest.

Taking Periodic Leaves of Absence from the institution in order to look more objectively at it, and to belong elsewhere for a while as a broadening experience.

Participating Actively in Democratic Processes by becoming well-informed, voting, and reaching out to educate and help others to exercise their rights and responsibilities as citizens.

useful to identify and to convict the wrongdoers. At the extreme, the government would engender unlimited development and use of intelligence equipment, including covert auditory and visual recording devices, weapons and other intimidation methods, prosecutions, incarcerations, and punishments. In short, we would declare all-out war on the "outlaws." We would become as thoroughly militarized as necessary to eradicate the bad elements in our society. In this extreme version, certain costs and dangers of repressive tactics become quite clear.

Such all-out repression would destroy the democracy we seek to protect. Our society would then become that which its antigovernment militants say we now are. Effectively, we would give truth to the lie. The U.S. Constitution, which is at the heart of our democracy, would be only a relic. We would have destroyed ourselves, thereby saving antigovernment militants the effort and assuring them of victory.

The common-sense reaction to this danger of self-destruction is to lessen the repression but to practice it in a more moderate fashion. Recognition that some repression is probably necessary, especially in the short run, should be coupled with the realization that it is a dangerous tool. Any repressive effort tends to inspire more militant rhetoric and action as well as to inhibit unlawful forms of protest. Many people who are already militant would increase their efforts, and many presently nonmilitant citizens, seeing their government practice harsh repression, would conclude that the government is indeed becoming like the militants say it is, and thereby become more militant themselves. The net effect could easily be more, rather than less, unlawful militancy. Historically, we have instructive examples from our government's attempts in the 1960s to repress Black militant dissidents, and from our conduct of the Vietnam war.

Inevitably, the use of repressive measures is a tricky business; the use of repression in a democratic society must be coupled with strong inhibitions against its use. Any increases in our repressive tactics against antigovernment militants would have to be matched by increases in surveillance and prosecution of government agents lest they exceed lawful limits on their powers. The checks and balances characteristic of a democratic government would have to be further mobilized. As a consequence, the "repressive solution" means expense not only in terms of direct expenditures for the repressive measures themselves but also expenditures to fund vigilant and inhibitory actions against these measures. Analogizing, it is as if we were to drive faster while applying the brakes harder at the same time, thereby surely generating more friction but compromising our forward progress.

In conclusion, while repression may be necessary to save lives, especially in the short run, it is hardly a first-rate solution. Rather, it is a dangerous, costly, and potentially quite divisive solution which, if carried to the extreme, would guarantee destruction of our democracy. Those who would regard repressive medicine as a cure in itself should be advised that "this medicine must be used sparingly as excessive use may cause more harm than the disease it is intended to cure." And in further service of truth in packaging, the warning should say, "Our only guarantee is that symptoms will persist or worsen if nothing is done except to use this medicine."

Negotiation

Though unappealing to "macho" mentalities, negotiation has a long and successful history of resolving disputes if used early enough in the conflict process. Its success depends considerably on ascertaining early signs of conflict as well as bringing an open mind, empathy, and goodwill to the negotiating table. Respect for opponents has a way of easing discussion and engaging them unless it is clear that an aggressor is already absolutely determined to dominate, as occurred when Hitler was not inclined at all toward sincere, peaceful negotiation and British Prime Minister Chamberlain misread him. Typically, negotiation does not work when matters have already gone very far. But when adversaries can be brought to the negotiating table early in the hostilities, it is possible to generate feelings of empathy and respect for one another.

Negotiators would do well to regard their "adversaries" as at least potentially constructive people with whom talking could be helpful. Carl Rogers, the psychologist whose principles of counseling extended far into other areas of discourse, posited an especially important principle for viewing interpersonal conflicts in need of peaceful resolution. As stated by Kirschenbaum (1995): Rogers

> ...acknowledged the powerful destructive forces within people but saw no evidence to suggest that they were *primary*. He saw negative *and* positive impulses existing side by side within the individual ... he saw when the therapist could provide the conditions of congruence, empathy, and unconditional positive regard, this helped the individual to accept both the positive and the negative feelings within himself. Once the individual could understand and accept all parts of himself and his inner experiences more fully, that person tended to choose more constructive courses of action (page 39).

The use of empathy in negotiation is a method for facilitating intragroup and intra-individual inhibitions against violence. It is much more difficult to behave violently toward people if you get to know them as fellow human beings and are in a position to become able to "feel for them." And when one shows empathy, it tends to beget empathy in others too. Ultimately the sense of empathy may carry the day. The reverse is also true. Perceived lack of empathy readily facilitates "negative" behavior, including violence and rebellion.

Intra-Individual Inhibitions against Violence

Leaders attract followers in many ways. On balance, the leader must be perceived as benefiting the followers in order for the followers not to leave. Even extreme forms of coercion and total lack of support for dissent cannot guarantee that a leader will keep followers if the followers are made thoroughly miserable by the leader. Two examples are offered here.

An older student, returning to study at the university he had left several years before, told his story about joining and then leaving a very large religious cult that demanded major personal sacrifices. He had achieved a high position of financial responsibility in the cult and attained a close personal relationship with the leader. But his years of hard work and devotion to the cause, which delayed his education and greatly restricted his freedom, were not enough for the leader. The leader demanded that he submit to an arranged marriage to be formally performed together with many others. Even this further sacrifice of his personal freedom was not enough for him to leave the cult. His own family of origin had been fraught with conflict and turmoil, and he greatly valued his place in his "new family" especially because he had such a close relationship with the "father." So he went through with the marriage, hoping that with time and his own dutiful efforts the marriage would become tolerable and, thus, confirm the far-seeing wisdom of the cult's leader. A couple of years passed during which he was thoroughly miserable with his arranged marriage and could not find grounds for compatibility. Finally, he left the marriage and the cult, albeit not without severe regrets for his relatively wasted years and the loss of his "father."

Floyd Cochran, the aforementioned national spokesman for the Aryan Nations, said he left the movement after a sacrifice they demanded got him thinking. As a prominent member of the Aryan Nations, he had avidly pursued his role as propaganda minister, recruiting many youths to the movement by giving them "just cause" for attacking minorities and others who were "racially inferior." As in Hitler's Nazi movement, the Aryan Nations was also dedicated to rooting out any "genetically inferior" members of their own "race" so as to make it "pure."

This theoretically satisfactory approach to racial purity foundered badly when the propaganda minister was told that his own son, who had a cleft palate (and therefore was imperfect) would have to be sacrificed for the cause. The minister not only then left the Aryan Nations but began to see that his former dedication had furthered atrocities. He went from a sense of right-eousness to a sense of having committed the most egregious sins. Whatever previous sense of guilt and inhibition that was kept at bay while he was a member was unleashed and became a tremendous, continual dedication to what he called "atonement." Everywhere he could, he made presentations unmasking the propaganda he had previously so fervently preached. The experience of having the cult's violence turned on his own flesh and blood served as a wake-up call. The movement had gone too far; it had threatened to kill someone precious to him.

These case examples illustrate that the "black holeism" tendency of deadly cults inevitably begins to destroy or lose their members. This cultish phe-nomenon of progressive pressure to conform and its backlash within the group partially explains how authoritarian institutions can become disabled from within.

Typically, when people become willing to become violent in a war against the government, (as emphasized previously) there is at least some reality basis for their inclinations. They feel, and often are, disenfranchised. Seldom are they the happy owners of highly successful and legal enterprises, nor are the majority well and broadly educated. The former propaganda minister of the Aryan Nations, who possessed only a GED himself, claimed that he was appointed to his major spokesman role only because he was so rare in his ability to speak a simple sentence "without having to consult a dictionary." He emphasized that the vast majority of his fellow members were not only poorly educated in the academic sense but lived in very isolated places where there were few voices of any kind, let alone people who would counter their ideology. And because individuals who are very ready to join a paranoid cult have paranoid tendencies themselves, one can imagine the difficulty of "getting through to" these people any message that would cause them to stop echoing the party line and reflect on other possibilities. Getting strong group emotional support for blaming "inferiors" is highly attractive. These considerations lead to recommending certain steps designed to make possible peaceful resolution.

How to Relate to Potentially Violent Antigovernment Activists

Take Their Complaints Very Seriously

Draw them out by listening with a ready ear. Empathize as much as possible with their own subjective feelings as well as any facts that they present which may support their claims. A sympathetic ear will facilitate some constructive relatedness that can help the militant person(s) get out of the black hole of their paranoid community. This approach does not mean humoring people, i.e., speaking or acting as though the listener is convinced that the complaints are valid in the sense of proven facts. It does mean, however, listening with an open mind, and being attentive to what may well be at least some substance to the complaints. This approach may also help engender more willingness to hear another point of view.

Encourage and Cooperate with Factual Investigations

Ralph Nader-like studies will tend to make actually legitimate complaints clear and believable instead of quickly judged "paranoid delusions." During Denver Model Cities hearings in the 1960s with citizens from poor areas of the city (Whitaker, 1970), some citizens complained that a supermarket chain charged more in the ghetto than in a wealthy neighborhood. A city council-man scoffed, saying, "How could the chain charge more in a poor area where people can't afford to pay as much?" As an advisor, I suggested that the offended citizens do an objective study, which they carried out meticulously. They were then able to show that, indeed, their claim was entirely justified. The "paranoid" complaints of the Black, Chicano, and poor White citizens then received more serious and sympathetic attention.

Provide, Where Interest Is Shown, Factual Information Related to the Complaints

When people experience a ready ear, they often respond with a ready ear. For instance, in the case of the Denver Model Cities citizen participation project, the Denver Black Panthers took on progressively more constructive and well-informed roles. And though some might carry a gun and seem ready for violent confrontation, overwhelmingly they did more studying and proposing peaceful projects than espousing violence. The very governments, city and federal alike, that had been labeled enemies became far more welcome as the processes outlined above were sensitively and sincerely implemented. Though a massive change in the U.S. presidency and executive branch dashed most of the funding prospects (Whitaker, 1972a), the spirit of constructive involvement persevered. Several former Black militants became important members of city government, and an education strategy begun by a formerly failed college student became the vehicle for many successful Chicano college graduates.

Educate

If we would inhibit evil, we must educate people to be good, and not simply try to repress evil. As Eisler (1996) has suggested, "…on the human level a far more useful way of looking at evil is as the absence of those qualities that make us uniquely human: our enormous capacity for consciousness, choice, and most important, empathy and love" (page 382). Traditionally, education has been defined as a formal academic process in which values as such are not taught. The mere mention of teaching values in school is objected to in the public school system on the grounds that it violates separation of church from state. But there is no need to select or use any religion to teach the values of a democratic society interested in survival.

The core values needed for a democratic society to survive and to be constructive in the world are respect for and empathy with other living beings and our natural heritage. Yet our schools in the U.S., let alone educational institutions in more authoritarian countries, do too little to prepare us for peaceful means of resolving conflicts. We should be especially careful to not emphasize the physical sciences at the expense of a liberal education. A broad education can teach respect for oneself and others through a wide array of subjects including the arts, humanities, and social sciences, and thereby the diversity of peoples and their contributions. Narrowly restricted education facilitates narrow mindedness, a crucial component of bigotry-motivated human violence.

A truthful education will also directly inhibit violence. What is most wrong with our gigantic violence entertainment industry is that it does not portray violence honestly. It eroticizes violence. As Eisler (1996) emphasized though, inherently, real violence is the opposite of sexual pleasure except that both may effect excitement. Furthermore, as Peter McWilliams noted (1993), the violence entertainment industry sanitizes violence although real violence is rarely sanitary. Consider here, for example, that favorite hate cult oxymoron "ethnic cleansing." McWilliams proposed a solution:

> All of this sanitized violence only makes real violence a more acceptable solution to problems. It's not that violence is shown, and that causes violence; it's that violence is shown as the *solution* to problems; *that* causes violence. "A single death is a tragedy; a million deaths is a statistic," said Joseph Stalin (who should know). If, however, the way in which each of these million died and the suffering they went through had to be viewed one at a time and in great detail, perhaps it would no longer be a statistic, and perhaps such tragedies would happen less often (page 590).

Harold Pagliaro (1996) has provided an excellent illustration of frontline combat in war, a group and institutional endeavor that otherwise is almost always shown as eroticized and sanitized entertainment in movies, television, and children's games. His book *Naked Heart* is as freeing as only the truth can be.

Truthful, realistic education in human relations is what is most needed in school curricula and in society at large. In its absence, we will continue to have a predominantly dominator mentality that adversely affects not only male-female relationships but all relationships involving positions of power. Otherwise, most of our institutions will continue to promote domination of others.

If we continue in serious pursuit of stereotypic masculine ideals of domination, inevitably we will exacerbate, rather than inhibit, fatal group and institutional aggression. But if we trade in the male stereotype model of domination which masquerades as the ultimate power, we can have a far more powerful model, the power to nurture and safeguard not only our lives and rights but those of others. Eisler's (1996) partnership model emphasizes nurturance, nonviolent conflict resolution, a more egalitarian social structure, mutual respect and freedom of choice in sexuality, empathy and unconditional love, pleasure bonding, and the enhancement of giving, nurturing, and illuminating life as the highest power. If we select the partnership model over the presently preeminent dominator model, we can certainly inhibit personal, group, and institutional lethal aggression.

Summary

This chapter proposes principles and methods useful for inhibiting group and institutional lethal aggression. It documents that all institutions have the potential for violence, as illustrated by various legally and societally approved professions such as law and journalism, by sports, by colleges and universities, and by the military. In the process, the relative effectiveness of their particular extra-institutional, intra-institutional, and intra-individual inhibitions is noted. The discussion then contrasts those legal institutions with antigovernment extremists, terrorists, and deadly cults, using the antigovernment Patriots in the U.S. and Aum in Japan as examples of the latter.

The Patriots and Aum appear to be very different in many ways but have certain characteristics which in combination define a cult: dependence on a leader, compliance with the group, avoidance of dissent, and devaluation of the outsider. The more authoritarian the leadership and the more coercive the conformity, the more likely it is that hostilities will be projected onto and acted out against outsiders. But members suffer losses themselves, including through training in cruelty that requires becoming insensitive to their own emotions and desires. Ultimately, as such groups become more ingrown and intolerant, they tend to turn on one another.

The readiness of such groups to attack the government arises in part from justified concerns such as feeling uncared for and not listened to while being stringently regulated and taxed by a government seen as wasteful and negligent of their needs. But the members tend also to share paranoid proclivities and show the too-human susceptibility to follow authoritarian leadership that promises to save them from some kind of doomsday. A cult's own vengeful brand of religion is used to compensate for feelings of persecution and low self-esteem while freeing members from inhibitions against committing violence. The people most likely to be recruited are alienated youths who find a "family" in the cult.

My blueprint for inhibiting institutional violence includes, but notes the considerable dangers of, repressive methods. Negotiation, if conducted early enough, can be very useful. Intra-individual inhibitions against violence, which are usually held in check by group pressures to conform, can be unleashed by even one dissenter, or by an individual's increasing sense of oppression, as illustrated by case examples. What is most fundamentally needed is early education in human relations and democratic living, with greater emphasis on partnership than dominator models.

Bibliography

Dees, Morris, *Gathering Storm: America's Militia Threat*, New York: HarperCollins, 1995, 254 pages.

As chief trial counsel for the Southern Poverty Law Center and its Militia Task Force, and an award-winning author, Dees knows what militias are about and he conveys his knowledge well. His years of investigative research enable him in this book to give richly detailed accounts of the militia movement both from the outside and the inside. The resulting picture is persuasive. The reader comes to understand that what we read in the newspapers or see on television is merely the tip of the iceberg. The movement's motivational impetus becomes clear in terms of its scapegoating nature and strong resemblance to the Nazi movement which has largely been reborn as a purer than thou "patriotism."

Deikman, Arthur J., *The Wrong Way Home: Uncovering the Patterns of Cult Behavior in American Society,* Boston: Beacon Press, 1990, 192 pages.

The author, a psychiatrist especially well known for his research on states of consciousness, shows clearly that cult behavior — dependence on a leader, compliance with the group, avoiding dissent, and devaluing the outsider — pervades the "normal" institutions on which we are dependent. He makes understandable the deadly extremes of authoritarianism that militia and terrorist cults fanatically pursue. Deikman's outstanding ability to illuminate the vicissitudes of dependency dynamics that underlie cult behavior is reminiscent of Erich Fromm's brilliant book, *Escape from Freedom*, that related the tragic lure of Hitler's Nazi ideology to its facilitation by social institutions in the pre-World War II era. Like Fromm, Deikman found that "the structure of cults is basically authoritarian; obedience and hierarchical power tend to take precedence over truth and conscience when they conflict, which they often do" (page 73).

Pagliaro, Harold, *Naked Heart: A Soldier's Journey to the Front,* Kirksville, MO, Thomas Jefferson University Press, 1996, 238 pages.

A distinguished professor of English literature gives an eloquent but literally and figuratively down to Earth personal account of his actual World War II front-line experiences as an 18-year-old infantryman. Presented in the humane context of his family experiences and values, the contrast is powerfully instructive. On the one hand, he is brought up to love and to revere life, and on the other he is forcibly trained to kill under the dictum of "kill or be killed!" A premonitory dream at age 14 depicted "exploding artillery shells that broke across the skies, lighting them in deep shadowed blazes of fire and shaking them with thunder. I remember the dream, as intense as hallucination, the live painting of a world gone mad" (page 3). The dream and reality become isomorphic, leaving no doubt that war is indeed a hellish nightmare utterly different from its vapid idealization.

References

Asch, S.E., *Social Psychology*, Englewood Cliffs, NJ: Prentice-Hall, 1952.

Bachman, W., *Law v. Life: What Lawyers Are Afraid to Say about the Legal Profession,* Rhinebeck, NY: Four Directions Press, 1995.

Barry, D., Outcast gladiators find a home: New York, *New York Times*, January 15, 1997, pp. A1, B6.

Beam, L., Leaderless resistance, *The Seditionist*, February 1992.

The Citadel's culture of abuse, *New York Times*, January 14, 1997, p. A14.

Cochran, F., Presentation on the Aryan Nations, Delaware County Community College, PA, November 6, 1996.

Crothers, C. T. and Matthews, A., Hazing days, *New York Times Magazine*, November 3, 1996, pp. 50, 51.

Cult in gas attack apologizes, but the Japanese are skeptical, *New York Times*, December 2, 1999, p. A8.

Dees, M. (with Corcoran, J.), *Gathering Storm: America's Militia Threat*, New York: HarperCollins, 1996.

Deikman, A.J. and Whitaker, L.C., Humanizing a psychiatric ward: changing from drugs to psychotherapy, *Psychother. Theor. Res. Pract.*, 16(2), 204-214, 1979.

Deikman, A.J., *The Wrong Way Home: Uncovering the Patterns of Cult Behavior in American Society*, Boston: Beacon Press, 1990.

Eisler, R., *Sacred Pleasure: Sex, Myth, and the Politics of the Body*, New York: HarperCollins, 1996.

Fromm, E., *The Sane Society*, New York: Henry Holt, 1990 (originally published 1955).

Gove, P., *Webster's Third New International Dictionary of the English Language Unabridged*, Springfield, MA: Merriam-Webster, 1966.

Higginbotham, A.L., Jr., *Shades of Freedom: Racial Politics and Presumptions of the American Legal Process*, New York: Oxford University Press, 1996.

Holmes, S. A., Income disparity between richest and poorest rises, *New York Times*, June 20, 1996, pp. A1, A18.

Howard, P.K., *The Death of Common Sense*, New York: Time Warner Books, 1996.

Kaplan, J., Ed., Adolf Hitler, in *Bartlett's Familiar Quotations*, 16th ed., Boston: Little, Brown, 1992, p. 676.

Kaplan, D.E. and Marshall, A., *The Cult at the End of the World*, New York: Crown Publishers, 1996.

Kirschenbaum, H., Carl Rogers, in *Positive Regard: Carl Rogers and Other Notables He Influenced*, Shuh, M.M., Ed., Palo Alto, CA: Science and Behavior Books, 1995, pp. 1-90.

Kriegel, M., Gentlemen, start your bleeding, *Esquire*, March, 1996. pp. 94-101.

Malcolm, J., *The Journalist and the Murderer*, New York: Knopf, 1990.

McWilliams, P., *Ain't Nobody's Business if You Do: The Absurdity of Consensual Crimes in a Free Society*, Los Angeles: Prelude Press, 1993.

Milgram, S., *Obedience to Authority*, New York: Harper & Row, 1974.

Okrent, D. and Lewine, H., Eds., *The Ultimate Baseball Book*, Boston: Houghton Mifflin, 1991.

Pagliaro, H., *Naked Heart*, Kirksville, MO: Thomas Jefferson University Press, 1996.

Pierce, W. (Andrew Macdonald), *The Turner Diaries*, Hillsboro, WV: National Vanguard Books, 1978.

Rivinus, T. M. and Larimer, M.E., Violence, alcohol, other drugs, and the college student, in Whitaker, L.C. and Pollard, J.W., Eds., *Campus Violence: Kinds, Causes, and Cures*, New York: Haworth Press, 1993, pp. 71-119. (Published simultaneously in *J. Coll. Stud. Psychother.*, 8(1/2), 3, 1993.)

Ruane, M.E., Cohen assails hazing by Marines, *Philadelphia Inquirer*, February 1, 1997, p. A1.

Silber, J., Students should not be above the law, *New York Times*, op-ed, May 9, 1996, p. A27.

Sims, C., Still furious at cult, Japan violates its rights, *New York Times*, August 27, 1999, pp. A1, A10.

Soldier tells of admission in double murder, *New York Times*, February 16, 1997, p. A19.

Southern Poverty Law Center, *False Patriots: The Threat of Antigovernment Extremists*, Montgomery, AL: Southern Poverty Law Center, 1996.

Sports Illustrated, Special NFL Classic Edition, Fall, 1995.

Whitaker, L.C., Social reform and the comprehensive community mental health center: the Model Cities experiment, Part I, *Am. J. Public Health*, 60(10), 2003-2010, 1970.

Whitaker, L.C., Social reform and the comprehensive community mental health center: the Model Cities experiment, Part II, *Am. J. Public Health*, 62(2), 216-222, 1972a.

Whitaker, L.C., Community mental health wars and black ownership, *Prof. Psychol.*, Fall issue, 1972b, pp. 307-310 and 321-323.

Whitaker, L.C., *Schizophrenic Disorders: Sense and Nonsense in Conceptualization, Assessment and Treatment*, New York: Plenum Press, 1992.

The Central Intelligence Agency and Lethal Violence 4

We have seen the best of our time: machinations, hollowness, treachery, and all ruinous disorders, follow us disquietly to our graves — William Shakespeare (1564–1616)

As soon as men decide that all means are permitted to fight an evil, then the good becomes indistinguishable from the evil that they set out to destroy — Christopher Dawson, *The Judgment of the Nations* (1942)

Does a covert agency of the U.S. government foster or damage the democratic spirit, ideals, and well-being of its own and other nations? Does the "gentlemanly game" of spying, together with sabotage and manipulation, intrinsically infuse its players with treacherous impulses and cause corrosive distrust and destruction throughout the world? Or is such clandestine work necessary to minimize evil in the world? What should a democratic government do?

In attempting to answer these and other questions, this chapter addresses

1. The early development and present formation of the CIA.
2. The CIA's more than 50-year history from 1947 to 2000, with emphasis on its cycles of destructiveness and reform.
3. The inevitable ethics questions about covert work.
4. The machinating mentalities necessary to carry out covert operations.
5. CIA mind control programs.
6. Efficacy questions regarding national and world well-being.
7. Prospects and recommendations.

The crucial question throughout is whether covert actions including spying, sabotage, and the manipulation of other nations has a net effect of enhancing or destroying lives in the U.S. and the world. Even *if* we might sometimes agree that the ends justify the means, do clandestine methods really achieve the ends of peace and well-being? While a conclusion is made difficult because of secrecy and the ubiquitous nature of the consequences of covert actions, at least partial answers are provided.

Early Development and Present Formation

Understanding the CIA requires knowledge of its origins, particularly how world affairs led up to its creation, and how it came to be an enduring independent executive bureau of the U.S. government. How has it managed to continue beyond the original reasons for its creation?

Early Development

What we know now as the Central Intelligence Agency (or CIA) had noble parentage. In 1940 the Axis powers — Germany, Italy, and Japan — were already ominous potential opponents of the U.S. in what was to be called "the good war." Clearly, so ran popular sentiment, the evil fascists had to be defeated. President Roosevelt, seeking to develop an intelligence gathering capacity that could help the U.S. meet an emergent war preparedness need, sent attorney and former general "Wild Bill" J. Donovan on a fact-finding mission to Europe. Donovan proposed that he be the director of a two-part centralized intelligence unit: the Office of Strategic Services (OSS) and the Office of War Information (OWI). The Japanese attack on Pearl Harbor on December 7, 1941 confirmed that U.S. intelligence operations were behind the times. Their covert nature was readily accepted amid the exigencies of such a desperate all-out war.

The OSS was created in 1942 to obtain information about enemy nations and to sabotage their war potential and morale. Its research and analysis section did valuable work, but did not get as much after-the-war publicity as the "cloak and dagger" section operatives who bravely infiltrated enemy territory and acted as liaisons with the underground in Nazi-occupied countries. A former OSS officer told me of his personal experiences of being parachuted behind enemy lines and helping to capture Nazi officials. Like his comrades, he felt entirely that he was performing good in the "the good war."

At the end of World War II in 1945, the Axis having been thoroughly defeated, both the OSS and the OWI were disbanded. But in 1946 President Truman established the National Intelligence Authority (NIA) within which the CIA was established in 1947. This was the same Truman who said "secrecy and a free, democratic government don't mix" (Kaplan, 1992, page 655). Given the seeming conflict with democracy implicit in granting extraordinary powers for clandestine operations, especially in peacetime, how could the president justify the further development of a highly secret, largely independent and nonaccountable agency with what were normally only wartime powers? Truman, together with Prime Ministers Clement Atlee (Britain) and W. L. Mackenzie King (Canada), provided an answer in their Declaration on Atomic Energy on November 15, 1945. They had to guard against: "Means of destruction hitherto unknown, against which there can be no adequate military defense, and in the employment of which no single nation can in fact have a monopoly" (as cited in Kaplan, 1992, page 655).

Besides his concern about the general availability of atomic weaponry, Truman was personally acquainted with a man who was correctly envisioned as capable of massive lethal violence not only toward other aggressor nations but also against his own people. As Josef Stalin was participating in peace negotiations with the Allies and the defeated Axis nations, his "good guy" status was still hostage to his history. As many as "...20 million people throughout the Soviet Union were annihilated in the first 30 years of Stalin's reign, not including the losses in war" (Goodman, 1997). Would the recent ally become a mortal enemy? The "Cold War" instantly replaced the hot war. Now the measures taken to protect the nation's security would be, like the Cold War itself, far more covert than overt. The thinking behind this strategizing has been expressed succinctly: "The CIA was founded to prevent another surprise attack such as occurred at Pearl Harbor" (Kessler, 1992, page 331).

Thus, the National Security Act of 1947 established the CIA as an independent agency within the executive office of the president. Of its five allotted functions authorized by Congress, the fifth, especially, left much room for interpretation "to perform other such functions and duties related to intelligence affecting the national security as the National Security Council may from time to time direct" (Richelson, 1995, page 13). Though this provision was intended only to authorize espionage, the CIA developed according to a maximalist interpretation authorizing covert action. "Because the legislation that set it up gave it little guidance, the agency had to invent itself along the way. There have been many false starts and many mistakes" (Kessler, 1992, page xxxv). The ambiguity of the legislation allowing maximalist interpretation resulted in the CIA becoming the primary U.S. government agency for intelligence analysis, clandestine human intelligence collection, and covert action; the latter included even attempts to overthrow other governments and to arrange at least indirectly for assassinations of their leaders.

One of the few stringent legislated limitations was that the CIA must only operate internationally, not collect information on the U.S.; the Federal Bureau of Investigation (FBI) had the domestic turf. During the long reign of FBI Director J. Edgar Hoover, the FBI and CIA were often at loggerheads. But the relationship became more complementary when William H. Webster became FBI Director after Hoover's death in 1972. The CIA and FBI even created a joint secret operation in 1980 to recruit Soviet spies in Washington. Beginning in 1981, when President Reagan signed Executive Order 12333, the CIA was given more latitude to operate within the U.S.: "...the CIA may operate domestically in order to collect 'significant' foreign intelligence, so long as the effort does not involve spying on the domestic activities of Americans" (Kessler, 1992, page 21). This "order," like its ambiguously stated "fifth function," left much room for interpretation; for example, was it justifiable to open the mail of thousands of U.S. citizens thought to have Soviet connections?

From its inception after World War II until the collapse of Soviet communism in 1990, the continued existence of the CIA had been justified primarily by the Cold War. During that period of over 40 years, the Cold War went through five phases: "confrontation from 1945 to 1955, coexistence and competition from 1955 to 1972, a period of détente from 1972 to 1979, renewed confrontation from 1979 to 1985, and a final period of rapidly easing tension from 1985 to 1990" (Flanders and Flanders, 1993, page 119). In 1997, the CIA had its 50th anniversary and continued to try to sell its role in the post-Cold War era.

Present Formation: The CIA in the 1990s

By 1992 the CIA had 22,000 full-time employees with a little over half working at the CIA's 258-acre compound in McLean, VA. The compound, and sometimes the entire CIA agency, is often referred to as "Langley," the name of a town that used to be there but is no longer on the map. The phrase, "The Agency" is used to refer to the whole of the CIA.

The language used by the CIA is rife with special terms, some of them cryptonyms, e.g., Project MKULTRA, which are secret designations for various individual persons or CIA projects. Others are euphemisms such as "neutralize" which usually means kill in this context — an extreme version of its ordinary designation of making inoperable or causing to have no effect. Other terms, such as "finding," also go beyond the readily assumed ordinary meaning. A "finding" in a scientific article or even in a detective's report typically means simply a discovery. But in CIA language it means a written determination by the President of the U.S. required before covert action may be undertaken, as in "a presidential finding that authorized the covert operation."

CIA language also includes many title designations of the kind that are common in bureaucracies operating behind a maze of mysterious jargon that defies easy understanding. As the *American Heritage Dictionary* (1992) puts it, together with an illustrative example, "bureaucratese" is "a style of language characterized by jargon and euphemism that is used especially by bureaucrats. 'Soviet *bureaucratese, especially the tongue-twisting acronyms and alien-sounding portmanteau words of the state security apparatus.*'"

Of the total of 22,000 regular CIA employees, 5000 constitute the Directorate of Operations, the most secretive, proudest, risk-taking, and troublesome CIA component. "By definition, it is the job of this directorate to break the laws of other countries" (Kessler, 1992, page 4). By 1992, 53 CIA *officers* had lost their lives in the service of the *Agency*. The count of officer deaths in the line of duty had risen to 58 according to the CIA headquarters plaque shown on a television special marking the CIA's 50th anniversary (C-Span's Washington Journal, 1997). There is no evident record of how many *agents,* persons recruited to act under control of an intelligence service, have been killed.

As of 1992, to collect foreign intelligence the CIA maintained stations in 130 countries with a staff of about 3300. Even friendly nations are spied upon, except Great Britain, Canada, and Australia. And CIA officers may be placed "under cover" in any U.S. government facility abroad except the Peace Corps. The remainder of the staff were located in 22 CIA offices in Washington, D.C., or in the CIA's domestic stations. In addition to regular employees, including CIA officers, the CIA had about 4000 agents.

The size of the intelligence budget has not always been clear. It was estimated in 1980 to be about $6 billion, and it was to be increased to more than $20 billion for 1985 during the Reagan administration (Woodward, 1987, page 193). Recently, "Many members of Congress want to reduce the intelligence community's $30 billion budget, or pry open more of its secrets" (Gerth, 1997, page A12). "The CIA itself spends about $3 billion a year, while the Director of the CIA (DCI) and the Secretary of Defense allocate most of the remainder to military intelligence services like the National Security Agency, which conducts electronic eavesdropping, and the National Reconnaissance Office, which builds spy satellites" (Weiner, 1997c, page A16).

On October 15, 1997 the CIA, under pressure from a Federation of American Scientists' lawsuit, stated that their current overall intelligence fiscal year budget was $26.6 billion. But it is still not known exactly how much is spent by each of the 13 agencies, listed in Table 4.1, that are covered under the spy budget which itself is buried in the Defense Department budget (Prying open the spy budget, 1997).

The Director of Central Intelligence (DCI) wears three hats: head of the CIA; coordinator of the other intelligence agencies in the government; and primary advisor to the president, through the National Security Council, on

Table 4.1   The U.S. Intelligence Community including the Central Intelligence Agency (CIA)

State Department's Bureau of Intelligence and Research
Energy and Treasury Department's intelligence components
National Security Agency
Federal Bureau of Investigation (FBI) counterintelligence component
National Reconnaissance Office
Defense Intelligence Agency
Army, Air Force, Navy, and Marine Corps intelligence elements
Other agencies, e.g., Commerce Department, that have intelligence components but are not
 full-fledged members of the intelligence community

foreign intelligence matters. Thus, the DCI has power over the intelligence community as a whole, including the CIA. The Deputy Director of the CIA (DDCI) is the first officer of the CIA itself. Both the DCI and the DDCI are appointed by the President of the U.S. with the advice and consent of the Senate.

Besides the president, the CIA is monitored by two congressional oversight committees (House and Senate); the President's Foreign Intelligence Board; a citizen panel that investigates CIA shortcomings and reports its findings to the president; and the President's Intelligence Oversight Board that is responsible for reporting any intelligence activities which appear to be illegal or improper. Finally, legislation passed in 1990 placed the CIA's Inspector-General on the same level of authority on the Agency's organization chart as the Director of Central Intelligence. But as former CIA Director Gates (1991-1993) pointed out (C-Span, 1997a) and as CIA Director William Casey clearly demonstrated, the DCI is not responsible to policy agencies but is really responsive to the president's own policies. For further information about the structure of the modern CIA, the reader is referred especially to Kessler (1992).

George Tenet, the current Director of Central Intelligence (DCI), the third in 6 years, has said the CIA would focus on 10 or 15 countries and increase their recent emphasis on combating terrorism, drug trafficking, and arms proliferation (Gerth,1997). One may seriously question whether the CIA's influence has actually increased terrorism, drug trafficking, and arms proliferation, as will be discussed later in this chapter.

Deputy Director of Central Intelligence (DDCI) John McLaughlin stated that during the Cold War 40 to 50% of the Agency's budget was spent in relation to concerns about the Soviet Union but that, since the end of the Cold War, only 20 to 30% is spent on Russia, and that the CIA has been "downsizing" by not replacing retiring or otherwise departing employees until a recent active hiring campaign (C-Span, 1997b), but it does not appear that the CIA has become substantially smaller. Former DCI Admiral Stansfield Turner said that the mission of the CIA has actually broadened to concern about 180 countries whose actions may impact on the welfare of the U.S. (C-Span, 1997b). At the end of the 20th century, the CIA was emphasizing recruiting "…women and ethnic minorities — particularly Asian and Arab Americans … and recruits with advanced degrees, foreign language proficiency, and experience in living and working abroad" (Landau, 1999, page A3).

The agency's utility as a spy organization has been criticized recently, including by many top former CIA officials. From 1990 to 1997 as inspector-general of the CIA, Fred Hitz' caseload increased fourfold. He filed classified reports on the CIA's connections with the Bank of Credit and Commerce

International, which has a record of operating as a criminal enterprise, and the CIA's ties to Guatemalan military members who have committed acts of murder, torture, and kidnapping. On October 2, 1997 this Inspector-General of the CIA, having served under five different directors, announced that he would leave the Agency to teach at Princeton University, where he was recruited to join the CIA 36 years ago (Weiner, 1997f).

As of the end of August, 1997, six top CIA positions were unfilled (Keeping track, 1997). George Tenet's appointment left vacant the position of Deputy Director of Central Intelligence for 8 months. Four new positions, created by Congress on October 11, 1996 to improve management of the CIA and the 12 other U.S. intelligence branches over which the Director of Central Intelligence presides, have never been filled. In essence, the CIA experienced considerable turmoil and morale problems in the 1990s but has been trying to change with the times.

Cycles of Violation and Reform

Since its inception the CIA has been a kind of legal criminal, authorized to break the laws of other countries but not its own. The many men and few women who were personally inclined, recruited, trained, and rewarded for breaking laws have not always observed this slippery distinction. Nor were their violations of U.S. law readily detected. Masters of disguise, deception, and cover-up, they may apply their skills in any direction. Inherently, therefore, the U.S. government and its citizens have dealt with a paradox of our own creation: how to promote criminal behavior without that behavior *excessively* compromising and damaging the democracy it was designed to defend. Table 4.2 shows alleged CIA institutional aggression from 1950 to 1995. Table 4.2 reflects, and the next sections of this chapter document, the cyclical nature of CIA violation and reform. The years from 1975 to 1980 and 1985 to 1990 mark periods of reform after major violations were revealed and oversight attempts, including congressional investigations, were instigated.

Table 4.2   CIA Institutional Aggression over the Decades

Date	Alleged CIA Behavior	Related Behavior/Remarks	Sample Ref.
1950	Recruited syndicate figures in France to form a "criminal terror squad" to force dockers to load arms in ships bound for Vietnam.	Syndicate allowed to refine heroin in Marseilles for shipment to U.S. with knowledge of CIA.	Pearce (1976), McCoy (1997)
1950– on	Opened and photographed mail of over 1 million civilian Americans without their knowledge or consent.	Associated activity included installation of surveillance devices, breaking into homes and offices.	Parenti (1983), Woodward (1987)

Table 4.2 (continued)   CIA Institutional Aggression over the Decades

Date	Alleged CIA Behavior	Related Behavior/Remarks	Sample Ref.
1953	Toppled Mohammed Mossadegh of Iran, a democratically elected leader, and installed Shah of Iran, Reza Pahlavi.	In addition to favorable oil concessions to U.S., Iran bought over $18 billion in weapons over next 2 decades from U.S.	Prados (1986), Moyers (1988)
1954	Overthrew Jacobo Arbenz of Guatemala, who had received 65% of the vote, thus violating rights of a friendly power.	CIA organized terrorists in Honduras who crossed over on June 18, 1954, to overthrow the Guatemalan government.	Herman (1982)
1954– on	Trained officers in Guatemala in terrorism and provided weapons, who then tortured, burned, strangled, and slaughtered political opponents for several decades.	Termed "Operation Success" by the CIA; all reform measures instituted by Arbenz were terminated, including the right to unionize.	Moyers (1988)
1957	Helped set up Savak, Iranian secret police, who tortured, mutilated, and killed regime's opponents.	Savak agents trained at USMC base in Quantico and at the CIA complex in Langley, VA.	Chomsky and Herman (1977)
1960	CIA planned assassination of Congolese nationalist leader Patrice Lumumba.	Before CIA plot was effected, Lumumba was murdered by rival faction.	Woodward (1987)
1960s	Recruited syndicate figures to assassinate Fidel Castro. Eventually, at least eight attempted assassinations, two with CIA-supplied lethal pills and hypodermic needle, were carried out over several years.	Planners included John Roselli, Sam Giancana, Santo Trafficante, Jr., Rafael "Chi Chi" Quinlero, Feliso Rodriguez, Frank Sturgis, and E. Howard Hunt.	Hinckle and Turner (1981), Myers, (1997), Prados (1986), Woodward (1987)
1960s	Worked with syndicate figures to develop Golden Triangle for opium growing in return for fighting Pathet Lao.	CIA's airline — Air America — transported opium to labs. Heroin was used by GIs in Vietnam and users in U.S.	Bellis (1981), McCoy (1997), Stanton (1976)
1960s	William Colby, ex-CIA Director, appointed bank official for Nugan Hand bank in Thailand.	Much of money from drug trade was laundered through this bank whose branch was close to Golden Triangle.	Sheehan (1988)
1960s	Worked with ITT who, threatened with being nationalized in Chile, toppled Salvadore Allende.	CIA spent $350,000 to bribe members of Congress in Chile and some $13 million to block election.	Simon and Eitzen (1986)

Table 4.2   CIA Institutional Aggression over the Decades

Date	Alleged CIA Behavior	Related Behavior/Remarks	Sample Ref.
1961	Bay of Pigs, planned and orchestrated by CIA DDO Richard Bissell, failed.	Cuban Missile Crisis of 1962 intimately connected with Bay of Pigs.	Blight and Lang (1995), Woodward, (1987)
1963	KUBARK counterintelligence interrogation manual published and widely distributed.	Presented coercive methods including sensory deprivation, hypnosis, use of threats of violence, and torture.	Declassified and redacted by CIA January, 1997
1965–1970	Organized secret MEO Army whose leaders were extensively involved in heroin production. CIA transported opium to clandestine labs through Air America. From 1965 to 1970, active heroin addicts in U.S. grew from 68,000 to 500,000.	Heroin ultimately used by GIs in Vietnam and individuals in U.S. White House surveys showed more than 3000 U.S. troops in Vietnam were addicted to heroin.	Bellis (1981), McCoy (1997), Marshall et al. (1987), Stanton (1976)
1968–1975	Operation Phoenix created by William Colby, first to assassinate suspected Viet Cong (VC) and VC sympathizers and then to assemble, incarcerate, and murder Vietnamese civilians.	For the first time in American history, quotas were set for the number of people to be "neutralized." From 1968 to 1971, over 40,000 civilians were murdered and thousands more were tortured.	Branfman (1978), Chomsky and Herman (1977)
1970s	Stockpiling of poison and venom previously banned by Presidential order.	Disregarded executive orders. Lethal pills previously used in assassination attempts.	Woodward (1987)
1970s	Bush was appointed head of CIA in 1976. Provided weapons and money to Angolan rebels, attempted to overthrow Jamaican government, and kept Manuel Noriega of Panama on payroll, who was deeply involved in drug trafficking. Eventually paid $160,000. Disregard of President Ford's (1976) ban on assassination which was reaffirmed by Carter.	In 1976 CIA created "Operation Condor" to monitor and assassinate dissident refugees in member countries (Argentina, Bolivia, Brazil, Chile, Paraguay, and Uruguay).	Corn (1988), Maas (1986), Morrison (1995)
1972	Ex-CIA operatives break into Democratic Party's headquarters in Watergate Hotel. James W. McCord retired from CIA's Office of Security 2 years earlier. CIA supplied operatives with CIA alias identities, a voice-alteration device, and a red wig.	Role of the CIA was downplayed in the most blatant threat to the democratic process in American history.	Kessler (1993), Parenti (1983), Woodward (1987)

Table 4.2 (continued)   **CIA Institutional Aggression over the Decades**

Date	Alleged CIA Behavior	Related Behavior/Remarks	Sample Ref.
1973	Worked with Chilean military to overthrow Allende, resulting in death of 30,000 civilians and President Allende himself.	Augusto Pinochet came to power. Over 20,000 political prisoners were killed between 1973 and 1976. Many more were tortured.	Faden (1996), Simon and Eitzen (1986)
1973	CIA's Technical Services Division destroys secret files on human radiation experiments.	Reported by former CIA official, Scott Breckenridge. Original order from Richard Helms, CIA Director, in 1972.	Faden (1996)
1975	Indirectly responsible for 25 to 30 bombings in Dade County, FL, in 1975 by Cubans trained by CIA to fight Castro. This group was also responsible for assassinations in Lisbon, Mexico, New York, and Washington, D.C.	Known as "Cuban Refugee Terrorist Network" whose collective organizations had up to 6000 members. Commentators argued that U.S. drug problem was largely due to CIA training of the terrorists with known drug distribution networks.	Herman (1982), Kruger (1980), Marshall et al. (1987)
1980s	CIA supports Chad Defense Minister Habrè in order to rid Chad of Quadafi's influence.	Habrè turns out, consistent with his past, to brutally suppress human rights in Chad.	Woodward (1987)
1980s	Opens up Golden Crescent to finance Afghan Mujahedin rebels in fight against USSR. Large-scale activities with arrival of CIA on Afghan-Pakistan border.	By 1986, 40% of heroin into U.S. was coming from Golden Crescent and 19% from the Golden Triangle, a switch from the 1960s and 1970s when CIA focused on Indochina.	Bellis (1981), Lifschultz (1988), Sciolino (1988)
1980s	CIA agent Lt. Col. Moses Klanzamation, deputy chief of Doe's personal guard, attempted to assassinate Liberia's leader, Samuel K. Doe.	Klanzamation, after confessing his CIA ties, was executed a week later.	Woodward (1987)
1980–1981	Carter White House was stocked with moles, spies, and informers who reported to senior Reagan advisors through CIA.	Reagan–Bush campaign officials, with help of CIA, contacted Iran directly, offering more arms than Carter and thus winning Iran's support. Hostages were freed after Reagan was elected.	Hoffman and Silvers (1980)
1982	CIA agents used electric shock device on suspects.	One suspect dies of torture. CIA agent was fired.	Woodward (1987)

Table 4.2   CIA Institutional Aggression over the Decades

Date	Alleged CIA Behavior	Related Behavior/Remarks	Sample Ref.
1983	In direct opposition to Boland Amendment enacted in 1982, which forbade public money for purpose of destabilizing Nicaraguan government, CIA obtained military equipment and arranged for destruction of oil facilities and storage tanks at Nicaraguan ports, in addition to mining Nicaraguan harbors. One British ship was hit by mine.	Termed "Operation Elephant Herd," CIA also prepared and distributed to Contras an assassination manual in violation of Executive Order 12333, which prohibited assassinations. Ignored 1986 World Court ruling that international law was violated and that the U.S. must cease and refrain from such activities.	Emerson (1988), Scheffer (1987), Woodward (1987)
1983	CIA hired pollster to conduct surveys and analyze data in upcoming Grenada election after U.S. invasion.	U.S.-backed Herbert Blaize won election and, as one of his first acts, asked Reagan to maintain 250 U.S. troops on island.	Woodward (1987)
1983	CIA published and distributed *Human Rights Exploitation Manual*.	Despite a disclaimer that most coercive techniques are improper, the manual details ways to induce aggression through prolonged heat, cold, and exertion.	Declassified and redacted by CIA in January, 1997
1984	Despite a second, stronger Boland Amendment which forbade the support of or involvement in operations in Nicaragua, Contras continue to receive money through trafficking in cocaine. Contras continued to receive arms from CIA support activities.	In 1986, at least 25 arms drops were made inside Nicaragua. Contras continued to conduct a campaign of terror. Cocaine use in U.S. increased 38% between 1982 and 1985, and crack cocaine use increased dramatically between 1985 and 1996, the height of the Contra arms-for-drugs trade.	Brody (1985), Chomsky (1985), Gutman (1988), Moyers (1988), Scheffer (1987)
1984	CIA Director Casey testified in Congress on CIA-distributed manual on "Selective Use of Violence" to "neutralize" Nicaraguan officials such as court judges, police, and state security officials.	The "Murder Manual" widely used in training and operations in CIA schools and covert operations which were not redacted in all editions read, "If possible, professional criminals will be hired to carry out selective jobs."	Woodward (1987)
1985	CIA proposed selling weapons to Iran despite opposition from Departments of Defense and State.	Iran, at that time, had numerous terrorist operations against U.S.	Woodward (1987)

Table 4.2 (continued)   CIA Institutional Aggression over the Decades

Date	Alleged CIA Behavior	Related Behavior/Remarks	Sample Ref.
1990	CIA learned that all but a few of East German recruits were double agents and were feeding false information.	Consistent with previous discovery that, in 1988, all of CIA's agents were actually working for Castro.	Morrison (1995)
1990s	Bank of Credit and Commerce International (BCCI) kept secret CIA accounts to finance Contras in Nicaragua and Mujahedin rebels in Afghanistan.	In return, CIA did not interfere with BCCI's involvement in heroin trade in Pakistan and cocaine trade in Central America.	Beaty and Gwynne (1991), Castro (1988), Schmalz (1988), Burns (1997),
1992–1995	Emmanuel Constant, a Haitian military junta thug, was placed on CIA payroll. Guatemalan colonel implicated in murder of U.S. citizen was retained on covert payroll.	CIA Director John Deutsch stated, "I believe that the U.S. needs to maintain, and perhaps even expand, covert action as a policy tool."	Morrison (1995)
1995	Possible spying on Japanese negotiators during automobile-export negotiations.	Some evidence of CIA as a tool in commercial espionage.	Morrison (1995)

Source: Collective Violence: Effective Strategies for Assessing and Interviewing in Fatal Group and Institutional Aggression, Hall, H.V. and Whitaker, L.C., Eds., CRC Press LLC, Boca Raton, FL, 1999. With permission.

Into the 1970s

Having been caught off-guard by the Pearl Harbor surprise attack, the U.S. quickly developed intelligence services during World War II. But with the Cold War and threats of Soviet takeovers immediately following World War II, the U.S. still found itself trailing both the British and the Soviets in intelligence. Thus, the newly formed CIA was set clearly on a mission to catch up to and, at least contain, the Soviets. What followed was authority for almost 30 years "to conduct covert activities including political, psychological, and economic warfare and paramilitary operations" (Flanders and Flanders, 1993, page 733). Under President Dwight D. Eisenhower, a 1954 report of the Doolittle Committee reinforced the CIA's authority with a mandate to "build a *covert action* service more ruthless and effective than the intelligence agencies of America's adversaries" (as quoted in Flanders and Flanders, 1993, page 733).

Failed missions, such as the U-2 spy plane incident in 1960 over the Soviet Union and the Bay of Pigs invasion of Cuba in 1961 tarnished the CIA's image but only around questions of CIA competence and control of covert activities, not questions of ethics or human safety or rights. It was not until the mid-1970s, when Congress spearheaded important reforms, that ethics questions came to the fore. Even then, Congress' concern was mostly about infringing on the lives of U.S. citizens and not about violating the rights of people in other countries, with the exception of assassination plots against foreign leaders. Congressional investigative committees, the Senate's Church Committee, and the House's Pike Committee were not formed to look into allegations of ethical and legal violations until there was public outcry precipitated by the press.

Press reports in May 1973 linked the CIA to a break-in and illegal search of the office of a psychiatrist who had been treating ex-government official Daniel Ellsworth, a pivotal figure in the Pentagon Papers. Investigation of what became known as the Watergate Affair led to disclosure of a secret document called the "Family Jewels," assembled within the CIA, which listed 700 possible abuses committed by the CIA since the Agency began in 1947. The list revealed acts of CIA participation outside its charter such as illegally opening the mail of U.S. citizens for 20 years, testing mind-altering drugs on unwitting subjects, surveilling domestic individuals and groups, including U.S. citizens opposed to the Vietnam War, and planning assassination attempts or plots against foreign leaders.

Several control measures were instigated as a result of these revelations. In January 1975, President Gerald Ford's administration appointed the Rockefeller Commission to look into CIA activities. Congress formed oversight committees in both the Senate and the House. In February 1976, President Ford issued an Executive Order (#11905) to prevent future intelligence activity violations. Under Ford, George Bush became Director of the CIA for a brief term in 1976 and 1977 with a mandate to restore confidence both within and outside of the Agency. During the next 4 years President Jimmy Carter and his CIA Director Stansfield Turner kept the CIA on a tight rein. Concomitant with this period of reform, the U.S. and the Soviet Union experienced a period of warming or détente in the Cold War from 1972 to 1979.

The 1980s

Pressure to increase covert activity increased in 1979 with the Soviet intervention in the Afghanistan War. By the early 1980s, U.S.–Soviet hostilities were intensifying under President Ronald Reagan, who called the Soviet Union an "evil empire" and gave support to the CIA for anti-Communist insurgencies worldwide. Thus, the CIA intensified and extended its activities to virtually the world at large. William J. Casey, who served as CIA Director from 1981 to 1987 under President Reagan, enlarged on the already aggressive mandate. He saw himself as a significant policymaker who was responsible to the president alone. The congressional committees and other oversight groups were bypassed as often as possible, resulting step-by-step in major violations of the CIA charter and the rights and responsibilities of legally constituted policymakers in the U.S. government.

While he was running for president, Ronald Reagan and the Republican platform had charged that President Jimmy Carter had made it virtually impossible for the CIA to conduct effective espionage, and that CIA Director Stansfield Turner was overly responsive to the Carter human rights campaign. Turner himself had once referred to President Carter as a "peacenik" (Woodward, 1987, page 7). Reagan and Casey "both had contempt for Jimmy Carter and what they thought was his weakness, his indecisiveness, and his unhealthy, hand-wringing anxiety" (Woodward, 1987, page 17).

William Casey fit the image of the covert operative. As Woodward (1987) has noted, he slurred his words with a speech pattern that sounded "like a shortwave broadcast, fading in and out" (page 14), "showed a hundred different faces to a hundred different worlds" (page 17), and "let nothing get in his way. He worked nights, weekends. It was a single-mindedness that had to be admired" (page 19). "He was said to love mystery, the cloak, and a little of the dagger" (page 30) and saw intelligence operations as "ruthless and cutthroat" (page 101). "The tough, cold, even hard Irishman was sure he knew right from wrong" (page 119).

As a member of the Office of Strategic Services in World War II and as a private citizen, Casey was used to living on the edge. His appointment was questioned when it was revealed that, as a 1% partner for his $95 investment in a potential pen development company, he taken $60,000 in tax deductions which the IRS was disallowing. "Casey had chalk all over his feet from playing close to the foul line most of his life" (Woodward, 1987, page 182). His political views, including strong endorsement of the "need for covert action," coincided with those of Ronald Reagan who was elected president in 1980. Allen Dulles, the DCI during the Eisenhower years, had noted "presidents always want a hidden way of doing things. That's how the CIA gets its clout with the White House" (Woodward, 1987, page 42). Thus, Casey appeared to be Reagan's ideal choice as DCI.

After he was elected, Reagan's campaign claims of imminent Soviet domination were unsupported by DCI Turner who did not estimate that the U.S. was "dangerously" behind the Soviet's in weaponry and preparedness for an all-out war. According to Turner, even after a first strike by the Soviets, the U.S. would have enough strategic nuclear weapons to destroy all Soviet cities with a population of over 100,000 (Woodward, 1987, page 56). But the new president insisted on more military spending and new weapons systems. The added expense during the Reagan years helped to quadruple the U.S. national debt. The stage for what became known as the Iran Contra Affair had been the 1980 Republican presidential platform which promised an aggressive CIA and stated, "We deplore the Marxist-Sandinista takeover of Nicaragua ... we will support the efforts of the Nicaraguan people to establish a free and independent government " (as quoted in Woodward, 1987, page 209).

Casey persistently dominated those around him despite early setbacks in his era and considerable opposition in Congress and within the CIA. His first choice of a DDCI, Max Heugel, failed to receive congressional approval because of income tax violations; the second, Bobby Inman, quit over disagreements with Casey, and the third, John McMahon, became someone Casey wished to avoid, in order to be as autonomous as possible. Though he had to include McMahon in the "paperwork loop," the latter appears to have had little power. "So Casey was not only running the Contra operation out of his office, as well as some of the fund-raising effort, he was running his own public-affairs office. He wasn't even telling McMahon what he was up to" (Woodward, 1987, page 408). Casey's orientation was reinforced by the president's dedication of a new $190-million, seven-story addition to the Langley headquarters, often called the Casey Memorial Wing (Woodward, 1987, page 408).

Feeling responsible only to President Reagan, Casey knew the president's policies but did not know what Reagan would actually do. The president's "wobbly seesawing … Yes … well … no" (Woodward, 1983, page 380) left room for Casey to operate as he chose, operationalizing what he sensed were the president's policies and ultimately forming policies of his own making, just as he had eagerly wanted to do when he accepted the position of DCI. While Casey was DCI, the CIA engaged in covert action by carrying out the Iran-Contra scheme without first obtaining a presidential finding, an absolutely legally required prerequisite for such action. Thus, Casey obviated his obligation to the president, as well as his duty to inform Congress. But Casey appeared proud of this complete circumvention of legally constituted authority. "To get the Ayatollah to fund the Contras was a strategic coup, a sting of unimagined proportions: having an enemy fund a friend. The DCI labeled this the ultimate covert operation" (Woodward, 1987, page 539).

The CIA's only direct action was to arrange the details of arms shipments (Kessler, page 92). But the CIA expedited matters indirectly, as it so often has. In this case, Lieutenant Colonel Oliver North arranged the actual carrying out of the operation through a self-financed arm of the National Security Council and National Security Advisor John Poindexter.

The Iran-Contra scheme had evolved from President Reagan signing a finding on December 1, 1981 providing the initial lethal assistance to the Contras to oppose Nicaragua's Sandanista government (Woodward, page 589). It ended with congressional hearings, the resignation of Poindexter, the firing of North, and Casey's death on May 6, 1987, the day after Congress began its hearings.

In a previous operation, Casey's secret work with the Saudi intelligence service to arrange the assassination of an arch-terrorist by car bombing, missed its target but killed at least 80 people, many of whom were innocent

(Woodward, 1987, page 587). Vastly greater destructive actions could be expedited through international arms deals. The CIA was known to place trust in Saudi arms dealer Adnan Khashoggi, the world's richest man, who courted governments and celebrities while he sold huge quantities of deadly weapons. Each of Khashoggi's three commercial-sized planes, outfitted far more lavishly than Air Force One, was fully staffed at all times with U.S. pilots and ready to fly anywhere in the world with less than an hour's notice (Kessler, 1986, page 4). Iran-Contra showed that CIA-expedited lethal actions could be carried out on a far greater scale involving the circumvention not only the laws of other nations but those of the U.S. itself.

Khashoggi had developed contacts with several U.S. presidents before Reagan, as well as with the CIA beginning at least as early as 1953 through Kermit Roosevelt when this grandson of Theodore Roosevelt had been head of the CIA's Middle East operations. Later, it was said of Khashoggi that "no one knew for sure where his CIA connections began or ended, magnifying his importance" (Kessler, 1986, page 64). His contacts with President Reagan included meeting him in person in February 1985 to negotiate the release of $180 million to the Sudan. Having become very well known both for his arms dealings and as a go-between in other massive money matters, he was a "natural" choice to arrange the complicated weapons for money and hostages scheme that eventually became known as Irangate. Kessler wrote:

> What emerged, according to sources, was the Iran arms deal, with plans to involve the Israelis, set up secret Swiss bank accounts, obtain bonds and letters of credit, trade arms for hostages as a way of establishing good faith, and solicit the approval of the U.S. government. It's likely that nobody else in the world could have pulled it off but Khashoggi... By doing a favor for the U.S., Khashoggi could win more friends for Saudi Arabia and enhance his own standing in all the countries (Kessler, 1986, page 309).

The man the U.S. depended on knew the plan would be revealed eventually and create a scandal. But he thought Reagan's gullibility was not his concern; of course, the president of the U.S. could not trade guns for hostages with Iran, the country that called the U.S. the "Great Satan." Khashoggi himself was caught up in the intrigue and suffered massive monetary reversals. He lost his status as the world's richest man but still had enough to support himself and lavishly entertain celebrities.

By the end of the Reagan–Casey era, the old CIA violations, first revealed by the press in the 1970s and elaborated upon in the "Family Jewels" document, had been superseded by more ubiquitously violating activities affecting entire nations and their relationships with one another. It was as if the reforms so belatedly and laboriously constructed in the 1970s had never existed. And instead of tallying the numbers of individuals killed as direct consequences of CIA activities, the toll of lethalities could only be estimated, at best, through complicated questioning starting with, "What if we hadn't done that?"

Has the vast, complicated web of CIA interventions saved more human lives than it has cost? Or has it facilitated greater destruction of human life through its massive system of intrigues designed to limit the spread of communism. While we cannot be sure of what would have happened without CIA interventions or exactly how many people died because of them, we do know that many of these interventions eventuated in tremendous numbers of fatalities. For example, as shown in Table 4.2, just within the period 1968 through 1976, Operation Phoenix resulted in the murder of over 40,000 Vietnamese civilians, and CIA work with the Chilean military resulted in the murder of over 20,000 political prisoners.

Revelations and Reservations in the 1990s

In 1990 Congress forced the CIA to establish an internal Historical Review Panel which was to propose declassifications of its secret documents. A historian, George Herring, who served on the panel for 6 years called it "a brilliant public relations snow job" (Weiner, 1997a). The panel did not meet at all between August 1990 and June 1994. In an editorial, the *New York Times* (Opening up C.I.A. history, 1997) noted, "All records from the agency's directorate of operations are exempt from Freedom of Information requests. Many of the documents the C.I.A. has made public over the years are meaningless because so much information is blocked out."

Furthermore, the CIA has destroyed many of its most important documents. For example, after promising for more than 5 years to make public the files from its covert mission to overthrow the government of Iran in 1953, the CIA said on May 28, 1997 that it had destroyed or lost almost all of them decades ago (Weiner, 1997e).

Inevitably, the CIA's long history of violations, cover-ups, exemptions from disclosure, and failed pledges to make information public have fueled not only tremendously deep and widespread distrust but also many specific conspiracy theories. For example, Representative Maxine Waters, a Democrat of California, and other Black leaders pushed for an investigation into allegations that the CIA knew of or promoted the selling of cocaine by Nicaraguan Contras in the U.S. in the early 1980s to raise money for their cause (Holmes, 1997).

Some revelations have been forthcoming, however. In September 1996 a summary of an investigation into the U.S. Army's School of the Americas (SOA) together with four pages of translated excerpts from its seven Spanish-speaking manuals, were released (Priest, 1996). The Defense Department summary noted that, to recruit and control informants, the manuals advised use of "fear, payment of bounties for enemy dead, beatings, false imprisonment, executions and the use of truth serum" (as quoted in Priest, 1996, page A1). In January 1997 two SOA training manuals in English were declassified and approved for release: "Counterintelligence Interrogation" (U.S. Army, 1963) and "Human Resource Exploitation" (U.S. Army, 1983).

Established in 1946 in Panama, and based in Fort Benning, GA since 1984, the SOA has trained Central and Southern Hemisphere nationals in the art of war. Among the 57,000 students it has graduated are many significant human rights violators; for example, over 40 Salvadoran officers responsible for major atrocities in Salvador's civil war. Those atrocities included the slaughtering of Archbishop Romero together with four nuns, six priests, and a housekeeper and her daughter.

In the process of revising the English-language manuals over the years and redacting them in readiness for release, some obviously torturous instructions have been lined through and replaced with qualifying remarks or other instructions that would seem to soften the treatment in what may have been a public relations effort. For example, Instruction E-27 originally tells the interrogator, "There should be no built-in toilet facilities. The subject should have to ask to relieve himself. Then he should either be given a bucket or escorted by a guard to the latrine. The guard stays at this side the entire time he is in the latrine." The revised version reads, "If there are no built-in toilet facilities, subject he [sic] should…" etc. Often, instructions which are more blatantly torturous have been entirely lined out, or disclaimers have been penciled in. For example, after elaborating on physically and psychologically coercive techniques that may, admittedly, result in permanent damage to the subject, a hand-printed comment appears, such as: "This technique is illegal and may not be used." Thus, the predominant residual emphasis is on more subtle psychological methods, but these changes in the manuals may not mean changes in the field in active practice.

Even with these "corrections," the 128-page interrogation manual and the somewhat briefer exploitation manual have provided a set of training guidelines that reads like a systematic 180-degree reversal of how to do beneficial psychotherapy. Some of the SOA methods — for example, sensory isolation, coercion techniques, and mind-altering drugs — are the same or similar to those used by psychiatrist D. Ewen Cameron in the CIA MKULTRA Project which it cites and which is discussed later in this chapter. As if to underline the antitherapeutic nature of all of the recommendations, the interrogators and exploiters are forewarned not to develop or permit any personal caring for their human subjects.

The thoroughly insidious nature of the entire SOA orientation is illustrated by how psychological research results are couched. For example, "The interrogator can benefit from the subject's anxiety. As the interrogator becomes linked in the subject's mind with the reward of lessened anxiety, human contact, and meaningful activity, and thus with providing relief for growing discomfort, the questioner assumes a benevolent role" (U.S. Army, 1963, page 90).

Reverend Roy Bourgeois, a Catholic priest of the Maryknoll order, has vigorously protested against the SOA for many years. In 1983, he and two associates secretly gained admission to its base in Fort Benning, were arrested, and sentenced to prison. His continuing campaign has been applauded by Representative Joseph Kennedy, II, a Democrat from Massachusetts who has attempted, with others in Congress, to close the SOA. But opposition has appeared to be strong. "A Pentagon spokesman says there has been no softening in the Defense Department's support for SOA, adding that military budget cuts and staff downsizing have intensified the need for the school, in order to maintain influence in the region" (Macklin, 1997, page D12).

As more documents are declassified, more and more apparent CIA-linked human rights violations come to light, substantiating Reverend Bourgeois' concerns. For example, the United Nations-instigated Historical Clarification Commission report of February 25, 1999 contradicted years of official denials of torture, kidnapping, and killings of thousands of civilians in the Guatemalan war, 1960 to 1996, in which it was estimated that 200,000 people were killed overall (Navarro, 1999). By lending direct and indirect support, including through the CIA and officer training, the U.S. Government helped the Guatemalan Government and allied paramilitary groups commit 90% of the war's 42,000 human rights violations, of which 29,000 resulted in deaths or disappearances.

Ethics Questions

A government that seeks to preserve itself and its people must devote a considerable share of its energies to its neighboring nations. Ideally at least, some portion of the energy goes into enterprises expressive of and intended to foster good will. Other portions are devoted to diplomacy and to arming itself against at least potentially warlike adversaries. Still another portion may be devoted to the covert enterprises of spying, including on one's "friendly" fellow nations, and sabotaging and manipulating other nations in clandestine fashion, including through propaganda and false information programs.

The actions of a legally constituted institution, when garbed in secrecy and not only authorized, but mandated, to break the laws of other countries, may have far more insidiously destructive consequences than an overtly destructive illegal institution that is readily subject to outside observation and regulation. Its beginnings may be noble in intent, but when its means and even its goals continue to be shrouded in secrecy, it may perpetrate death in the guise of goodness and, by means of its covert authority, it may also result in such corrosive distrust as to alienate its own citizens as well as those of other nations. In the case of a democratic nation, heavy reliance on covert actions may seriously undermine or even destroy the very democracy it is supposed to protect. In essence, the clandestine nature of the CIA, together with its mandate to break laws while striving for plausible deniability virtually guarantees it will not be fully accountable and that it will violate even its own charter.

The motto of the CIA, borrowed from the Bible, is "know the truth and the truth will set you free." But this motto, like many of the euphemisms used by the CIA, is unidirectional; the CIA appears truly interested in uncovering the truth about others while maintaining secrecy for itself.

Often, the CIA has aided and abetted murderous actions by recruiting others to do the actual killing, including assassinations. For example, a CIA guerrilla-warfare training manual advised the Nicaraguan Contras on "selective use of violence" to "neutralize carefully selected and planned targets such as court judges, police, and state security officials, etc." (as cited in Woodward, 1987, page 444). The manual also stated: "If possible, professional criminals will be hired to carry out selective jobs. This was embarrassingly reminiscent of the CIA's hiring of John Roselli, a member of the Cosa Nostra, to assassinate Castro in the early sixties" (Woodward, 1987, pages 445 and 446). The question of "neutralizing" enemies, as well as the CIA's sacrificing or endangering its own officers and agents and friendly associates, whether directly or, more often, through the enlistment of others, is at the heart of the ethical and governmental issue of whether or not the CIA should exist.

Rationales and Rationalizations

Lethal violence is most likely to be condoned in overt war. Even then, certain rules of decency are supposed to apply. But one extreme answer to the ethics question regarding lethal and paralethal violence is that "all is fair in love and war." As for war, there are both hot and cold wars, the latter intended ostensibly to prevent the former. And as for love, frequently, the spy or saboteur must get close, sometimes in a very friendly way, in order to "recruit" agents, which means getting people to become traitors to their own countries. "The most effective tool of recruitment was not cash or thumbscrews or blackmail or ideology — but simple friendship" (Thomas, 1996, page 182).

Cultivating friendships for this purpose has certain possibly lethal consequences. Although the CIA officer, the recruiter, may be at some risk, the recruited agent, the traitor, is at much greater risk. Some governments, apparently excepting the U.S., execute traitors who are discovered. For example, the Soviets executed as many as 20 of its traitors after CIA officer Aldrich Ames, who became a traitor himself, identified them for the Kometét Gosudárstvennoi

Bezopásnosti (KGB). And, periodically, cases involving other government retributions come to light. Recently, an Iranian Air Force colonel was hanged in a prison near Teheran after he was discovered gathering information for the CIA (Iranian hanged, 1997). But the clandestine nature of all of this "double-dealing" makes it difficult to ascertain the full measure of the lethal consequences even for the particular traitors, let alone the more insidious, ubiquitous, and often long-term lethal consequences promulgated by the spying business overall. Still, one may hold to the rationale that all is fair in love and war, at least when national security is at stake.

The case of spy and double agent Aldrich Ames (Earley, 1997), to be discussed in detail later, illustrates fully the deadly results of cultivating close "friendships" in order to recruit agents who thereby become traitors to their own countries. Closeness can be fostered in the doctor-patient relationship wherein patients' institutionalized trust and susceptibility, based on the ostensibly "helping and healing" nature of the relationship, can lead to the destruction of their brains and any semblance of mental well-being, as will be illustrated later in the case of psychiatrist D. Ewen Cameron and CIA Project MKULTRA (Weinstein, 1990). Or the CIA may be capable of destroying its own, as will be illustrated in the case of a U.S. Army major (Morehouse, 1996). Finally, in addition to damage and death directly attributable to violence against them, CIA leaders as well as operational officers may become severely disturbed by their lives in the agency, as will be illustrated in the case of Frank Wisner (Thomas, 1996).

How does the CIA actually provide rationales for its extraordinarily off-limits behavior? That depends, in large part, on the abilities of its individual members to provide and accept rationales in keeping with the moral standards of gentlemanly conduct. The early CIA leadership was drawn predominantly from Ivy League universities: Harvard, Yale, and Princeton. During some years in the 1950s, the CIA recruiter at Princeton University was William Lippincott, the dean of students. Another recruiter was Yale crew coach Skip Walz. Frank Wisner, who earned both his undergraduate and law school degrees at the University of Virginia when it was likened to the private Ivy League schools, became a high-ranking CIA officer in its formative years. Observers noted:

> With his moralistic background, Wisner may have been bothered at some level by the dirty work of spying, but he never showed it. The ability to swallow one's qualms, to do the harder thing for the greater good, was regarded as a sign of moral strength by men like Wisner. At meetings with his staff, he seemed moved less by squishy scruples than by practical necessity. "We talked about assassinations," said Jim McCarger, one of Wisner's top aides. "Wisner's attitude was that the KGB was better at it" (Thomas, 1996, page 37).

Wisner retired in 1962. But swallowing qualms appears to have played a major role, cumulatively, in his becoming haunted and experiencing cycles of increasing depression. "Old ghosts flitted through Wisner's addled mind" (Thomas, 1995, page 319). In October 1965 he shot himself. "Wisner's death saddened but did not shock his colleagues" (Thomas, 1996, page 320).

Aldrich Ames claimed that at "The Farm," a CIA training site, "you were told that you were now part of an elite service, that you were selected because you were one of the best and brightest, and that your job was paramount to the very survival of the U.S. Because of these things, you were entitled to lie, cheat, deceive. You did not have to obey laws in any foreign countries" (as quoted in Earley, 1997, page 39).

Whereas CIA officer Aldrich Ames took matters a step further by becoming a "mole" in the service of the Soviet Union, CIA officer David Whipple maintained his clandestine but "loyal" adherence to his training: "We don't think of it as living a lie. We think of it as a necessary thing.... You have to protect your identity in order to remain effective.... It's as if you were a slightly different person" (as quoted in Kessler, 1992, page 9).

Duane Clarridge, recruited as an officer by the CIA in 1954, has been the highest-ranking American spy directly and personally involved in espionage, war, counterterrorism, and intrigue to make his life public. For 33 years, he epitomized the CIA's clandestine activities. In his book, *A Spy for All Seasons: My Life in the CIA* (1997), he objected to the "serious limitations imposed by the U.S. legal system on the efficacy of a Clandestine Services effort" (page 408) and the "handwringers" who claim that by collecting information on terrorists and the proliferators of weapons of mass destruction, narcotics and international crime, the CIA becomes "one of the bad guys." Clarridge stated:

> This is absurd. But you do have to deal with undesirables to penetrate the organizations or states involved to obtain information. Mother Teresa, for all her wisdom, unfortunately, doesn't have it. What is disturbing is the hypocrisy on this issue of some in Congress, the executive branch, the media, academia, and, most disgraceful of all, the current CIA leadership. The CIA is lambasted by these worthies for dealing with "scumbags" to acquire secret intelligence to protect American lives and property, whereas no such condemnation is leveled at the FBI, the DEA, and local law enforcement agencies, which deal routinely with criminals (called paid informants rather than agents) to capture and convict other criminals (page 409).

The real issue here is not merely whether the CIA has to deal with undesirables, but whether killing and other harmful acts are committed with impunity. Actually, dealing with undesirables has often resulted in such acts.

William Casey, Director of the CIA during the increased covert activities era of the Reagan administration, in which Clarridge was particularly active, invoked, for the sake of endorsement, the words of General, and later first President of the U.S., George Washington: "For upon secrecy, success depends in most enterprises of the kind, and for the want of it, they are generally defeated, however well planned and promising" (as quoted in Woodward, 1987, page 210). Casey went on with a further rationale: "It is much easier and much less expensive to support an insurgency than it is for us and our friends to resist one. It takes relatively few people and little support to disrupt the internal peace and economic stability of a small country" (as quoted in Woodward, 1987, page 211). Thus, ease and economic expediency were offered as suitable rationales. President Reagan's CIA Director Casey also proclaimed his right to be free of substantial oversight by elected officials other than the president. Casey stated, "The business of Congress is to stay out of my business" (as quoted on the television program "20th Century" (Arts & Entertainment), 1997).

Former CIA Director Gates put the matter bluntly — working for the CIA requires "scams and tricks" and having "strange and unsavory bedfellows" (C-Span, 1997c). But unsavory behavior by oneself as well as one's close associates raises qualms, whether openly admitted or not.

Qualms and Quibbles

Claims and rationales for the "necessity" of covert actions have been countered by qualms even within the CIA, including among its highest officials. Admiral Bobby Ray Inman, who served directly under DCI Casey as DDCI, found it troubling that "covert operations seemed to get started when the White House and the State Department were frustrated with diplomacy ... the painstaking steps of negotiation and endless meetings, proposals and counterproposals.... The secret covert action provided a shortcut ... the comfort of action, the feeling that there was a secret way to get things done..." (Woodward, 1987, page 187). CIA officers in training sometimes quit as they experienced misgivings about the nature of covert operations.

Furthermore, highly placed CIA officers have looked down on the low-life spies beneath them. Rick Ames documented this prejudice by citing former CIA director Dulles' attitudes toward the spy, in this case Benedict Arnold, vs. the spy's superior who was British Major John Andre. Ames said, "Having been both a case officer and a spy, I can tell you clearly.... The agency's leadership, as opposed to the rank and file, has consistently denigrated and despised the spy. One of Allen Dulles' favorite lines was Sir Francis Walsingham's line about how he had gone out and hired a low fellow to spy. Meanwhile, Andre is described as the model of professionalism" (Ames, as quoted in Earley, 1997, page 204).

Another qualm-raising argument is that the CIA's recruitment of spies to become agents in the service of the U.S. relies on persuading foreigners to become traitors to their own countries. Does persuading someone to become a traitor cultivate a traitorous spirit in oneself, the persuader, albeit a denied or compartmentalized part?

Yet another criticism of CIA ethics is that the Agency has contracted with people known to be criminals, by the standards of U.S. law, to carry out covert actions on behalf of the U.S. Is there something contradictory about hiring criminals to do the dirty work for a good cause? Perhaps, once started down the road of covert action, there is no telling where, how, or when, if ever, the repercussions will stop.

In the pursuit of "plausible deniability," the CIA may further cover over the covert actions. But the covers on top of covers may result in far greater distrust and hostility years later. A CIA cover-up of covert aircraft testing in the western U.S. in the1950s and 1960s led people to believe that their sightings of unidentified objects in the skies were alien spaceships (Wise, 1997). Recent revelations of that cover-up have fed the already widespread suspicion that our federal government is not honest with its citizens. Former CIA Director Stansfield Turner has said that the CIA is too secretive for its own good; when cover-ups are brought to light, they provoke more investigative interest (C-Span, 1997c).

The media are often asked, in the name of national security, not to reveal CIA activity but to put themselves in a quandary. It is difficult, for example, for respectable newspaper publishers to know where to draw the line. The *Washington Post* considered and reconsidered whether to publish a story about a covert operation involving U.S. submarines picking up messages in Soviet underwater cables. *Post* board chairwoman Katherine Graham reasoned, "If intelligence agencies were trying to overthrow governments, we probably should publish, but how could the U.S. gather too much intelligence? Listen too much? The Soviets did it to us. Even if we were ahead in the various technologies, should we wait for the Soviets to catch up?" (Woodward, 1987, page 534).

Machinating Mentalities

"Feelings were the natural enemy of the CIA operative" (Woodward, 1987, page 48)

The War against Feelings

Many people drawn to covert work in its most aggressive and clandestine forms are characterized by machismo: "a strong, sometimes exaggerated sense of masculinity-stressing attributes such as courage, virility, domination of women, and aggressive manliness." The adjectival form is illustrated by a quote from Arthur M. Schlesinger: "*he was a mindless activist, a war lover who found macho relish in danger and felt driven to prove manhood by confrontation*" (*American Heritage Dictionary of the English Language*, 3rd ed., 1992).

The macho orientation and morbid behavior are closely associated in terms of "protest masculinity" which presents as bravado and aggressive impulsivity and serves as a cover-up for a lack of deep masculinity (Whitaker, 1987; 1996). The macho orientation short-circuits careful reflection and demands actions to prove one's manhood. Men who lack a strong, secure sense of masculinity readily become compulsive courters of danger. They are compelled to provide or be provided with tests of masculinity but remain insecure about their masculinity even if they "win."

Macho men must try to dominate women in contrast to cultivating equality-based partnerships with them, and they must deny and forcibly reject all signs of "femininity" in themselves. Typically, macho men regard women as inferior, and they are usually homophobic. The CIA has been extremely male dominated in terms of numbers and authority, and its largely macho orientation shows in the language used as well as its actions. Woodward (1987) documented examples. President Reagan repeatedly denigrated Libyan political leader Qaddafi as fay (which actually means a fairy, elf) and remarked, "Qaddafi can look in Nancy's closet anytime" (as quoted, page 509). Lieutenant Colonel Oliver North, who conducted much of the Iran-Contra affair, remarked that "it was time to kill the cocksucker terrorists" (page 412). Observing that DDI John McMahon apparently had an inhibiting effect on his boss, DCI William Casey, the State Department's Tony Motley "wondered whether McMahon maybe had something on Casey." Motley had once said jokingly, "McMahon had somehow caught Casey sucking cock!" (page 375).

While macho personalities seem drawn to morbid forms of risk-taking, even death-defying or death-courting exploits, the fear of involvement in such activity cannot be admitted, sometimes even to oneself. Accordingly, macho men are also drawn to drugs that would help them anesthetize and deny fear. In the case of CIA operatives who are not supposed to use illicit drugs but are trained to perform in extremely dangerous situations, alcohol has been the drug of choice. Heavy drinking is said to be so characteristic in the CIA Operations Directorate that nothing but extremely gross interference with observed work functions is cause for special intervention. For example, Aldrich Ames habitually imbibed heavily even on duty, but was never taken aside for reasons of his problem drinking.

Even problem use of drugs other than alcohol may be observed but discounted. Operatives who became traitors to the U.S. became so after internal security lights should have been flashing. "The CIA knew Edward Lee Howard had a drug problem but prepared to send him anyway to Moscow, where he began working for the Soviets. The agency knew that William P. Kampiles also had a drug problem but allowed him access to the top-secret manual for the KH-11 spy satellite, which he promptly sold to the Soviets" (Kessler, 1992, page 324).

Disregard for internal security generally has been a major problem within the CIA. Polygraph (lie detector) tests have been omitted or downplayed in major traitor cases including that of CIA officers Aldrich Ames and David Barnett, as well as Karl Koecher, a Czech Intelligence Service officer who became a CIA employee. Thus, the CIA's expertise in conducting and detecting covert operations, seemingly paradoxically, is not applied within its own organization; professional level self-monitoring is lacking. However, the laxness of its self-monitoring is not difficult to understand when viewed in the light of the personalities and ethos involved. The right to break rules, as long as there is "plausible deniability," often seems to permeate the mentality of the CIA.

> Instead of improving security, the CIA's response over the years to embarrassing spy cases has been to try to cover them up by opposing prosecutions that would make its mistakes public. Thus, the CIA's blasé attitude about security is a form of self-protection, a way of insulating CIA officers from accountability. The attitude is fueled by directors of Central Intelligence who consider the subject of security to be both dreary and beneath them (Kessler, 1992, page 331).

The macho orientation in spies has a particular characteristic twist. Their clandestine operations are by definition not directly confrontational. Instead, plotting, deception, stealth, and craftiness are needed to accomplish missions. The thrill is in the secrecy as well as the action of derring-do. As Thomas (1995) noted in his book *The Very Best Men*, the CIA preferred to hire college men who gave the appearance of gentlemen; they were certainly not impulsive criminals or the kinds of men who go to bars looking for a fight. They were often good fraternity men or members of gentlemen's secret societies who "played by the rules," though sometimes rules of their institution's own making. Many were sports teams members who were, accordingly, well disciplined at following the rules of the game. In the CIA, often the rules have been of the Agency's own making, and breaking rules is not only acceptable but needed for effective covert action. To protect themselves and the Agency, officers should strive for what has been termed "feasible deniability." Ideally, of course, officers as well as any agents they have recruited should not be caught, but if they are, the Agency may have to deny any connection in an effort to maintain its own deniability in the face of accusations. Therefore, the spy may have to be a loner.

Because war and the "blood sport" of hunting require killing and deception, they may very readily lend themselves to other forms of deadly covert action. As discussed also in Chapter 2, sports, as well as most competitive games, may be regarded as sublimated warfare (Whitaker, 1997) involving deception as well as, at least, modulated aggression. After all, chess was invented as a substitute for war. All sports involve tactics that are designed to be deceptive and evasive: end runs in football, fakes in basketball, curve balls in baseball, and so on. These tactics are licit parts of the game, i.e., within the rules. Sportsmen and gentlemen play by the rules, and both sides in a game of sport are required to abide by the same rules.

The CIA also abides by rules, although they are more often secret and allow lethal consequences. Those traditional archenemies, the Russian KGB, and its opposite, the CIA, have tacitly observed certain rules to avoid lethal consequences, such as not executing each others' own spies, though many double agents, i.e., traitors to their own countries, have been executed by their own governments. Thus far, the U.S. has preferred incarcerating rather than executing its own officers caught spying against the U.S.

So, in the overwhelmingly male world of the CIA, a man can transfer experiences in sports to being a CIA officer and feel somewhat at home, except for two major differences: visibility and independent oversight. In organized sports, spectators are welcome to watch, comment on, debate, and discuss all of the action, and umpires or referees and lines people scrutinize every aspect of the game to maximize fair play. In contrast, CIA officers are often not only allowed but required to engage in foul play and to keep secret almost everything they do. Theoretically, the CIA is subject to independent oversight but it is difficult to ensure.

How do generally intelligent, well-educated, and typically "well-raised gentlemen" come to like this work and to tolerate the inherent emotional conflicts? Part of the answer is drug use, with an emphasis on alcohol.

Covert action with the intent to do harm, including to those one befriends, requires denial and distancing of feelings in the face of very emotionally provocative experiences. Typically, emotions in such situations become too strong to be managed simply by an acute denial reaction, even when blunted by drugs. What is needed is a personality already thoroughly inculcated in denial of emotion. The covert operative must be already capable of a certain coldness and distance learned in his early years. Fear and stalwart denial of feelings is aided by being learned early enough to be reliable in later "dangerously emotional" situations; the operative must not give himself away by being genuinely emotionally expressive. Drugs, including alcohol, can help to suppress any residual proclivity to becoming emotional.

Other parts of the answer include automatic, unreflective obedience to authority, and perceiving the enemy as less than human. These two characteristics are essentially two sides of the same coin. If an individual is extremely concerned with obeying and satisfying an authoritarian leader, then other people count for very little. Thus, an unreflective, unemotional, obedient follower can far more easily kill another human being than can a reflective, independent person, because the latter empathizes with and "feels for" the potential victim.

Heroes

The CIA's heroes, as well as its traitors, appear overall to have been successful at warring against their feelings and avoiding genuine emotional intimacy, though sometimes at great cost in terms of personal relationships and their own emotional well-being. In *A Spy for all Seasons*, Clarridge (1997) disclosed his own subtle but profound early training in denying emotion: "Although not stated, it was made clear that emotional gestures and speech were signs of weakness and to be avoided" (page 27). This training probably contributed to his social reticence. "There was no question that I could do the schoolwork, but I didn't do nearly as well with the social work of growing up. I was a rather shy and withdrawn child — I played with other kids, but never formed the great boyhood friendships that other children did" (page 25). In his adult years, like so many of his colleagues in the CIA, he became a heavy drinker.

Evan Thomas' book, *The Very Best Men* (1995) has provided biographic accounts of four CIA operatives who performed feats of derring-do in the relatively free-wheeling era of the 1950s and early 1960s. The quotes cited in the remainder of this section are from his book. Besides damaging others' lives, "for Wisner, Bissell, Barnes, and Fitzgerald, the personal cost was high as well. The careers of two were ruined; one killed himself; only one lived past the age of 62. They could not see that the mortal enemy was within, that they were being slowly consumed by the moral ambiguities of a life in secrets" (page 12). Nor were these four men unusual in their eventual disenchantment. Most of the 66 former CIA officials interviewed by Thomas readily acknowledged that there were more CIA failures than successes.

Initially, idealism characterized these and many other leading CIA officers. They were consumed by the moral ambiguities because they were virtuous, highly educated gentlemen reared by their parents and their universities to be idealistic. "Patriotic, decent, well-meaning, and brave, they were also uniquely unsuited to the grubby, necessarily devious world of intelligence" (page 11). Confident of the rightness of their actions at the outset but naive about consequences, they headed boldly into tragedies of their own and others' making. Yet, perhaps they had at least some prescience of the fate of adventurous violation. Thomas quoted the old "Whiffenpoof" drinking song sung by Yalemen with their arms linked:

> We're poor little lambs who've lost our way…
> Little black sheep who have gone astray…
> Gentlemen songsters off on a spree
> Damned from here to Eternity

Romantic, even comradely, idealism was seldom linked to the ability to tolerate deep feelings, unless in the form of an intense yet emotionally distant rather than really emotionally vulnerable manner. "Frank Gardiner Wisner had grown up in a world that was, like the one the CIA would help create, secretive, insular, elitist, and secure in the rectitude of its purpose…. In later years, Wisner was regarded, even by intimates, as a remote figure; capable of charm and warmth, yet somehow not quite all there" (page 17). He showed what was regarded as moral strength: to swallow his qualms and to "do the harder thing for the greater good." He impressed others as a very strong man in command. A manic-depressive, his high energy wore out his men, and by his late 40s he was more floridly manic. For 6 months in 1958-1959 he was psychiatrically hospitalized at Sheppard-Pratt where he was given electroconvulsive shock treatments (page 162). It was his end as head of clandestine services. What others had observed as "a certain fatalism in his character" (page 70) was consistent with his committing suicide in later life.

Desmond Fitzgerald, the second of the men biographed by Thomas, exemplified, if anything, an even more extreme version than Wisner of the macho, emotionally distant, highly educated, and seemingly fearless gentleman so idealized in that era. He was described by those who knew him as cold and "not one to reveal his feelings" (page 49). As a well-connected 31-year-old lawyer, he enlisted in the Army as a private, instead of taking a safe rear-echelon job, and became a combat officer. At 34, he joined the CIA. Wisner placed him in charge of the Office of Policy Coordination's Far East Division and he ran secret armies in Tibet and Laos. Later, he was made director of all clandestine operations for the CIA, to which he brought esprit and high standards. Fitzgerald "wanted his spies to be at once intellectual and macho. His idea of perfection, said one of his case officers, was a Harvard Ph.D. who could handle himself in a bar fight" (Thomas, 1995, picture caption near page 127). Although his romantic notion of what could be achieved by an individual was upset by the development of weapons of mass destruction, he persisted with covert projects that would subvert rather than directly confront. Like Wisner before him, Fitzgerald became worn out. In 1967, at age 56, while playing tennis in 97° July weather he collapsed with a fatal heart attack (page 333).

Tracy Barnes, the third man, may have been even more extremely macho than Wisner or Fitzgerald. Barnes' relish of risk from an early age may have been related to being "on his own" as a child whose mother favored his older brother. His mother's father had committed suicide. After Groton, Barnes matriculated at Yale where he was known to court death by speeding in his car. Looking back on his life, his widow said, "Tracy invited danger. He couldn't wait for it." She remembered that on the Monday morning after Pearl Harbor, he enlisted without waiting for breakfast" (as cited in Thomas, 1995, page 75). Others observed, during his World War II service, that he went out of his way to tempt fate. John Bross, the senior prefect in Barnes' class at Groton who got him a position training commandos to drop behind German lines, thereby preventing his almost certain death as a would-be waist gunner in the air force, said "I rather got the impression that he wanted specifically to look death in the eye" (page 76). Consistent with his clearly macho orientation, "Personal feelings were not to be spoken of at Barnes' dining room table" (page 174) and, according to his children, "On the tennis court, he could come close to tantrums. He created an atmosphere that was so intense it became unpleasant" (page 175). Like Richard Bissell who became his boss in clandestine operations, he was an extremely impatient "doer," rather than reflective.

As a CIA officer, Barnes was surrounded by fanatical devotion to deviousness, for example, in the form of E. Howard Hunt who became known in later years as one of the Watergate burglars. The 1950s atmosphere even promoted the wildest, most unregulated actions. Accordingly, "Barnes was willing to try just about anything. There was little to hold the CIA back. Congress provided almost no operational oversight, while handing out what amounted to a blank check of unrestricted funds. The press was docile, caught up in the thinking that to quibble would be unpatriotic" (page 85).

Richard Bissell was another Groton and Yale alumnus like Tracy Barnes, and he liked Wisner and Fitzgerald whom he had gotten to know at Georgetown dinner parties. The Georgetown crowd was known for betting, games, striving to appear carefree instead of workaholic, and heavy drinking. A member remarked, "I never went to a Sunday night supper when someone didn't get embarrassingly drunk.... Just to unwind. It wasn't maudlin. No one threw up. We just drank a hell of a lot. A martini was like a glass of water is now" (page 103).

As a boy, Bissell was, in his own words, "shy and timid, a perfect foil for teasing" who relied on his mother as "my refuge from the cruel world" (page 89). He was known as the smartest man in Washington, largely for his work on the Marshall Plan and the U-2 spy plane, when he was appointed head of CIA clandestine services in replacement of the mentally disabled Wisner.

Bissell took special interest in a top-secret project code-named MKUL-TRA, dedicated to experiments to turn human beings into robots, which is discussed later in this chapter and, beginning in 1960, to assassinate Cuban leader Fidel Castro. Failed plots involving the Cosa Nostra to kill Castro by poisoning his cigars or his drinks, and later the Bay of Pigs invasion of Cuba, became well-publicized fiascos which, together with the U-2 spy plane discovery, helped bring down Bissell.

The DCI, for most of this free-wheeling period, was Allen Dulles who served from 1953 to 1961 under Presidents Eisenhower and Kennedy. "Dulles does not seem to have been in the least troubled by the ambiguities of intelligence work. He was a man capable of an amiable encounter with the enemy and the Devil; he learned to deal comfortably in perfectly bad faith, without ever violating a personal sense of moral rectitude and decency," wrote his biographer Peter Grose (1994, page 73). According to Louis Auchincloss who had worked in the same law firm as Dulles, "Allen was shrewd — but cold as ice" (as cited in Thomas, 1996, page 73).

Traitors

The Aldrich Ames case is a thoroughly documented example of the most insidious development of the spying mentality. While "straightforward" spying is itself fraught with dangers to everyone involved, these dangers are multiplied when the "patriotic" spy begins to spy for the enemy. Yet such a personal transformation is just a further logical step in a sequence already characterized by treacherous behavior.

"Rick" Ames' father, who had worked for the CIA, told him, "You and I know that lying is wrong, son…. But if it serves a greater good, it is okay to lie. It is okay to mislead people if you are doing it in the service of your country, but it is never okay to lie or mislead people for your own personal benefit" (cited in Earley, 1997, page 31). Decades later, the younger Ames would explain that he had sold information to the Soviets for the sake of his wife (whose extravagant tastes he seemed to share). As a CIA officer trained to "recruit" foreigners to betray their own countries, it was both natural and traitorous for him to betray his own country.

Ames' childhood and adolescence had much in common with others in his vocation. He recalled a combination of idealistic high standards and discomfort with feelings: "We did not speak much about feelings…. The idea was that individual integrity and worth was of paramount importance…. Stoicism was the virtue…" (cited in Earley, page 26). Perhaps he was attempting to fill the emotional void by stuffing himself with food paid for with money stolen from his father, in "solitary greed" (page 28) before regular family dinners. His later alcoholism may have had the same function of denying and displacing emotional needs. His role model became the "Saint," a fictional James Bond of the day who rescued damsels, smoked cigarettes, drank highballs, and solved mysteries.

After his father revealed that he worked for the CIA, Rick obtained a summer job with the CIA making counterfeit money. By then, his father's career was floundering and, as Rick and two of Rick's three siblings would do later, he became an alcoholic. Rick had become, according to those who knew him, a "sincere" liar who "got his kicks from fooling people" (page 33). After flunking out of college in his second year and experiencing blackouts from binge drinking, he continued his interest in acting but began drinking heavily on a regular basis, deteriorated in his living habits, and returned home where his father got him a regular job with the CIA.

At the CIA's training site called "The Farm," Rick's proclivities were furthered by being trained to focus on identifying a person's vulnerability or weakness and to "befriend" the person in order to recruit him or her — the same approach used by deadly cults as discussed in Chapters 1 and 2. His heavy drinking, often with his instructors, fit with the Directorate of Operation's macho image. "You have to realize that hard drinking had been an accepted part of the CIA culture for many years. James Angleton was famous for getting loaded every day at long lunches. There was still an element of macho pride in being an officer who could go drink-for-drink with other men" (Ames, as cited by Earley, page 112).

Meanwhile, his heroic idealism continued side by side with his machinating mentality. On his honeymoon with his first wife, he saved two boys from drowning. But that idealism did not diminish "…what is at the core of the intelligence officer's world — betraying another person's trust in you" (Ames, as cited by Earley, page 43). Given the nature of his formative years, his reliance on the anesthetic effects of alcohol to still emotional needs and qualms alike, the "ethical vacuum" of CIA covert operations, and the mandate to encourage betrayal, it is not surprising that as Earley notes (1997) through Shakespeare: "The villainy you teach me I will execute, and it shall go hard but I will better the instruction" (*The Merchant of Venice*).

Although not very good himself at recruiting Soviet officials who could be induced to betray their countries, Ames' attainment of a senior position in the CIA Directorate of Operations gave him access in 1983 to files that showed the Agency's penetration of every aspect of the Soviet system. There, he learned of the specific operations and the names of the Soviets recruited to spy within the Soviet intelligence establishment. These "moles" or "double agents" were traitors to their own country and were dependent on the CIA to help protect them from exposure. Now Ames was in a position to "blow the cover" off these traitors. By becoming a mole or traitor himself, Ames could be of great value to the Soviets and be paid handsomely for his betrayal of the Soviet moles and the U.S. If discovered, the Soviet moles would, in all likelihood, be executed, while, as a traitor to the U.S., Ames would, at most, be imprisoned for life.

Ames' decision to betray his country and, in effect, give the death sentence to the Soviet moles, appears to have been based on disillusionment and greed, as well as facilitated by his own machinating mentality. Ironically, his own idealism helped foster the disillusionment. He had become revolted by evidence of CIA abuses as well as the ignoring of accurate information gathered by the CIA in favor of political expediencies that helped to gain and protect presidential offices.

He was especially impressed by the damage done by James Jesus Angleton, the CIA's former chief of counterintelligence. Angleton was a legendary mole hunter who in the early 1960s was an increasingly alcoholic and conspiratorial man who would puzzle over counterintelligence cases while having 4-hour lunches at an elite restaurant and downing serial martinis (Thomas, 1995, page 307). His destructive use of authority included a "hostile interrogation" of double agent Yuri Nosenko who was still working for the KGB and turned out to be a genuine defector in the service of the CIA and the U.S. The interrogation lasted 4 years and 8 months. It included sensory and social isolation, near starvation, disorientation, sleep deprivation, massive shots of Thorazine and other psychotropic drugs, phony lie detector tests, and being told he was going crazy and that everyone who had known him had abandoned him. Ames was struck by the actual insanity as well as immorality demonstrated by Angleton and his men.

Furthermore, it was apparent that the CIA could not control one of their own who was engaged fanatically in destructive and demoralizing witch hunts. By the mid-1960s, still the chief of counterintelligence, Angleton was hopelessly preoccupied with what he believed was a "monster plot" by the Soviets to plant a mole in the CIA and he, thereby, made it difficult for the CIA's Soviet Division to recruit agents. Even the high-ranking Desmond Fitzgerald, noted earlier in this chapter, could not get Angleton to attend important late afternoon meetings when the chief of counterintelligence may have still been out drinking his lunch. Fitzgerald, himself preoccupied with CIA plans to kill Castro, was aware that Angleton's paranoia was corrosive to the Agency but was doubtful that CIA Director Helms would support any effort to curb Angleton in the spring of 1967. As already noted, the exhausted Fitzgerald died of a heart attack in July of that year. Ironically, having caused much of Fitzgerald's anguish and deadly fatigue, Angleton wrote the man's widow, "I have just received the breaking of hearts message. To me Des was a man of rare spiritual harmonies" (cited in Thomas, 1995, page 333).

Disillusioned, heavily in debt, and having learned that the CIA was an organization that could fail to monitor or control even extreme behavior destructive to itself, on April 16, 1985 Ames walked into the Soviet embassy and began a liaison with the KGB that was not discovered until 1995. Meanwhile, he was known to be alcoholic, had compromising lie detector test results, and had an ostentatious, extravagant life style, since at least the summer of 1986, that contrasted starkly with his modest salary.

Surveillance of his actions was apparently minimal until very near the end. Eight years after he had first become a double agent, he was able, on June 13, 1993 to carry a shopping bag with seven pounds of CIA intelligence reports right past CIA guards as he left work. None of the guards asked to look inside the bag. Even after being placed under intense surveillance by the FBI, Ames got away with making at least two successful "dead drop" deliveries of information to the Soviets. It was not until October 6, 1993 that the FBI began to discover what turned out to be a wealth of definitive evidence against Ames, who was thereby forestalled from collecting another $1.9 million being held for him in Moscow.

Arresting Ames on February 21, 1994 had required a very elaborate and expensive set of investigations by the CIA and the FBI. In addition, the CIA's inspector general, Fred Hitz, later required 12 investigators, a review of 45,000 pages of documents, and 300 interviews. His 486-page classified report blistered the CIA for "sleeping on the job and not catching Ames much earlier" (Earley, 1997, page 333). This report and the Agency's failure to follow it's recommendations resulted in congressional investigations and President Clinton signing a directive that gave the FBI more power in relation to the CIA.

Altogether, Ames identified for the Soviets at least 20 of their officers who had become agents for the CIA. Most of them were subsequently arrested and many were executed. Ames was sentenced to life imprisonment while his wife Rosario, who knew the source of their wealth in later years, was sentenced to 5 years in prison. Jeanne Vertefeuille of the CIA, who actually did much to reveal Ames' treachery, summed up her impression: "As I see it, the money was never important to him, until he met Rosario … it was a combination of his weakness and Rosario's materialism that caused him to do it" (as quoted in Earley, 1997, page 351).

Other men who were traitors to the U.S. in recent years have been somewhat less troublesome to the CIA's image. Marine Sergeant Clayton Lonetree confessed spontaneously to a CIA officer in 1986 to having been recruited by the KGB as a spy. And two former FBI agents were sentenced to prison in the 1990s (FBI agent who spied, 1997). But Ames was a CIA insider, one of their own. And the CIA was aware of its own past excesses. Vertefeuille said, "We *all* agreed that we would not act in any Angletonian fashion" (Earley, 1997, page 224).

After Ames was caught, an even higher-ranking CIA officer, Harold J. Nicholson, was apprehended in November 1996 and sentenced in June 1997 (CIA traitor, 1997). He had been selling secrets to Moscow since 1994. Like

Ames, his excuse for severely endangering and even causing loss of lives was needing to get financial support for his family. But whereas Ames made millions, Nicholson reaped only $300,000. In view of his cooperation, Nicholson, age 46, was given a sentence of 23 years and 7 months, calculated to make his release possible before he turned 70 (Weiner, 1997b). Unlike the Ames case, Nicholson's compromising lie detector results were given very careful attention. Prior to the Ames and Nicholson cases, moles had not been caught purely on the basis of detective work. "Every spy caught by a U.S. intelligence service in recent history had been nabbed because of a snitch" (Earley, 1997, page 224). It had been traitors betraying traitors.

Mind Control Programs

The prince of darkness is a gentleman — William Shakespeare (1564-1616)

MKULTRA and Dr. Cameron

In 1953, the CIA Project, code-named MKULTRA, began a top secret mind and behavior influence program. It was run overall by Sidney Gottlieb of the Chemical Division who had a Ph.D. from Cal Tech and labeled himself one of the "Dr. Strangeloves" of the technical services staff. Project MKULTRA may be the best single example of the complete failure of the adage, "the ends justify the means." In the case of the MKULTRA endeavors, not only were the means illicit, but the ends were seldom, if ever, achieved, just as the Nazi medical experiments on helpless victims contributed little of scientific value, unless one includes the later psychological studies of the perpetrators. It took until 1977 for the general public, through a *New York Times* front page article in August of that year, to learn anything of the secret 25-year, $25-million project that the CIA operated in the 1950s.

Gottlieb was "a pleasant man who lived on a farm with his wife, ... drank only goat's milk and grew Christmas trees, which he sold at a roadside stand" (Thomas, 1996, page 211). He and his staff were devoted to harming minds as well as bodies. Their deadly endeavors involved using drugs on totally unknowing citizens, including even CIA-affiliated scientists, one of whom leapt out of a window after unwittingly ingesting LSD. MKULTRA's early emphasis on LSD experiments was inspired by a false intelligence report that the Soviets were trying to buy up the world's stock of LSD. Throughout the 1950s the CIA covertly tested LSD on unwitting subjects, including in whorehouses they ran in the Greenwich Village section of New York City and in San Francisco where customers were slipped powerful drugged drinks. CIA case officers watched through one-way mirrors and joked about "operation

Midnight Climax" (Thomas, 1995, page 212). The results contributed no new knowledge of mind control.

As was often the case with CIA projects, MKULTRA also contracted with nongovernmental institutions and individuals. In revelations made possible by the Freedom of Information Act in 1977, the CIA's mind control programs involving 185 nongovernmental researchers in 80 institutions, including 54 colleges and universities, 15 research foundations, 12 hospitals and clinics, and 3 penal institutions came to light.

D. Ewen Cameron was a Canadian biological psychiatrist whose work was modeled on the disease concept of mental disturbance with ambition to "conquer the disease of schizophrenia" and to rise to world prominence. He was one of three North American psychiatrists invited to Nuremberg, Germany after World War II to evaluate war criminal Rudolph Hess.

Cameron considered the impact of the holocaust in a 1946 paper called "Frontiers of Psychiatry" in which he used the case of Nazi Germany to exemplify how a society poisoned the minds of its citizens through propagating anxiety. But instead of really rejecting authoritarian methods of influence, he chose to perform experiments on unwitting patients in his care, although with the ostensible aim of countering authoritarian regimes as exemplified by the fascists and communists, and finding methods to improve society. "Thus, Cameron's solution to the ills of society was simple: experts should decide who can parent and who should govern. These experts must develop methods of forcefully changing attitudes and beliefs" (Weinstein, 1990, page 99). Thus, the ultimate irony: the would-be rescuer became the same kind of perpetrator himself, directing medical experiments not unlike those of the Nazi doctors who experimented cruelly on their hapless victims.

Having learned about Dr. Cameron's experiments, the CIA used a front organization to fund his work from 1957 through 1960 in order to gain access to the results of his experimental "treatment" of patients at the Allan Memorial Institute of Psychiatry of McGill University, Montreal. The Canadian government also helped fund this research.

Cameron was, at various times, president of virtually all of the world's major psychiatric organizations. Shielded by secrecy and his own world renown, and never really challenged by colleagues, though they knew something of the aggressive treatments he forced on unwitting patients, Cameron was never brought to justice. He died in 1967, 10 years before his "experimental" work came to public attention.

Cameron used frequent, often extremely intense electroconvulsive treatments (ECTs) known as Page-Russells, plus debilitating psychiatric drugs, sensory isolation, and "psychic driving" consisting of seemingly interminable forcing of verbal messages on the patient. All of these "treatments," each capable of producing lasting damage by itself, were used in various combinations in the relentless pursuit of what Cameron called "depatterning," which was likened to the brainwashing attributed to Communists in Asia. In essence, the purpose of such treatment was to deprive the subject, as thoroughly as possible, of his or her mental faculties.

Psychiatrist Harvey Weinstein's book, *Psychiatry and the CIA: Victims of Mind Control* (1990), has provided a detailed account of Cameron's pseudo-scientific, thoroughly iatrogenic treatment of nine of the Cameron victim-patients, including Dr. Weinstein's father, Lou, who initially presented only an anxiety disorder related to an episode of suffocation in childhood. But Cameron repeatedly hospitalized and subjected this previously highly successful man, against his will, to treatments which so grossly shrunk his faculties as to reduce him to an essentially vegetative condition for the rest of his life. For example, in one 3-month hospital stay, Lou Weinstein was put into drugged sleep continuously for 54 days, given at least 23 ECTs, subjected to "psychic driving," and "depatterned" to a state of complete regression. Some temporary success at instituting regression had been achieved, but the psychiatric team had to be sure to institute a deeper, longer-lasting regression. An excerpt from a psychiatric resident's notes clearly indicates the process and the goal:

> Last week he was deeply confused, incontinent, and we plan to keep him on sleep for 10 days prior to driving. He has, however, come out of his confusional state rather rapidly. He is beginning to be oriented, and no longer incontinent. We are then reinstituting Page-Russels twice a day until incontinence is reached, which we hope we will be able to accomplish in 48 hours, and will place him on isolation and on driving immediately (as quoted in Weinstein, 1990, page 41).

Like Cameron's other patients, Lou Weinstein was finally discharged, his treatment having broken his brain, his spirit, and his finances. In turn, those who really cared about him were permanently damaged also, in no small part because the damage and its causes, would never be acknowledged by the responsible parties.

It took nearly 3 decades for the patients to gain a settlement, from the CIA. It was only then, October 3, 1988, by which time there were only seven surviving ex-patients cum plaintiffs, that they were given, collectively, US$75,000, or about CAN$100,000 each. Even then, the response of the CIA through its spokesman, Bill Devine, was quite illustrative: "Any settlement, if approved, does not represent a concession of liability on the part of the agency" (Weinstein, 1990, page 270).

While the denial of liability serves as a legal defense against any further lawsuits, it also serves to perpetuate the psychological damage to the patients. People who have been severely traumatized are best helped by defining the trauma and its causes and by providing the victims with full acknowledgment of responsibility by the parties actually responsible or, at least, their agents. Denial serves, psychologically, to continue and even to worsen the hurt.

How can such atrocities be inflicted, covered over for decades, and be psychologically perpetuated? Is the responsibility merely that of an individual, or is there a collective responsibility? Is it enough to discover and stop the individual perpetrator? These are questions that ought to be paramount in all cases of grievous wrongs, especially where institutions are directly involved.

Thoroughly understanding the individual perpetrator and his or her actions necessitates knowing the developmental and contemporaneous contexts. Without such thorough understanding, we will only react simplistically, and not in ways that will prevent future atrocities. Thus, we need to know both about the individual and the gestalt of formative influences.

Cameron studied and operated within a psychiatric system that was predominantly authoritarian and gave credence to a wide array of potentially quite harmful but much vaunted physical treatments (Whitaker, 1996). Egas Moniz, a Portuguese neurologist, was co-winner of the Nobel Prize in 1949 "for his discovery of the therapeutic value of prefrontal lobotomy in certain psychoses." Eventually, the prestige and popularity accorded this surgical procedure caused 50,000 persons to have their brains irreversibly damaged to the point of permanent dementia. The practice was stopped not so much by the sober, genuinely scientific independent evaluations that made clear that its harmful effects were not compensated by benefits, but by the introduction of powerful major tranquilizers that came to be called "antipsychotics." These neuroleptic drugs, including the phenothiazines, now account for tens of millions of cases of irreversible brain disease, including millions of cases of tardive dyskinesia, but together with new variants of antipsychotics, are still considered the treatment of choice for schizophrenic disorders. These and other treatment procedures illustrate the "persistence of shrinking" (Whitaker, 1996) which is based on a kind of reductionistic fallacy that continues to permeate the field of biological psychiatry. In essence, such treatment is aggressive on the part of the treater, passive on the part of the patient, and targets symptoms that appear disruptive, usually at the expense of long-term results of benefit to the patient. Its motto sometimes seems to be, "If your brain offends you, we will damage it in an effort to banish your offensive symptoms."

Having studied and practiced in this atmosphere, most of Cameron's characteristic treatments were not so much radical departures as they were exaggerations of the then contemporaneous trends. For example, ECTs were widely used, despite the fact that patients' brains were evidently damaged to the point of causing amnesias. But Cameron increased frequencies of ECT administration. And, often, he used "Page-Russell" ECTs, which were up to 75 times "normal" dosage (Kessler, 1992, page 308). Cameron combined ECT with both approved and experimental drugs and forced drugged sleep and sensory isolation on his uninformed patients.

At least 100 patients were subjected to brainwashing according to Cameron's prescriptions. An evaluation of his results on 79 patients hospitalized from 1956 to 1963, who had reached the third stage of depatterning, showed many "complications" including persisting amnesia and, therefore, brain damage, in 60% of these patients. Altogether, Cameron performed almost 10 years of ever-increasing and intrusive experimentation involving brainwashing procedures with no one intervening (Weinstein, 1990, page 142). The results of Cameron's endeavors yielded no valuable scientific knowledge and, according to Dr. Sidney Gottlieb, neither did the MKULTRA Project of which it was only a small part (Weinstein, 1990, page 143).

In one way, Cameron's actions were unremarkable. Hadn't he done vastly less damage than if he had performed lobotomies? Or if he had been forcing massive, long-term doses of neuroleptics on virtually anyone diagnosed schizophrenic, as was common practice? Over 50,000 lobotomies and millions of cases of neuroleptic-induced brain damage dwarfed the damage he did or could do as an individual. Besides, wasn't he, like Moniz, trying to forge a breakthrough treatment for the "mentally ill?"

Cameron had a covert purpose. He was not just trying to help his patients. In fact, the patients were individuals in some cases who did not present severe psychological or psychiatric disorders. One such patient was a young woman physician looking to become a psychiatric resident. Cameron said she appeared "nervous," required her to have a medical examination at Royal Victoria Hospital, affiliated with McGill University and Allan Memorial Institute, and then subjected her to his depatterning experiments (Weinstein, 1990, page 166). She, too, became brain damaged.

What lessons, then, can be learned from Cameron's destructive experiments and similar medical atrocities? Weinstein offered this sad realization:

> It is the silence and resistance to truth that makes us all vulnerable. I am haunted by the silence of my colleagues who worked at the Allan Memorial Institute in the 1950s and did not speak up; I am appalled by their continued silence in the 1980s when the truth emerged. Medicine has a history of engaging in evil undertakings when the motivation can be reframed so that the outcome is couched under the rubric of "for the greater good." The nontreatment of syphilis by the U.S. Public Health Service, the experimentation of the Nazi doctors for the good of the Fatherland, the irresponsible destruction of psychiatric patients under the guise of "curing their schizophrenia" — all of these found willing adherents, physicians who would carry out the work for a larger philosophy of good intention. Phillip Zimbardo, a social psychologist at Stanford University, terms this phenomenon the "structure of evil." The actors engage in evil for a "good" reason (page 285).

Certainly in the case of Cameron, the road to hell was paved with ostensibly good intentions. Cameron had become very like the Nazi doctors whose experiments on hapless victims were supposed to enhance society. The means, and not just the ends, may be crucial. And, very clearly, authoritarian means guaranteed destructive outcomes.

These and other endeavors undermined and even permanently ruined the lives of citizens the agency was supposed to protect. The means had come to severely damage the democratic goals it was supposed to serve.

Psychic Warriors

In the 1970s, it was known that the Soviet Union had been involved in "remote viewing" and related parapsychological studies. Sometime in that era, the Stanford Research Institute in California was conducting a program funded by the U.S. government which became the point of origin for similar studies conducted by the Defense Intelligence Agency (DIA), a part of the intelligence community overseen by the CIA. The U.S. research unit, begun in early 1974, was first code-named Sun Streak and later Stargate.

David Morehouse (1996), the distinguished Honor Graduate of many army training programs, was recruited for the unit in early 1988 after he was accidentally shot during an infantry exercise and began experiencing paranormal phenomena. The bullet entered deeply into his helmet but did not pierce his skull. Nevertheless, it was this head trauma that opened the door, as it were, to his being trained as a "psychic warrior." His story is remarkable both for its revelations of the content of this top secret research and for what happened to him personally in the process.

The head trauma precipitated an ability or a curse, depending on circumstances, manifested in visions that were revelatory or nightmarish. One theory was that the conduits normally left closed at birth were damaged, that they had been forced open and were not reclosable. Morehouse, then an Army Ranger commander, was seen as someone whose new-found ability could be furthered by training. He was advised by some in the Army not to join the paranormal training program but was invited by others despite their acknowledgment that such training had been damaging for some trainees. What was he to do about his often frightening experiences? Morehouse's wife wanted him to get professional help. In response, "Levy," the head of the paranormal unit made a cautionary prediction. Ironically, because Morehouse took the would-be cautious route and joined the unit instead of seeking professional help, he only temporarily avoided the predicted outcome. Levy said:

> I'll tell you what the doctors will do. They will very carefully document his descriptions of the visions, perhaps even ask him to draw sketches. They will

put him through some simple tests. They will classify him as delusional, maybe even psychotic. And then they will prescribe all sorts of drugs, They will want to control his visions with a chemical straightjacket. They will not be understanding; they will not care; and his career will be over. The best you could hope for would be a medical discharge for psychological disability. Not a very fitting end to an otherwise exceptional career is it? (Morehouse, 1996, page 98).

Training in "remote viewing" took place in austere, sensorily deprived environments of the kind that make for hypnotic or trance conditions. Having achieved the needed brain wave frequency, which the viewer did more readily with training, the viewer became removed from his or her Earthly body and entered "the ether," an altered state of consciousness whereby the viewer became able to transcend ordinary time and space. Often the aim was to investigate a specific place or event. Though disembodied, as it were, and therefore never harmed bodily, sometimes the viewer was traumatized by his or her experiences; for example, a visionary visit to Nazi concentration camps or to burning Iraqi oil fields in the Gulf War.

Meanwhile, the process was monitored via a variety of physiological measuring devices and, usually, another experienced remote viewer. On coming back to ordinary consciousness, the trainee would make notes and sketch what he or she had seen in the space and time travels.

According to then Major Morehouse, the government pumped tens of millions of dollars into paranormal research in half a dozen private and as many state and federal research centers across the U.S. But, due to the secrecy level and the nature of the research, those affiliated with it were feared, ridiculed, scoffed at, mocked, and ostracized, and were set apart apparently so as not to be a really accountable part of the intelligence community. His story illustrated the lengths to which the CIA has gone to develop superior intelligence gathering methods and to which it went, apparently, to stop one of its officers from divulging its secrets, even when the secrets had already been largely disclosed by others. Morehouse said:

I had to define clearly what I was about to do. First I considered whether telling my story would endanger the national security of the U.S., the country I loved dearly and had sacrificed for. I concluded that it would not. The Cold War was over. A year ago our Soviet counterparts had told the entire world what they had been doing for the past forty years in the paranormal arena. I wasn't giving away launch codes or the names of top-secret operatives. I was telling a story about psychic spies, whose existence was already an established fact (Morehouse, 1996, pages 190-191).

What followed initially were threats and phone taps. Cassette tapes of his conversations with various people started showing up in his mail, as did little cardboard packages or envelopes with no return address. Next, his home was broken into and his office ransacked. Then, he ascertained that he was being followed as he drove his car, and he had a blowout independently diagnosed as, "This here tire's been cut to blow" (page 200). After these strategies failed to neutralize him, he was charged by an Army prosecutor with trumped-up allegations. Further on, he and his wife and children again had their home invaded, this time after unknown persons moved his generator into the garage and dispelled a potentially deadly gas into their living quarters. Next, he was psychiatrically hospitalized and, except for a woman psychiatrist who took him seriously (and later lost her position over doing so) and refrained both from diagnosing him as having "biological problems" and drugging him, he was regarded as needing psychiatric drugs.

Brought before the directors of Walter Reed Hospital's psychiatry department, it was decided eventually that Morehouse would be medically retired, as no longer fit to do what he had been trained to do, and too emotionally unstable to wear a uniform. After the retirement process had begun, he was visited, in the presence of his wife and children, by a major from Sun Streak who asked to speak with him alone. But his wife stayed with him. The visiting major informed the soon to be ex-Major Morehouse that he could not let Morehouse destroy the unit with any claims and that he, the major, would do anything necessary to protect it. The visitor ended the conversation ominously with, "Oh you have no idea who's swinging, my friend. You really don't have any idea at all. And you remember this, in this world, even when you can see who's swinging, you'll never see the one that gets you" (Morehouse, 1996, page 224). The visitor then winked, turned, and walked away.

A few days later, Morehouse relapsed, falling back into the "ether" and experienced being slashed and screeched at. He awoke from this "nightmare" finding his body, face, and bedclothes covered with blood, pages torn from his notebook, and sketches made on the pages in his blood. A single razor blade was found stuck in the table next to his bed. Neither he nor hospital personnel could account for the incident.

Subsequently, he was given Halcion, Prozac, and a number of other psychiatric medications to stop what were regarded by the "biological" psychiatrists as hallucinations, and then transferred to the psychiatric ward at Ft. Bragg's Womack Army Hospital where the authorities were to proceed with a court martial. Ironically, at Womack, the treatment of Major Morehouse, who had not been a drug abuser, consisted almost entirely of giving him prescribed drugs and having him sit through classes for drug abusers.

> The drugs I was given were overwhelming — a cupful every day by the time I left the hospital. I was on forty milligrams of Loxitane (a powerful antipsychotic), sixty milligrams of Prozac (an antidepressant), six milligrams of Cogentin (to offset the tremors caused by the Loxitane), and thirty milligrams of Restoril (a tranquilizer). Most mornings these drugs knocked

me to the floor. Although I didn't have any dissociative episodes or trips into the ether, I spent every day in a fog (Morehouse, 1996, page 231).

In this condition and without any actual defense by an attorney, contrary to his normal legal rights, he had no opportunity during preparation for the court martial hearings to speak for himself, and there were no responses to requests by him or his wife to other authorities. Depositions, which he paid a private attorney $5000 to obtain, and which he felt would have destroyed the government's case, were never used. Nevertheless, he was able to resign in view of the weakness of the prosecution's case, albeit with none of the usual benefits: retirement, unemployment compensation, the VA loan on his home, the right to be buried in a military cemetery, and even access to the American Legion. Thirty days after agreeing to resign his commission in the Army "for the good of the service," the charges against him were dropped, his resignation was accepted, and an "other than honorable" discharge was bestowed upon him. No evidence had been presented in his behalf.

The senior psychiatrist who had believed Morehouse's story suffered also. She later told him that the government, via her supervisors, had ordered her to change his diagnosis to psychotic and delusional, alter his records, and to give him drugs. She had refused as far as possible, giving him the smallest possible dose of antipsychotic drugs. She was subsequently forced to resign, after 12 years of government service, was professionally destroyed, and she too lost all her benefits, including a pension.

Whereas even the very existence of the Stargate (formerly Sun Streak) program had been denied, the CIA, in cooperation with the Defense Intelligence Agency, started a carefully planned and executed media blitz revealing the government's psychic research and, purportedly, *former* psychic warfare program. It was apparently time to do so for purposes of self-interest.

Morehouse recalled that, as a young captain, the Army's deputy Chief of Staff for intelligence (the highest-ranking intelligence officer in the Army) told him and two others, "The CIA does nothing, says nothing, allows nothing unless its own interests are served. They are the biggest assembly of liars and thieves this country ever put under one roof and they are an abomination" (Morehouse, 1996, page 249).

Efficacy Questions

How can a democratic government not only permit but support the kinds of covert and, in the last analysis, often lethal programs that have been carried out by the CIA for over 50 years? As noted earlier, the CIA had noble parentage. Democratic nations were defending themselves in a hot war against tyrants who blatantly broke the rules not only of diplomacy but of war itself.

As the old Spanish proverb says, it was necessary to "fight fire with fire." But, since World War II, the U.S. has been directly subjected to very little active fire. Yet, during the 1960s, for example, the CIA committed massive murders and tortures through the Phoenix program, as noted in Table 4.2.

Part of the answer is that the general populace has had a positive image of the CIA even after the Church and Pike Congressional hearings in the 1970s which disclosed extreme CIA violations. A 1979 Opinion Research Corp. opinion poll showed that 62% of U.S. citizens had a favorable opinion of the CIA; only 24% had an unfavorable opinion, while 14% had no opinion. But, unfavorable opinions were highest among citizens who were college educated and had higher incomes (Kessler, 1992, page 9). By implication, positive imagery of the CIA would be lessened if people were better educated in general and, perhaps, about the CIA in particular. For an agency like the CIA to continue to exist within an essentially democratic society, most of the populace must support the concept of covert activity, although without necessarily knowing its exact nature or outcomes.

But, besides the question of its political acceptability, there are many important substantive questions about the CIA's actual effects. While the answers to these questions cannot be complete because much of the CIA's activities remain shrouded in secrecy, considerable knowledge is now available.

How efficacious has the CIA been in accomplishing its stated missions of predicting and controlling important events affecting national security? The CIA failed to predict both the Korean War and the end of the Cold War; it failed to accomplish its mission in the Bay of Pigs fiasco which led to the Cuban missile crisis (the closest we've come to nuclear destruction); and its attempts to assassinate foreign leaders have been both outside of the bounds of its charter and ineffective. And, as noted earlier in this chapter, apparently most CIA veteran officers have come to believe that most of their missions were failures, sometimes because the information they have gathered has been ignored in favor of political expediency. On the other hand, the CIA is inclined to take credit for the end of the Cold War and for avoiding an all-out "hot war."

Has the CIA actually promoted the well-being of the U.S. and its people? While it may claim to have done so, it has also clearly violated the rights of U.S. citizens as well as the laws and rights of citizens of other countries. And it has contributed substantially to distrust and paranoia among the people of the U.S. as well as other nations. Its clandestine nature has been antithetical to the democratic spirit that it is supposed to preserve and protect.

Perhaps, the bottom line question should be whether, overall, the CIA has actually promoted freedom and well-being among the world's nations and their citizens? The results are mixed at best. The CIA's methods may have been expedient in some cases, but the methods themselves have exacted a high price in human life and well-being, and conveyed the opposite of the democratic spirit. Often, through the CIA, the U.S. has equated freedom with its own capitalistic system and promoted rightist autocrats rather than allowing the citizens of other nations to determine their own leaders and governmental systems. In some cases, as exemplified by information in Table 4.2, the CIA and the U.S. have committed what can be termed second-order genocide.

Overall, the CIA has probably "succeeded" at many missions, albeit at the expense of massive destruction of human lives and well-being, corrosive distrust of the U.S. and its "democratic" government, and the sacrifice of more enlightened and longer-term goals in the service of what is increasingly a one-world economy and culture. For example, as the foremost seller and exporter of weapons in the world together with France, the U.S., through the CIA, has been helping to perpetrate lethal violence. These weapons have begun to come back into the U.S. through weapons importers and other nations that are or have been allies who received them from the U.S. originally. The U.S. Congress has even considered a measure that could place 2.5 million more rifles and pistols onto its streets (The surplus gun invasion, 1997). What goes around comes around.

Prospects and Recommendations

It would be naive to believe that the CIA will soon be scaled down or eliminated. CIA supporters can point to the rapidly accelerating growth in technology, including weapons systems and detection methodology that are or soon will be available to most nations. Supporters can argue that the U.S. had better be not only the most advanced nation technologically, but that it must slow down or stop sophisticated potentially hostile actions against it. Furthermore, methodology to invade personal privacy has become so common that there are threats to personal security everywhere. For a price ranging from $75 to $450, depending on the particular personal facts the purchaser wishes to acquire, information brokers will obtain an individual's bank balance, salary amount, investment funds amounts, credit card number, telephone records, or 10-year medical history (Bernstein, 1997).

In view of the acceleration of information technology and what is perceived as the CIA's inadequacy to analyze and monitor world developments, Congress' House Permanent Select Committee has wanted to increase secret intelligence spending by at least 5% which would raise the overall intelligence budget to over $30 billion, its biggest budget in 5 years (Weiner, 1997d). Thus, if anything, the CIA budget and operations may be increased in the near future.

Let us suppose that a great deal of valuable intelligence has been gathered by the CIA over its first 50-plus years. Must the actions of the CIA be kept secret lest national security be severely compromised? Allegations of a link between the CIA and the introduction of crack cocaine into Los Angeles in the 1980s have been subjected to independent investigation within the CIA and by congressional oversight committees. John M. Deutch (1977), the former DCI, has endorsed making the results of these investigations unclassified; he suggested that making these documents available for public scrutiny will help the CIA's image and thus help gain the necessary public support to further its missions: fighting terrorism, countering weapons proliferation, and serving as our nation's first line of defense.

George F. Kennan (1997) has stated "It is my conviction, based on some 70 years of experience, first as a government official and then in my 45 years as a historian, that the need by our government for *secret* intelligence about affairs elsewhere in the world has been vastly overrated" (page E17). He sees spying as inducing extensive counterintelligence operations by other nations and thinks that most of what is needed can be acquired openly and without deadly competition.

Clearly, every effort should be made to limit harmful covert operations and to monitor those that are planned or performed. The overwhelmingly most important measures the U.S. can take to protect its own security and to help other nations to become free are to empathize with the needs and feelings of its own citizens and those of other nations, and to respond with constructive, not clandestine actions. The U.S. Peace Corps programs have been enormously effective in these ways. Not coincidentally, the Peace Corps, purportedly, is the only U.S. organization abroad which has not been infiltrated by the CIA.

The constructive spirit of the Peace Corps communicates the best message we can give other nations and ourselves. This federal government organization, set up in 1961, trains and sends U.S. volunteers abroad to work with people of developing countries on projects for technological, agricultural, and educational improvement. Its message of peace, goodwill, and good deeds is ethical, efficacious, economical, and trustworthy. Many similarly spirited organizations exist. Let us make every effort to proliferate such efforts as these and we will have far less need for the unethical, generally ineffective, expensive, clandestine, and often lethal activity that so readily alienates other peoples and our own citizens.

In conclusion, our national priorities should be reset by publicizing destructive actions for what they are and promoting constructive projects at home and abroad. We must remember that the best way to counter the threat of one-world technology is to cultivate one-world empathy.

Summary

The Central Intelligence Agency (CIA) had its roots in World War II in the form of the Office of Strategic Services (OSS) and the Office of War Information (OWI) with the noble mission of defeating the Axis aggressors. Its continuance into the next century has had a series of justifications ranging from the Cold War to terrorism. The question throughout is whether the CIA's secrecy and violations, which have compromised democracy and been associated with lethal violence, benefit the causes of peace and well-being for the U.S. and the world at large.

The CIA's structure and history of cycles of reform and violation were presented together with discussion of the group and individual mentalities comprising its culture. The ethical dilemmas inherent in its structure and mission are illustrated by its actions and personalities. The tolls taken on democracy, people throughout the world, and its own personnel are weighed against the possible benefits of covert, frequently paralethal projects to protect the U.S. and promote world peace.

While much needed evidence is still unavailable, recently available materials suggest a very high cost in human lives and the democratic spirit in addition to a yearly budget approaching $30 billion. Many observers, including former high-ranking CIA officials, have concluded that the CIA has had a low level of effectiveness overall in accomplishing its stated mission. Another question then ensues: would the U.S. and the world at large benefit more from programs that positively foster human well-being, such as the Peace Corps, that not only do not violate democratic ideals but promote them by example? The overwhelmingly most important measures the U.S. can take to protect its own security and to help other nations to become free are to empathize with the needs and feelings of its own citizens and those of other nations, and to respond with clearly constructive, not dangerously clandestine, actions.

Bibliography

Earley, P., *Confessions of a Spy: The Real Story of Aldrich Ames,* New York: G.P. Putnam's Sons, 1997.

This is the story of a CIA spy who became and was ultimately discovered to be a "mole," a spy operating as a double agent against his own government from within its own intelligence establishment. The man the media called "America's most damaging traitor" was said to be responsible for the deaths of as many as 20 Soviet informers whose own mole status he revealed. The book is also a personal portrait of the inherently duplicitous spying mentality. Even as a traitor, Ames felt that he had remained faithful, in his words, to "…what is at the core of the intelligence officer's world — betraying another person's trust in you" (page 43).

Kessler, R., *The Richest Man in the World,* New York: Time Warner, 1986.

This book shows that violence is golden. Its subject, the weapons broker Adnan Khashoggi, became the world's richest man as an unstinting practitioner of sociopathy accepted and aided by myriad governments, celebrities, industries, and even a university unable to decline his gifts. He came to the attention of the CIA partly through the Iran-Contra affair. Khashoggi's public relations skills made ready accomplices among the famous who were willing to overlook his and their own contributions to lethal violence throughout the world, a perfect example of the effectiveness of this advice:

> The prince must … avoid those things which will make him hated or despised; and whenever he succeeds in this, he will have done his part, and will find no danger in other vices — Niccolò Machiavelli, *The Prince*

Kessler, R., *Inside the CIA,* New York: Pocket Books, 1992.

The author, who had the CIA's cooperation, gives a guided tour of the agency and an evenhanded account of the structure and operations of the CIA since its beginnings in 1947. He found the CIA "sloppy" in its early years but basically effective as well as essential to national security into the 1990s. Kessler is critical and laudatory by turns, depending on the specific CIA project. His book is an especially good account of the complicated structure of the CIA itself, its relationships with the broader intelligence community, and its oversight by the president, congress, and other governmental and nongovernmental groups.

Thomas, E., *The Very Best Men,* New York: Simon & Schuster, 1996.

A story of the early "glory days" of the CIA from its beginning in 1947 until its decline in the mid-1960s, as related through the careers of four daring officers who tried to contain the Soviet threat. Thomas' vivid biographical accounts bring to life the personalities and the complex webs woven in the paradoxical processes of using trickery and violence to try to serve democracy.

Weinstein, H. M., *Psychiatry and the CIA: Victims of Mind Control,* Washington, D.C.: American Psychiatric Press, 1990.

An excellently told story of 9 Canadian citizens, out of over 100 unwitting patient-victims, who were "treated" and experimented on by world-famous psychiatrist D. Ewen Cameron. Financed in part by the CIA as a component of Project MKULTRA, his work was also endorsed by the Canadian government. It is told by the psychiatrist son of one of the victims. Like other unwitting patients, the author's father was subjected to ruthless experiments with drugs, electric shock, sensory isolation, enforced sleep, and auditory "driving" of messages into his brain. The "patients" all got worse to the point of irreversible, at least largely incapacitating, harm. This extreme violation of the traditional injunction, "physician, do no harm" was only faintly acknowledged and recompensed decades later after many years of heroic legal and journalistic efforts. Weinstein's book is an effective object lesson in the synergistically powerful destructiveness of authoritarianism and unaccountability.

References

Arts & Entertainment "20th Century", September 17, 1997.

Beaty, J. and Gwynne, S. C., The dirtiest bank of all, *Time*, July 29, 1991, pp. 42-47.

Bellis, D. J., *Heroin and Politicians: The Failure of Public Policy to Control Addiction in America*, Westport, CT: Greenwood, 1981.

Bernstein, N., On line, high-tech sleuths find private facts, *New York Times*, September 15, 1997, p. A1.

Blight, J. and Lang, J., Burden of nuclear responsibility: reflections on the critical oral history of the Cuban missile crisis, *Peace and Conflict*, 11, 225-264, 1995.

Branfman, F., South Vietnam's police and prison system: the U.S. connection, in *Unlocking the CIA*, Frazier, H., Ed., New York: Free Press, 1978, pp. 110-127.

Brody, R., *Contra Terror in Nicaragua: Report of a Fact-Finding Mission, September 1984–January 1985*, Boston: South End Press, 1985.

Burns, R., Former senator to review gulf war investigations. Associated Press report, *Honolulu Advertiser*, May 2, 1977, p. A6.

Castro, J., The cash cleaners, *Time*, October 24, 1988, p. 65-66.

Chomsky, N. and Herman, E. S., The United States vs. human rights in the third world, *Mon. Rev.*, 29, 22-45, 1977.

Chomsky, N., *Turning the Tide: U.S. Intervention in Central America and the Struggle for Peace*, Boston: South End Press, 1985.

C.I.A. traitor, saying he wanted cash for family, gets 23 years, *New York Times*, June 6, 1997, p. A19.

Clarridge, D. R., *A Spy for All Seasons: My Life in the CIA*, New York: Scribner, 1997.

Corn, D., Bush's CIA: The same old dirty tricks, *The Nation*, August 27–September 3, 1988, pp. 157-60.

C-Span Washington Journal, September 16, 1997.

C-Span, September 17, 1997a.

C-Span, September 9, 1997b.

C-Span, September 16, 1997c.

Deutch, J. M., *New York Times*, May 18, 1997, p. E17.

Earley, P., *Confessions of a Spy: The Real Story of Aldrich Ames*, New York: G. P. Putnam's Sons, 1997.

Emerson, S., *Secret Warriors Inside the Covert Military Operations of the Reagan Era*, New York: G.P. Putnam's Sons, 1988.

Faden, R., *Final Report of the Advisory Committee on Human Radiation Experiments*, New York: Oxford Press, 1996.

F.B.I. agent who spied is sentenced to 27 years, *New York Times*, June 24, 1997, p. A14.

Flanders, S. A. and Flanders, C. N., *Dictionary of American Foreign Affairs*, New York: Macmillan, 1993.

Gerth, J., New C.I.A. chief picks veteran staff, *New York Times,* July 22, 1997, p. A12.

Goodman, W., The tragic human toll of the early Stalin years, *New York Times,* July 14, 1997, p. C13.

Herman, E., *The Real Terror Network,* Boston: South End Press, 1982.

Hinckle, W. and Turner, W., *The Fish is Red — The Story of the Secret War Against Castro,* New York: Harper & Row, 1981.

Hoffman, A. and Silvers, J., An election held hostage, *Playboy,* 35(10), 73-74, 1980.

Holmes, S., Call for C.I.A.-cocaine inquiry is renewed, *New York Times,* May 15, 1997, p. B15.

Kaplan, J., Harry S. Truman, in *Familiar Quotations,* 16th ed., Boston: Little, Brown, 1992, p. 655.

Keeping track: empty posts at C.I.A., *New York Times,* August 25, 1997, p. A15.

Kennan, G. F., *New York Times,* May 18, 1977, p. E17.

Kessler, R., *The Richest Man in the World,* New York: Time Warner, 1986.

Kessler, R., *Inside the CIA,* New York: Pocket Books, 1992.

Kessler, R., *The FBI,* New York: Simon & Schuster, 1993.

Kruger, H., *The Great Heroin Coup,* Boston: South End Press, 1980.

Landau, J. S., CIA's mission: Seeking next generation of spies, *New York Times,* November 12, 1999, p. A3.

Lifschultz, L., Inside the kingdom of heroin, *The Nation,* 477, 492-496, 1988.

Maas, P., *Manhunt,* New York: Random House, 1986.

Macklin, W., In the name of protest, *Philadelphia Inquirer,* August 4, 1997, pp. D5, D12.

Marshall, J., Scott, P.D., and Hunter, J., *The Iran-Contra Connection,* Boston: South End Press, 1987.

McCoy, A., Part I: CIA Covert Actions and Drug Trafficking. *North Coast Express,* 5,16, 1997.

Morehouse, D., *Psychic Warrior: Inside the CIA's Stargate Program: The True Story of a Soldier's Espionage and Awakening,* New York: St. Martin's Press, 1996.

Morrison, D., Recollections of a nuclear war, *Sci. Am.,* 273, 42-46, 1995.

Moyers, B., *The Secret Government: The Constitution in Crisis,* Washington, D.C.: Seven Locks Press, 1988.

Myers, L., After CIA offered $150,000, mob said it would kill Castro for free, Associated Press report, *West Hawaii Today,* July 2, 1997.

Navarro, M., Guatemala study accuses the army and cites U.S. role, *New York Times,* February 26, 1999, pp. A1, A10.

Opening up C.I.A. history, *New York Times,* Editorial, May 30, 1997, p. A28.

Parenti, M., *Democracy for the Few,* New York: St. Martin's Press, 1983.

Pearce, F., *Crimes of the Powerful,* London: Pluto Press, 1976.

Prados, J., *Presidents' Secret Wars,* New York: William Morrow, 1986.

Priest, D., U.S. instructed Latins on executions, torture, *Washington Post*, September 21, 1996, pp. A1, A9.

Prying open the spy budget, *New York Times*, Editorial, October 17, 1997, p. A34.

Richelson, J. T., *The U.S. Intelligence Community*, 3rd ed., San Francisco: Westview Press, 1995.

Scheffer, D. J., U.S. law and the Iran-Contra affair, *Am. J. Int. Law*, 81(3), 696-723, 1987.

Schmalz, J., Bank indicted for money laundering case, *New York Times*, October 12, 1988, p. A56.

Sciolino, E., Fighting narcotics: U.S. urged to shift tactics, *New York Times*, April 10, 1988, p. A56.

Sheehan, D., *Inside the Shadow Government*, Washington, D.C.: Christie Institute, 1988.

Simon, C. P. and Eitzen, D. S., *Elite Deviance*, Boston: Ally and Bacon, 1986.

Stanton, D., Drugs, Vietnam and the Vietnam veteran: an overview, *Am. J. Drug Alcohol Abuse*, 3, 557-570, 1976.

The surplus gun invasion, *New York Times*, Editorial, September 9, 1997, p. A26.

Thomas, E., *The Very Best Men*, New York: Touchstone, 1996.

U.S. Army, *Counterintelligence Interrogation*, 1963.

U.S. Army, *Human Resource Exploitation*, 1983.

Weiner, T., C.I.A.'s openness derided as a "snow job," *New York Times*, May 20, 1997a, p. A16.

Weiner, T., C.I.A. traitor severely hurt U.S. security, judge is told, *New York Times*, June 2, 1997b, p. A24.

Weiner, T., House panel says C.I.A. lacks expertise to carry out its duties, *New York Times*, June 19, 1997c, p. A20.

Weiner, T., Research group is suing C.I.A. to reveal size of spy budget, *New York Times*, July 22, 1997d, p. A16.

Weiner, T., C.I.A. destroyed files on 1953 Iran coup, *New York Times*, May 29, 1997e, p. A19.

Weiner, T., Veteran C.I.A. official quits but will finish investigations, *New York Times*, October 3, 1997f, p. A13.

Weinstein, H. M., *Psychiatry and the CIA: Victims of Mind Control*, Washington, D.C.: American Psychiatric Press, 1990.

Whitaker, L.C., Macho and morbidity: the emotional need vs. fear dilemma in men, *J. Coll. Stud. Psychother.*, 1(4), 33-47, 1987.

Whitaker, L.C., Social inducements to paralethal and lethal violence, in *Lethal Violence 2000: A Sourcebook on Fatal Domestic, Acquaintance and Stranger Aggression*, Hall, H., Ed., Kamuela, HI: Pacific Institute for the Study of Conflict and Aggression, 1996, chap. 5.

Whitaker, L.C., The persistence of shrinking: remembrance of things not so past, *J. Coll. Stud. Psychother.*, 11(3), 47-59, 1996.

Wise, D., Big lies and little green men, *New York Times*, August 8, 1997, p. A27.

Woodward, B., *Veil: The Secret Wars of the CIA 1981-1987*, New York: Pocket Books, 1987.

Lethal Violence by Entire Governments

5

We have seen, in the sequence of Chapters 2, 3, and 4, a progression of forms of destructiveness wielded by organized groups and institutions. The sequence began with the account in Chapter 2 of ordinary destructiveness in legally authorized ordinary institutions within the U.S., a democratic nation. Chapter 3 exemplified nongovernmental subgroups, operating on the fringe of or outside of the laws of their democracies, that threaten or actually commit subversive acts of violence, such as the deadly Japanese-based cult called Aum, and the Aryan Nations in the U.S. Chapter 4 exemplified how a democratic government may institute and charge a government agency, the Central Intelligence Agency in this case, with the task of breaking laws in the course of its duty, albeit supposedly limited to breaking the laws of other nations.

This book's exploration of institutional destructiveness culminates in this chapter addressing authoritarian governments that, at their most extreme centralization of power are called totalitarian. It is here that Winston Churchill's aphorism is most telling: "Democracy is the worst form of government except for all those other forms that have been tried from time to time." Churchill defined democracy succinctly, in contrast to the other authoritarian forms: "It is the people who control the Government — not the Government the people" (as quoted in Humes, 1994, page 28).

The Facts of Democide

As noted in Chapter 1, R. J. Rummel, in his book *Death by Government* (1997), has carefully studied, documented, and characterized what he has called "Democide: The murder of any person or people by a government, including genocide, politicide, and mass murder" (page 31). People are marked for genocide by their indelible group membership, meaning their race, ethnicity, religion, or language; politicide by their politics or political purposes; and mass murder refers to the indiscriminate killing of people by their government. While wars themselves account for massive destruction of human life, it is democide, committed most often under the cover of war, that accounts for vastly more lethality.

Rummel has established a great deal of factual knowledge about democide and his findings are worth careful study by anyone seeking to lessen human destructiveness. For pupuses of this chapter, however, only an overview, suited to later exploration of other facets of this form of human perpetration of violence, is presented here.

Governments perpetrate enormously more lethal violence than individuals or dissident groups within nations. The amount of death by government corresponds so closely with their degree of authoritarianism that other causes on this macroscopic level of explanation appear almost trivial. The general findings are that the more authoritarian the government, meaning the more it requires unquestioning obedience from its subjects, the more such a government has waged war against other governments and the more it has killed its own people.

As Rummel notes, whereas wars waged by governments against other governments are given far more attention in history books than democide, the latter phenomenon accounts for about four times as much lethality as wars per se. By categorizing governments into democratic, authoritarian, and totalitarian according to the degree to which their authority can or cannot be questioned by its citizens, Rummel has shown definitively that the degree of centralization of power accounts accurately for the extent to which a government kills its own and others. When this rough categorization is fine-tuned as it were, even the relatively small amount of lethal violence committed by "democratic" governments is shown to be related to their lesser degrees of democracy than other democratic governments. Thus, "about 90 percent of the citizens killed by democracies have been killed by marginally democratic Spain (during the 1936-1939 civil war), India, and Peru (during its struggle against the Shining Path guerrillas)" (Rummel, 1997, page 24).

Accounting for wars, defined as any military action in which at least 1000 persons are killed, from 1816 to 1991 there were none between democracies, 155 between democracies and nondemocracies, and 198 between nondemocracies, for a total of 353 wars in this period of history. So the correlation between authoritarianism and killing in war per se is also firmly established.

Comparing the amount of killing in war itself and killing by democide for the period 1900 to 1987, the approximately 170 million killed by democide dwarfs the number killed by international war per se, that is apart from those people killed by democide during wartime. Rummel points out that "most democides occur under the cover of war, revolution, or guerilla war, or in their aftermath" (page 22). For example, while it is estimated that between 40 and 60 million were killed in World War II, the vast majority were victims of democide, as when Hitler's Nazi regime alone murdered 20 million in acts of democide, such as against Jews, the handicapped, mentally ill, homosexuals, and Slavs among others.

Paralleling the close correspondence between authoritarianism in government and killing in the actions of war, authoritarian governments have accounted for all but 1% of democide deaths, with totalitarian governments (the most extremely authoritarian) killing several times as many people by democide than the merely authoritarian. In essence, "for all this killing in this century, democide and war by democracies contributes only 1 and 2.2%, respectively, to the total" (Rummel, page 17).

It would be difficult to argue against Rummel's conclusion that when the elite have absolute power, war or democide follows a common and seemingly inevitable process, and that democratization of nations is needed to prevent mass killings of humans by other humans. He emphasized that power in government is ever changing, so that a democracy can readily shift into an authoritarian regime. Therefore, we can conclude at this stage of exploration that it is not enough to have achieved a democracy, even a thoroughly democratic government; instead, a democracy must be cultivated and maintained, and no constancy can be assumed.

Dynamics of Power and Freedom

Suppose that we accept Rummel's well-grounded findings and their implications. Then the path is clear: recognize, as Professor Rummel has proven, the truth of Lord Acton's aphorism: "Power corrupts and absolute power corrupts absolutely," which Rummel has presented in terms of his "Power Principle: power kills, and absolute power kills absolutely" (page xvi). The way to prevent lethal violence is through democratization, to make sure that power is shared *and* that people take their democratic responsibilities to heart. But here is the rub. It is not easy to follow this undeniably sage advice.

The responsibilities that must be assiduously carried out tend to be neglected. Neither the powerful nor the weak are readily inclined to do their parts to actively sustain democracy, whether on the national or international levels or in personal relationships. In the latter case, as discussed in Chapter 2, Riane Eissler proposed partnership between equals as providing the most constructive and harmonious personal relationships. Like R.J. Rummel, who proposed analogously that nations should cultivate more egalitarian partnerships both domestically and internationally, Eissler is right. How can we implement their superb advice?

Attempts to democratize totalitarian governments have met with powerful resistances both from above and below. The powers above, the power elite, have been loathe to give up or even begin to share their power and the privileged status that goes with it. And those below have so often clung to their powerlessness, and avoided the responsibilities that must go with power to make it constructive, that even revolutions that give "power to the people" often result in yet another version of totalitarianism.

One of the clearest examples of what I would call the "Wasted Power Principle" is that of Russia. The revolution of 1917 in totalitarian czarist Russia, which was itself marked by massacre, resulted in the 1922 formation of the Soviet Union, a nation that holds the all-time record for sheer numbers of murders: nearly 61 million. Rummel estimated that over 42 million people were murdered during the dictatorial reign of Joseph Stalin alone during the period 1929 to 1953. Thus, the Russians and neighboring peoples went from the frying pan into the fire as the egalitarian ideals propounded by the Soviets were cruelly mocked by their practices.

For sheer *efficiency* of murder, Adolph Hitler's dictatorship from 1933 to 1945 is unexcelled, with over 20 million murdered by his Nazi regime. As mentioned in Chapter 1 and as will be discussed further on in this chapter, that murderous saga was effected very gradually through incremental dehumanization facilitated by legislation against human rights, including the rights of Jewish people, of whom 6 million were murdered.

Authoritarian Personalities and Governments

What causes people to aggregate power to themselves and to use their power arrogantly to harm people rather than to help them? And what causes people subjected to such treatment to permit themselves to be treated that way, to submit to autocratic leaders like Hitler or Stalin or China's Mao Tse-tung?

As noted earlier, the sociologist and later psychoanalyst and social psychologist Erich Fromm contributed profound understanding of this dilemma of the dually entered-into abrogation of resonsibility in his book *Escape from Freedom* (1969), which was published originally in 1941 when puzzlement and anguish about the Nazis peaked. He explained that freedom can be frightening and totalitarianism tempting. So the tyrant and the subjected agree to dance together, to collude, the tyrant eager for power over others and the subjected glad to be free of their frightening freedom. Thus is played out dominance-submission, the sadomasochistic kind of relatedness whereby neither party successfully confronts and resolves the sense of aloneness and alienation that initially stands in the way of being free to be constructive for oneself and others. Fromm succinctly characterized the challenging responsibility of freedom by citing a Talmudic saying:

> If I am not for myself, who will be for me?
> If I am for myself only, what am I?
> If not now — when?

The dominance-submission or sadomasochistic bond provides and sustains some sense of belonging and meaning via enforcement of the relationship. While in this condition of relatedness, neither party has the courage to confront and resolve their fears of aloneness and insignificance. Both are held in the relationship by fear rather than love. Being able to control another against the other's (at least ostensible) will is the tyrant's narcotic, while the narcotic of the oppressed comprises not having to accept responsibility for their lives and feeling significant in their suffering. As will be exemplified in the case of Hitler, each party to the contract plays the other's role vicariously through identification with the other party. The dance is deadly because no true resolution is possible therein; the relationship is dependent on destructiveness as the medium of exchange.

Inevitably, the tyrant is contemptuous of his subjects and the humiliated subjects require other persons to feel superior to, to be contemptuous of. Thus is born not only war, which displaces the hostility to outside nations, but also the much more common form of murder called democide. Because the hostility cannot be expressed openly to those in power, it must be directed at the less powerful. Typically, then, "out-groups," be they stigmatized groups actually within a society or country or geographically outside, become targeted for abuse as scapegoats. They become depicted as inferior to the in-group; they are less worthy according to the stereotypes thrust upon them. Accordingly, the "ins" attempt to dominate the "outs" just as they themselves have been abused. Bullying becomes a mass movement fostered, sustained, and accelerated by bigotry.

Authoritarian personalities and governments are notable for their dogmatic beliefs, their having highly certain answers to the most difficult of questions. If they are religious in any sense, they have the answers and cannot abide other answers. "Belief in God" takes on a narrow, constricting orientation that permits no doubt or inquiry so that other orientations are righteously dismissed out of hand. Atheism can be an equally authoritarian position if no other points of view, whether agnosticism or belief in God, are tolerated.

Perhaps, in Rummel-like fashion, some researcher will document how many deaths have been perpetrated by rigid theists and how many by rigid atheists. We do know that many millions of humans have been righteously killed in the name of God and many millions by righteous atheists. We also know that where governments accept and appreciate diversity of belief and inquiry, that they resist war and democide to such an extreme that their contribution to mass murder is negligible compared to their righteous authoritarian counterparts.

In terms of science, the authoritarian approach falters in dealing with the human element in its equations. We have seen in Chapter 3 how the deadly cult Aum has attracted those with only education and training in the so-called hard sciences and not the social sciences or humanities. The tolerance of uncertainty needed to cultivate understanding in the social sciences is weak in authoritarian personalities and groups. When the topics are sociology, psychology, psychiatry, and anthropology, for examples, what emerges in theory and practice by authoritarian persons and groups is dependent on and contaminated by the initial misconceptions of prejudice. Pseudoscience or "scientism" replaces real science.

Authoritarianism fails to achieve an adequate sense of reality because it fails to tolerate dissent. Diversity of opinion, while often difficult to appreciate in the short run, provides greatly needed checks and balances as well as valuable alternative approaches. In clinical terms, authoritarianism sacrifices reality testing and, inevitably, therefore, its own long-term self-interest.

Human Destructiveness as Folly

Historian Barbara Tuchman has focused on destructive human behavior in terms of her concept of folly as pursuit of policy contrary to self-interest, the result of self-deception. In her book, *The March of Folly* (1984), she gave three criteria for such folly: (1) it must have been perceived as counterproductive in its own time, (2) a feasible alternative course of action must have been available, and (3) the policy is that of a group rather than an individual ruler, and it persists beyond any one political lifetime (pages 5 and 6). "If pursuing disadvantage after the disadvantage has become obvious is irrational, then rejection of reason is the prime characteristic of folly" (page 380). The results of folly are self-destructive as well as destructive of the well-being and interests of others.

Unlike the emphasis on the destructiveness of authoritarianism that is so marked in the works of Rummel (1997) and Fromm (1973), the focus on folly does not distinguish the type of governmental regime. Tuchman claims that monarchy, oligarchy, and democracy produce folly equally. But if we consider destructiveness strictly in terms of directly lethal behavior and not paralethal behavior, then Rummel is definitive epidemiologically and Fromm is definitive psychosocially.

The particular value of Tuchman's contribution is her documentation of the timelessness and universality of folly and her demonstration of how no era or place is safe from human self-deception and its indirectly or directly destructive consequences. Therein we can find ways to understand how to avoid folly. For example, she asks why, in democracies as well as in authoritarian regimes "…we invest all our skills and resources in a contest for armed superiority which can never be attained for long enough to make it worth

having, rather than in an effort to find a modus vivendi with our antagonist —
that is to say, a way of living, not dying" (page 8).

Such cautionary reflection may not seem practical, if we consider only
the short run. But in the long view of history it makes sense when we realize,
as documented in Chapter 1, that the world's rapidly escalating armamen-
tarium has been closely correlated with the 20th century's stunning surpass-
ing of previous centuries in the rate of lethal human behavior. Are
democracies playing a crucial paralethal role by engaging themselves and
other governments in the arms race? If we remember from Chapter 1 that
France and the U.S. are the world's greatest exporters of weapons, we may
have to look at not just the immediate killers but also at those who, as
weapons pushers, may be insidious contributors to violence just as drug
dealers contribute to drug use.

What Tuchman calls religious mania is both a paralethal and direct
contributor to violence. Although religious beliefs may inhibit lethal violence,
religious mania insists on beliefs against natural evidence gained through
first-hand observation or through genuinely scientific investigation. As a
result, actions may be taken on the basis of delusions, for example, that ethnic
or religious cleansing is needed so that persecution and war are justified.
Thus, religion is often used to dehumanize "nonbelievers," whether they are
people not belonging to the "in" group at all or people within who dissent.
Religious mania turns religions into deadly cults.

How is it possible for religion, ostensibly based on virtue, to be used
destructively? Tuchman reminds us:

> In the search for meaning we must not forget that the gods (or God, for
> that matter) are a concept of the human mind; they are the creatures of
> man, not vice versa. They are needed and invented to give meaning and
> purpose to the puzzle that is life on Earth, to explain strange and irregular
> phenomena of nature, haphazard events and, above all, irrational human
> conduct. They exist to bear the burden of all things that cannot be com-
> prehended except by supernatural invention or design (pages 45 and 46).

Thus, religion can be, and often is, a mental manipulation by one or more
people to aggregate power, fraudulently obtained, and to subjugate other
people. And when the adherents and their leader commit atrocities, they can
claim that their actions are in the service of "God" who, ironically, is scapegoated thereby. *The sure signs of a malignant religion are a form of exclusivity
that proclaims that only its adherents are worthy, and a willingness to excuse
its own destructiveness in the name of "God."*

Tuchman illustrates such use of religion by documenting the succession
of six popes from 1470 to 1530 who turned spirituality on its head by their

immoral, greedy, corrupt, and calamitous political acts, including war against "infidels," to the dismay of truly devout Catholics and the considerable destruction of the Church itself. Given this perspective, Protestantism was inevitable.

Hostile exclusivity, as in religious mania or ethnic mania or political mania, and so on, is so shortsighted as to qualify as folly, pursuit of a policy contrary to self-interest, particularly when the policy is lauded and popular long after it has been clearly shown to be self-destructive. The late 17th-century persecution of the Huguenots in France set in motion by Louis XIV resulted in destructive consequences for all concerned. The hard-working Huguenots had benefitted France more than their minority status, as one tenth of the population would suggest. But that persecutory policy "...was greeted with the greatest enthusiasm and still lauded 39 years later at the King's funeral as one of his most praiseworthy acts" (Tuchman, 1984, page 19). The government tried to force the Huguenots to convert to Catholicism, to the considerable resentment of Catholics who saw forced conversions as perjury and sacrilege. The King's soldiers were induced to rob, beat, rape, and generally abuse this religious minority to the extreme and, at the same time, forbade them to leave the country. Huguenot pastors who continued to preach were broken on the wheel. Other nations, realizing that Huguenots would help them prosper, gave incentives to the Huguenots to escape France, resulting in considerable gain to the other nations and great loss to France.

If we substitute Jews for Huguenots, then Tuchman's account is analogous to what happened in Nazi Germany which in its folly effectively destroyed a particularly valuable segment of its own human resources except for those who escaped and then contributed much to other nations, including helping those nations defeat the Nazis. Of course, Nazi Germany's 20th century folly and destructiveness were far more immensely barbaric compared to that of France's, even though the latter's crudity and cruelty were momentous for that era of the 17th century. Although so many such lessons were evident from the history of previous centuries, the 20th century has been witness to a much more strident march of folly.

Folly is often not evident in the short run when, in fact, a governmental or other group regime may be popular and strengthened in its power. Its harshly dominating ways, its reliance on the stick of subjugation rather than the carrot of caring, may persuade people to join the movement out of fear and their wish to be associated with power. Just as the reign of Louis XIV was generally acclaimed for decades, Hitler, too, was acclaimed and venerated by millions for decades. But the tide tends to turn against tyrants in the long run. Why is this so?

The forceful arrogating of power, whether by a single person, a group, or a government, sets in motion an insidious process of self-destruction. Beginning with the most obvious cause, the subjects begin to resent the ruler, more and more so if they are treated arrogantly, and they must delude themselves to a degree to forestall expressing their resentment at a "dangerous" target, to wit the ruler. As a result, the ruler now is in charge of a populace with a defective sense of reality which must affect their work and judgment. Second, and somewhat less obvious, the suppression of dissent serves to make the ruler unaware of conditions that do or will threaten the regime, effecting a progressive blindness to hazards to his regime and ways to keep it going. Third, those who are harshly treated require a "safe" target for their resentment, so scapegoats must be provided, particularly in the form of "outsiders." Consequently, such regimes tend to war on other groups or governments and to find and persecute some — usually more and more — would-be insiders who are the newly labeled undesirables in service of a never sated scapegoating appetite. Both the persecuted within and the warred-upon outsiders become enemies of the regime. Such enemies may be killed but the list grows due to the continual need for scapegoats until no one, including the leader, is safe from being scapegoated and destroyed.

In essence, the harshly oppressive regime destroys itself eventually both from within and outside its original purview, no matter how much territory it conquers in the oppressive process. Its cancerous spread has no inherent boundaries; it can destroy others, but in the long run it destroys itself inexorably from within. The self-correcting dynamics of egalitarian or democratic societies have been made unavailable by the authoritarian regime's own doing.

Even a seemingly benign society may come close to destroying itself to the extent that it allows a part of its government to ignore and to distort reality. Tuchman exemplifies this folly with the British loss of America. By villifying the colonists, including some of its leaders who were the most friendly to the British government, such as Benjamin Franklin, and treating them as much less important than other citizens, they brought forth a revolution which effectively cut off their greatest source of prosperity.

What then became in the 18th century the U.S., a democratic nation, committed its own folly with stubborn escalation of the Vietnam conflict even in the face of increasingly massive dissent that threatened to tear the nation apart. The folly of the French in trying to sustain a colonial hand in Vietnam, which it first colonized in the 19th century, was taken over gradually by the U.S. From 1954 to 1975, having failed already in a vain 8-year effort to support French domination, the U.S. "supported" a weak South Vietnam resistance to the North Vietnam Communists.

Many false assumptions, blatantly contradicted by considerable evidence, were endorsed by and guided by those who became known as "the best and the brightest" U.S. leaders. On the whole, these false assumptions were based on emotionally attractive ethnocentric premises. Asiatic people were regarded as inferior but were assumed to want to be taught the U.S. brand of democracy. The leaders' continuing de facto defense of colonialism was a defense against the threat of being branded Communist in the maniacal aura of McCarthyism which, ironically, was fanatically dedicated to destroying independent thinking and freedom of speech, the hallmarks of democracy. Fearful of "giving in to the Communists" and fearful for their own reputations and security, one president after another together with their top aides pursued a hopeless, egregiously destructive war that was long-labeled euphemistically "the Vietnam Conflict."

Although the CIA had clearly indicated the falsity of crucial assumptions, including that of a "winnable war," Allen Dulles, the head of the CIA from 1953 to 1961, became caught up in the fear of McCarthy:

> The witch-hunts of McCarthyism, of the House Un-American Activities Committee, the informers, the blacklists and the fire-eaters of the Republican right and the China Lobby, the trail of wrecked careers, had plunged the country into a fit of moral cowardice. Everyone, in and out of office, trembled to prove his anti-Communist credentials. The anxious included Dulles, who, according to an associate, lived in constant apprehension that the McCarthy attack might turn next upon him. Less intensely, it reached up to the President, as shown by Eisenhower's silent acquiescense in McCarthy's attacks on General Marshall (Tuchman, page 259).

The craven cowardice of U.S. elected leaders and appointed officials alike in the 1950s was in the service of a bogus maniacal morality driven by egocentricity and ethnocentricity. Thus, morality was turned upside down, with fear and destructiveness in the guise of patriotism and honor.

The Vietnam War resulted in the U.S. suffering 55,000 killed and 300,000 wounded while Vietnamese casualties on both sides ran into the hundreds of thousands. In 1975, North and South Vietnam were reunited under Communist control, representing the final failure of three decades of U.S. policy in Southeast Asia (Flanders and Flanders, 1993, page 621). Although President Franklin Roosevelt, the CIA, and top military officials warned against U.S. involvement in Vietnam, every succeeding president from Harry Truman through Richard Nixon became actively involved in pursuing the hopeless endeavor. But even Roosevelt had been under the sway of the prevailing ethnocentrism, believing that, regardless of the Vietnam peoples' history of long devotion to self-government, they would not be ready until prepared under Western tutelage (Tuchman, 1984, page 235). Thus, a kind of arrogance, a psychological blindness, in this case belief in the superiority of one's own ethnic or racial status, was a decisive factor in this relentless pursuit of policy against the interest of the pursuer, as well as being destructive of other people.

The depth and extremity of this ethnocentrism is illustrated by the fact that, among the 45,000 French bureaucrats who were in Indochina, a 1910 survey showed that only three could speak a reasonably fluent Vietnamese. As Roosevelt had noted correctly, the French record in Indochina was the most exploitative in Asia (Tuchman, 1984, page 237).

Ironically, the stubborn refusal of the U.S. to grant the independence Vietnam so clearly insisted on, from the French domination onward, is analogous to the British loss of America. Both were attempts to keep colonies in their colonial subjugation, and both flew in the face of careful prognostications of consequences. In 1946, French commander General Leclerc, assigned to accomplish the reconquest of Vietnam, told his political advisor, "It would take 500,000 men to do it and even then it could not be done" (as quoted in Tuchman, 1984, page 244). Both his estimate and prediction were perfect; 20 years later, 500,000 U.S. soldiers were actually in the field fighting a losing battle. Britain's Lord Barrington had argued that if Britain made war on the colonies, "the contest will cost us more than we can ever gain by success" (as quoted in Tuchman, 1984, page 254).

The governmental mechanics of the U.S. persistence was crucially reliant on a kind of lopsided intelligence discussed in Chapter 3 in the case of the deadly cult called Aum which has relied so heavily on men gifted only in the hard sciences. Such men have great facility for developing powerful weapons and terrifying strategies but their formulas lack consideration of the human factor. In the case of the U.S., Robert McNamara personified this approach, depending on mathematical formulas that left out the difficult or impossible to quantify. He assured victory at a Pentagon briefing with the statement, "We have the power to knock any society out of the 20th century" (as quoted in Tuchman, 1984, page 285).

The lesson we can learn from history — that might doesn't make right — is magnified by the 20th century's scientific development and use of increasingly destructive weapons for conducting atrocities. Japan's Aum and U.S. aggression in Vietnam are but two examples discussed thus far of a blind arrogance firmly entrenched in ignorance of the humanities and the social sciences. What may be called the human factor — an essential, mysterious, at best mathematically messy factor — is missing from their equations. Given their enormous inability or unwillingness to sense the reality of the human spirit, their aggressive reckonings become symptoms of extreme mental and emotional defect, the madness of human destructiveness.

The 20th century's greatest scientific mind, however, managed, after making possible the development of the atom bomb, to recognize and recommend a solution for this madness:

> It is not enough to teach a man a specialty. Through it he may become a kind of useful machine but not a harmoniously developed personality. It is essential that the student acquire an understanding of and a lively feeling for values. He must acquire a vivid sense of the beautiful and of the morally good... He must learn to understand the motives of human beings, their illusions, and their sufferings in order to acquire a proper relationship to individual fellow-men and to the community... This is what I have in mind when I recommend the "humanities" as important ... Albert Einstein in the *New York Times*, 1952 (as quoted in *Essential Einstein*, Eddington, A. B., Ed., 1995, page 62).

Lest we ourselves engage in reductionistic explanations of such a complex, long-lasting, and mysterious folly as the Vietnam War, we need to explain further the complexity of the destructive mentality needed to sustain irrationality, and particularly for an individual to successfully persuade others that he is rational, even in the face of grossly contradictory evidence.

The crucial failure to enter the human factor into the equation begins at home with the individual being sure of his own rationality. To think that human irrationality can be safely left out of the equation is to be unaware of and denying of one's own irrationality, unable to take into account another's irrationality in any genuinely knowing or empathic sense. This failure of awareness of human irrationality, which includes both one's attitude toward the self and others, results in delusion. A person's supposed "rationality" then is actually only pseudorational and his science, when it comes to predicting human emotions and behavior, is "as if" science or pseudo-scientific. It is irrationality cloaked in ostensibly scientific clothes, proverbially "the emperor's new clothes."

The fact that the U.S. was dealing in Vietnam not only with foreigners of another "race" than Caucasian, with whom some bigots called "slopeyes" and "gooks," made empathy difficult to achieve anyway. But empathy could have been wrested from the history of World War II when the British reacted with enormous defiance to being bombed by the Nazis in the London blitz, or imagining what U.S. citizens would have felt and done had they been bombed on their own land.

Instead, the U.S. kept bombing Vietnam at an increasing rate despite lack of success in turning the tide, reaching an annual rate at the end of 1966 of 500,000 tons, a higher bombing rate than against Japan in World War II. Instead of becoming more docile as "rational" prediction assured, Hanoi then became insistent on a bombing cessation as a requirement for even beginning negotiation, whereas previously North Vietnam had sometimes expressed stronger interest in negotiating. McNamara's prediction failed also to recognize that, unless nuclear weapons were used, the bombing could not knock North Vietnam out of the 20th century. North Vietnam not only survived but later took over South Vietnam. Bad science reigned.

So what drove the massive unwitting irrationality that was needed to persist in the face of glaring error? What was needed was a synergistic combination of supporting factors. One was secrecy and deception as practiced commonly by the government and the military in times of war, as excused by "national emergency." This factor gave freer rein to the macho mentality. Unchecked, the macho mentality is dedicated to winning at any cost, even if that cost is loss of life, a form of irrationality typically shared between antagonists in war, with neither side being willing to back down from their "righteous" cause. The proof of righteousness itself is winning; backing down is considered not only weak but wrong because winning, and only winning, proves that one is right. Fully developed, the formula states that, "God is on the side of the righteous, so the righteous will prevail." Given this "truth," it follows that losing shows that one is evil.

In contrast to this rigid assumption that one's power must be used to vanquish and dominate, dissenters finally came forward in sufficient numbers to halt the madness. They had a very different view of how power should be used. For example, as Tuchman notes, James Thomson, who had been on the Far East staff of the State Department in 1966 wrote the *New York Times* that there had always been "constructive alternatives" and, in an echo of Burke, who had pleaded for rational use of power by Britain in their regard for the American colonies, 'that the U.S. as the greatest power on Earth had the power to lose face, the power to admit error, and the power to act with magnaminity'" (Tuchman, 1984, page 341). Tuchman has suggested, in addition to Lord Acton's dictum that power corrupts — with which she has agreed — that power breeds folly and the power to command often causes failure to think and the fading of responsibility.

In the case of the U.S., after nearly 30 years of covert and overt aggressive actions in Vietnam and other parts of Indochina, Tuchman has proven her point that democracies, too, can engage in folly — in this case, massively lethal folly. The U.S. did so by aggregating power to the federal government and the military and stifling dissent both from within the enclave of power and from its citizens outside. In essence, then, even a long-established democracy can be a perpetrator of lethal violence when it disallows these basic freedoms without which a democracy ceases to be: the rights to be told the truth and to voice dissent. Thus, Rummel's generalization that the solution to violence is freedom of the people is upheld.

The Case of Adolph Hitler and Nazi Germany

Why Study Hitler and the Nazis?

The Nazi regime is probably the single most compelling illustration of Tuchman's "fading of responsibility" as well as R.J. Rummel's (1994) claim that "power kills; absolute power kills absolutely," and, "the more power a government has, the more it can act arbitrarily according to the whims and desires of the elite, and the more it will make war on others and murder its foreign and domestic subjects" (pages 1 and 2).

Careful examination of extreme examples of a phenomenon and its context often provides a full-fledged display of the phenomenon's causes and composition. Hitler, arguably, is the most extreme example of a destructive person. His "teachings" still appeal to much of the world; for example, the deadly cults discussed in Chapter 3: the Japan-based Aum, and the Aryan Nations in the U.S., and innumerable other hate groups. As noted previously, while the substance of such bigotry is remarkably unchanged and stubbornly unyielding to facts, the technology is keeping pace. The small cells characteristic of Aryan supremacy groups sometimes comprise only a few or even one person; the otherwise lonely new terrorists get much of their indoctrination from the numerous computer-accessible hate group lines on the worldwide Internet. Distanced, impersonal affiliations often appeal to alienated and paranoid-like lone wolves who can relate only through hate. This arrangement satisfies both those individuals and the more clearly group-affiliated paralethal perpetration-provocateurs of hate crimes who remain safely out of accountability's way by not doing the killing themselves. Hitler never killed anyone himself either.

By the end of the 20th century such lone wolf atrocities committed in the name of Hitlerian ideology so accelerated as to be labeled "leaderless resistance" in the era of lone terrorism (Thomas, 1999). In accord with Hitler's own pseudoreligious appeals by which he ascended to the mythical status of God, his new era converts sometimes arrogate a high priest status for themselves modeled on the supposed deed of Phineas in the Old Testament slaying an interreligious couple. As put forward by Richard Kelly Hoskins, a former member of the American Nazi Party, God, in his forbidding any mixing of the races, rewarded Phineas with an everlasting priesthood (Thomas, 1999). Such murderers, either collectively or as lone wolves, become immortal disciples of the immortal Hitler. Thus, the study of Hitler and the Nazi era is vital to understanding the present and the future of this continuing madness.

Some of the information needed for a detailed depiction of the formation of Hitler's personality in terms of his family origins and childhood is still missing or uncertain. Yet, so much useful and substantially verified factual information is now available that we have more pertinent knowledge of Hitler than we do the majority of other historical figures. And although there is inevitable scholarly disagreement about the importance of various findings and their interpretation, the mentality underlying Hitler's destructiveness has become largely understandable and illustrative of the mentality of human destructiveness in general. Thus, given the extremity of his destructiveness, and the richness of the scholarly findings and interpretations, we can advance the discovery of the madness of human destructiveness from the example of Hitler.

Ron Rosenbaum's book, *Explaining Hitler* (1998), thoroughly explores the remarkable interest in, ambivalence about, and controversies over trying to elucidate and interpret the horror that was Hitler. While not all the "facts" are sufficiently verified, some investigators and would-be explainers are averse to explaining, as if Hitler is beyond the pale of any human personality, as if he was not part of the human race. Or, they surmise that explaining him would exonerate him; as if to understand is to forgive. Another difficulty is that each investigator-interpreter sees the phenomenon from a different viewpoint, rather like the proverbial viewers of an elephant who, each viewing from a different vantage point, declare their view to be the only valid view. Such unwittingly partial views easily lend themselves to false disputes and controversies as well as reasonable disagreements.

Finally, a crucial difficulty is the tendency to dismiss out of hand those observations and interpretations that one is simply not qualified to understand. Historian Robert Waite's "Afterword" to psychoanalyst Walter Langer's *The Mind of Adolph Hitler* (1973) spoke to this failing as exemplified by himself not being equipped as an historian-investigator to fathom psychodynamic functioning:

> Whatever psychological insights that have been brought to our endeavor have generally come from "common sense." But we begin to feel helpless when the subject with whom we are dealing just doesn't behave sensibly. …Simply to conclude such conduct is strange and irrational and inexplicable — or that the man seemeth beset by unknown demons — is not really very useful (page 228).

Since Hitler was an extremely irrational personality, whose appeal has always been to the unconscious and irrational, inability to fathom the contradictory depths of his character leaves the would-be interpreter unable to explain what is most important. What is of value in the nonpsychodynamic accounts, nonetheless, is the immensely important discovery and verification of facts, albeit often without adequate explanation. For example, Waite's book *The Psychopathic God* (1977) made a vital contribution to factual knowledge, and he corrected some mistakes Langer made from an historical point of view.

The following discussion represents an attempt to take into account these difficulties and to integrate some of the excellent investigation and interpretation in the vast and growing literature on Hitler and the Nazi regime that began when he rose to power in the 1930s. By profiling the destructive mentality of Hitler particularly, and the general psychosocial conditions which both facilitated him and which he helped engender, we can more comprehensively define the mentality of human destructiveness.

Psychological Understanding of Hitler

Germany had been widely regarded around the world as a cultured and enlightened civilized nation notable for high attainments in science, music, literature, and many other constructive endeavors. But, while the German culture that preceded the Nazi regime was not barbaric according to the standards of the time, it did share in the common prejudices and bigotry of many "civilized" nations. That basic dehumanization, carefully accelerated, had such deadly consequences that Hitler and his Nazi regime hold the historical record for killing efficiency.

As discussed previously, Erich Fromm's concept of authoritarian personality and society in *Escape from Freedom* (1969) provided an important part of an urgently needed explanation of Hitler and his Nazi regime when it was originally published in 1941. He showed the workings of sadomasochism in the authoritarian character who never regards himself as equal to anyone, but must be either dominant or submissive. At the extreme, as was Hitler, the authoritarian person must humiliate or be humiliated.

In August 1941, a few months before the the U.S. entered World War II, the Office of Strategic Services (OSS) director, "Wild Bill" Donovan, responded eagerly to psychoanalyst Walter Langer's offer to contribute an in-depth psychological analysis of the Nazi dictator. *The Mind of Adolph Hitler: The Secret Wartime Report* (1973) was used by the OSS during World War II, but not made available to the public until 1972.

Langer enlisted the help of fellow psychoanalysts in the difficult, time-pressured task of analyzing someone they could know only through others' observations. Langer himself was not altogether happy with the result, particularly because too little was known at that time about the young Adolph's formative childhood years which Hitler had gone to great lengths to conceal and distort. The psychoanalysts did know that Hitler, born in 1889, was shiftless up until age 25, appeared to have no sense of identity or direction, worked enough only to live in conditions of filth and squalor in his early adulthood, and showed no ambition except for dreams of being a great artist. While anti-Establishment and vocal about society's shortcomings, Hitler was short on accomplishments of his own.

The psychoanalytic study group decided early that this extremely alienated man was a "neurotic psychopath" (Langer, 1973, page 26), a term suggestive of both inner torment and extreme unscrupulousness and destructiveness. At another point, Langer wrote that Hitler's mental derangement was schizophrenic-like. (The concepts of psychopathic personality and schizophrenic disorder are discussed later in this chapter.) Clearly, considering the wealth of information they gained from interviewing people who had known Hitler, and from his speeches, writings, and various other communications, Hitler displayed the kind of grandiosity that is associated with the most severe mental disorders.

Annointing himself the "Chosen One" (as quoted by Langer, page 45), he claimed utter omniscience and omnipotence, that he was all-knowing and all-powerful like God. He conceived of himself as a second Christ, a supposed improvement on the first; but unlike the Christ who suffered and was crucified, Hitler was "called on by Providence" to rid the world's population of its impurities through unrelenting brutality, the hallmark in Hitler's mind of masculinity. Disdaining intellectuals and serious study of history, he disregarded the fact that Christ was Jewish and that most early Christians were Jewish. Violating historical truth, he depicted Christ as worthy only for his supposedly anti-Jewish behavior. Hitler charismatically fashioned himself not only as dictator but an immortal religious figure who was to be worshipped, after his physical death, atop a 70-story mausoleum that would last at least a thousand years, as would the roads he built; and still more monuments would be built honoring him in never-limited grandeur.

Finally, faced with the limitation of certain defeat, he declared that he was too good even for his chosen people, the "Aryan race." As he ran out of people to destroy, his ultimate aim was not merely to destroy the ever-increasing types and numbers of "inferior peoples" and a sizeable minority of Aryan Germans, but also to destroy all of his chosen people, the totality of the Aryan race and himself as the Allies closed in.

Inability to tolerate criticism or to admit his personal weaknesses was crucial to Hitler's destroying others and himself. Instead of achieving genuine self-discovery, he strenuously denied his sense of inferiority and unworthiness and projected these attributes onto others. The inexorable course of his extreme paranoid projection was to try to exterminate all of his desperately needed and, therefore, ever-increasing numbers and kinds of "inferior" enemies. Such inexhaustible need results over time in attempts to destroy everyone, and utimately oneself. Those he could not draw to him by mesmerizing, he tried to conquer militarily. Hitler was like the "black hole" in astronomy, sucking in everyone to death, together with himself — a kind of star in gravitational collapse.

Many observers realized that Hitler was a madman, meaning he was morbid both in terms of his irrationality and destructiveness, but little was done about treating him as such despite his two blatant mental breakdowns at ages 20 and 29 as well as pronounced psychiatric symptomatology observed throughout his adult life. The Harvard physician and psychologist Henry Murray:

> …toured Germany with his family during the summer of 1937 and wrote home of having had a "close view" of Hitler at the Wagner festival in Bayreuth. "He is an unimpressive, harassed man … who seems to me to be beyond his depths. He is under the constant care of a Munich psychiatrist of the old school. Symptoms: severe depression & nightmares (insomnia) — probably of persecution. To think that the peace of Europe hangs on the electro-chemical system in that cranium (as quoted by Robinson, 1992, page 229).

Conceivably, Hitler could have been treated successfully by a more psychodynamically oriented practicioner but the task was daunting. Sigmund Freud's early but then estranged Swiss protege Carl Jung was such a possibility, although his apparent sympathy toward the Nazis and anti-Semitism was a double-edged sword capable of both attracting Hitler and nullifying Jung's effectiveness. Henry Murray, pondering this dilemma, "…was sensitive to the evidence of anti-Semitism in Jung's thinking; but he knew as well that the Old Man regarded Hitler as a dangerous paranoid and had refused to take him as a patient" (Robinson, 1992, page 230).

What was needed before any psychotherapy could be effective was not the massive humoring his idolators gave him in ever-increasing doses, but an environment that would refuse to play host to Hitler's externalization or "acting out" of his internal conflicts. The challenge would have been like getting an alcoholic to stop drinking so that, in a resultant sober condition, psychotherapy could be effective. Instead, Hitler was both actively and passively aided and abetted to lead Germany into massive destructiveness. In this light, Hitler is merely one of countless people who, encouraged to vent their venom, ultimately turn into destroyers of others as well as themselves. Simply depending on mental health practitioners to treat people with severe personality disorders, in the hope that that alone will keep them from being destructive, is costly for all concerned, including society as a whole (Whitaker, 1996).

Meanwhile, as Chancellor of the Third Reich from 1933 to 1945, he dominated the minds and behavior of millions of people who obeyed him as if he were infallible. How could someone so aberrant by the usual standards of sanity do that? How could he get people to believe him? Many mutually supportive conditions were needed to override his and others' doubts in himself.

As George Victor has convincingly portrayed in *Hitler: The Pathology of Evil* (1998), Hitler was driven by such a sense of alienation, meaninglessness, and dread of inferiority that he desperately, fanatically "believed" in his own powers, exaggerated to the degree of his underlying fear. But his belief had to be contagious rather than absurd. Ordinarily, people who declare themselves to be Jesus Christ or, in this case, better than Christ, are quickly regarded as psychotic.

In addition to strenuous fanatical belief in his omniscience and omnipotence, he had to be highly intelligent in terms of the standard meaning of the term. And there is plenty of evidence that he was. Many direct observers documented his superior intelligence. For example, "He has an extraordinary memory... All kinds of facts and figures relevant to the problem flow from him without the slightest hesitation or effort, much to the amazement of those about him" (Langer, 1973, page 70).

Hitler's intelligence extended to virtually every domain relevant to gaining and maintaining political and military power. Langer "briefly summarized" that intelligence under 27 headings spanning 6 pages (pages 71 to 76). Hitler paid careful attention to the masses generally and to women and youth particulary, and used hypnotic ways of relating in both group and individual settings, first empathizing with people so as to cast his spell over them. Langer's headings #22 and #23 note "Hitler's ability to repudiate his own conscience in arriving at political decisions has eliminated the force that usually checks and complicates the forward-going thoughts and resolutions of most socially responsible statesmen.... Equally important has been his ability to persuade others to repudiate their individual consciences and allow him to assume that role.... As Goering has said 'I have no conscience. My conscience is Adolph Hitler'" (Langer, 1973, page 75). Similarly, Adolph Eichmann, who had a central role in killing six million Jews and never showed even the least compunction in the planning, organizing, and executing of the Holocaust, stated in his recently published memoirs, "Now that I look back, I realize that a life predicated on being obedient and taking orders is a very comfortable life indeed. Living in such a way reduces to a minimum one's own need to think" (as quoted in Cohen, 1999).

Hitler as Master of Propaganda

> All propaganda has to be popular and has to adapt its spiritual level to the perception of the least intelligent of those towards whom it intends to direct itself — Mein Kampf (My Battle), 1933, Vol. 1, chap. 2.
>
> The great masses of the people ... will more easily fall victims to a big lie than to a small one — Mein Kampf, 1933, Vol. 1, chap. 3.

Hitler, the frustrated artist, advanced lying to an art form, and he was a "pathological liar," a liar who believes in his own lies. His only alternative, given his inability to assess himself realistically, was to sink into the abyss of his passivity and despair, into a frank psychosis. In short, he had to lie to himself to maintain and bolster his own superman image, to stay on top, albeit precariously, of his sense of utter worthlessness and meaninglessness. In order to convince others, he and his propaganda ministry used all the tricks of the trade, including what may be the invention and use of more euphemisms than any other dictatorial regime (see Table 5.1).

By empathizing with others to ascertain their darkest and most destructive thoughts, Hitler could then relieve them of their constraining human decency by preaching to them the righteousness of their violent inclinations, thereby filling the void where their consciences had been with himself as their "conscience." In this way he not only humored them out of their guilt sensibilities, and with it their freedom and responsibility to think for themselves, but induced in them a savage euphoria.

A master propagandist himself, he commanded a propaganda ministry that erased all doubts of his magnificence. His hypnotic methods included arranging his talks to the masses for the end of the day when they were too tired to think critically and were most receptive to being relieved of their guilts, responsibilities, and need to think.

Hitler also appealed to other, quite independent people in power, most particularly to those like himself who insisted on avoiding being regulated by others and who shared his scapegoating and contempt for minorities. The American industrialist Henry Ford was an admirer of Hitler's synthesis of intelligence and anti-Semitism. As Asimov (1981) noted: "Adolph Hitler kept a framed photograph of Henry Ford on his desk and Ford kept one of Hitler on his desk in Dearborn, MI. Hitler had used in *Mein Kampf* some of Ford's anti-Semitic views, and he had always welcomed Ford's substantial contributions to the Nazi movement" (page 219).

The Two Hitlers

In extreme contrast to his propagandized image, Hitler was in most respects not only different but opposite. Although he was intelligent in the traditional sense of the word, and even partially intelligent in what is now often referred to as emotional intelligence, and a superb actor as well, his weak physique, physiognomy, and dark hair failed grossly to fit the tall blond superman Ayran ideal. In 1923, the most eminent eugenicist in Germany, the University of Munich's Professor Max von Gruber, gave this assessment:

> It was the first time I had seen Hitler close at hand. Face and head of inferior type, cross-breed; low receding forehead, ugly nose, broad cheekbones, little eyes, dark hair. Expression not of a man exercising authority in perfect self-command, but of raving excitement. At the end an expression of satisfied egotism (quoted in Langer, 1973, page 52).

Table 5.1   A Glossary of Euphemisms Peculiar to the Nazi Regime

The great enemy of clear language is insincerity. (George Orwell)

Advisor for Jewish Questions: Nazi title for its representatives sent to expedite deportation and death.

An Act for Relieving the Distress of Nation and Reich: The assumption of dictatorial power by Hitler.

Care centers: Places where children, taken from their foreign laborer parents, were starved to death.

Change of residence, preventive detention, protective detention, and re-education into the discipline of work: Incarceration in concentration camps, often with death as the likely result.

Convalescent camps: Places where concentration camp inmates too sick to work were sent to die.

Eastern regions of Germany: Poland.

Euthanasia, mercy killing, and final medical assistance under the auspices of the Community Foundation for Institutional Care: Killing.

Forced labor therapy: Deliberately working incurable patients to death.

Health resorts and *charitable foundations for institutional care*: Death camps.

Infant homes, specialist children's wards and *infant concentration camps*: Facilities for killing German children.

Insuring its neutrality: Invading and occupying Belgium and Holland.

Jewish communities fund: Money and property confiscated from the Jews, as was used directly to deport and exterminate them.

Law Against the Overcrowding of German Schools: Denying an education to Jewish children.

Law for the Restoration of the Professional Civil Service: Elimination of Jews and people with partial Jewish ancestry from the government.

Negative population policy, disinfection, deportation, evacuation, relocation, resettlement, forced labor, housecleaning, special treatment, and *the final solution*: The Nazi extermination program.

Pacifying: Razing a city or town to the ground.

Protecting it: Invading and occupying Denmark and Norway and looting art and other property in occupied countries.

Protection of the German people: Suspending constitutional protection of Germans and their property.

Retirement villages: Places where Jews were sent to die by starvation and freezing.

Shower rooms: Gas chambers.

Strengthening the solidarity of the German people: Abolishing political parties.

Transit and the earlier term *special treatment* which it replaced when the latter euphemism had become notorious: Extermination.

Traveling for free: What Bulgarian Jews were told regarding plans to deport them.

Voluntary surrender and *transfer to Aryan possession*: Stealing from Jews, as when the SS or Gestapo arrested them at home and took whatever property they fancied.

Source: Adapted from Victor, G. *Hitler: The Pathology of Evil*, Brassey Publishers, Dulles, VA, 1988, pages 112-114, and 119.

His voice was rasping and broke into a shrill falsetto when, as so often happened, he became aroused. In his early days, while ascending to power, his diction was especially poor. And instead of presiding in a purely German dialect, he spoke in a mix of Austrian and high German.

His origins also contradicted his propagandized image. Hitler was born in 1889 in Austria to a father who was illegitimate himself and who fathered an illegitimate child. Hitler feared his father might be partly Czech and Jewish, and he had relatives who were mentally and physically handicapped. He had nagging concerns that he might be "dangerously" close to the Slavic, Jewish, and handicapped "inferior" peoples he had to destroy as representatives of (his own) "poisonous blood."

As a young man, his only venture into a love relationship had been with someone he never identified himself to but called "Stephanie," thought to be a Jewish-sounding name. Sexually, he was anything but the virile superman. Usually limited to looking at pornography, he was seldom if ever potent, and required a woman to abuse him, including apparently having the woman urinate or defecate on him, perversions clearly expressive of his masochistic side. "Sex seems to have been the only activity in which he openly expressed his self-loathing, telling his partners he was unworthy of them and begging them to say degrading things about him" (Victor, 1998, page 156).

While ostensibly submitting to a woman and making himself vulnerable, he was actually giving orders. Like so many Nazis, Hitler regarded women as inferior, lustful, and therefore evil. In private, he expressed the same views as in Nazi publications wherein propagandist "...Rosenberg described women as a vegetable-like, inferior species, and Streicher described them as stupid, lustful, and deceitful" (Victor, 1998, page 151).

His inability to enjoy or even tolerate genuine physical intimacy was reflected in his abhorrence of being physically examined and of massage. As many researchers have documented, several women, whose involvement made them miserable, actually committed or at least attempted suicide. The real but typically hidden Hitler was anything but comfortable with sexuality; he was fervently antisexual. His frequent nightmares, extreme insomnia, and such heavy reliance on drugs as to cause early aging and physical deterioration were signs of being at war with himself as well as others.

Two rejections by the Vienna Academy of Fine Arts had devastated his only constructive career ambition. What remained for him was to turn his personal psychosis into a mass madness that could validate him. Addiction to violence ensued, a long, viscious downward spiral along the lines of deviation amplification as formulated in the second law of cybernetics:

Hitler's struggle to free himself from his conscience succeeded; he became a person of extreme destructiveness and took much of Germany with him. When the self-hatred that propelled his rise to power turned to killing scapegoats, his guilt increased, and he needed still more scapegoats. Eventually, all of Germany was his scapegoat (Victor, 1998, page 216).

At very nearly the end, on learning that "…thousands of Berliners, mostly women, children, and wounded men, sought refuge in subways and other tunnels … Hitler ordered the tunnels flooded" (Victor, 1998, page 214). How can Hitler's "black hole mentality" be classified diagnostically?

As discussed earlier in this book, the terms psychosis and insanity — and we can include schizophrenia — have been reserved for individuals, not groups. The individual who manages to convince others — in Hitler's case millions of others — receives the "consensual validation" that is lacking for the individually deranged person. But as Fromm asserted, we should recognize also the phenomenon of *"folie a* millions," the mass madness of the masses believing in massive lies that brook no contradiction by evidence.

Was Hitler Mad or just Bad?

Diagnosing or labeling an individual or a group as deranged makes sense only in terms of morbidity: (1) the mental and emotional deficits of the person(s) which predispose them to premature death, i.e., their being afflicted and (2) their actions that inflict disease and death on others, i.e., their afflicting. Considering the first criterion, Hitler may have effectively postponed his own demise; he may have avoided early suicide or further lonely, individual psychosis by persuading followers to join him in his delusions of persecution and grandeur.

But, even if we insist on only individual, nonshared morbidity as a necessary condition to designate Hitler as deranged, we must admit that he merely postponed and did not finally succeed at avoiding premature death or a lonely derangement except for the few people who committed suicide with him in his bunker. And, clearly, Hitler was grossly deranged in terms of the second criterion.

If we look at signs and symptoms for schizophrenic disorder, which is predominantly type (1) morbidity and which Langer (1973) considered, a case can be made for his having been what at the time was called "schizophrenic character" (Schafer, 1948). But let us now take a modern view.

According to the American Psychiatric Association's (1994) *Diagnostic and Statistical Manual of Mental Disorders*, 4th ed. (DSM-IV), at least two of the following five symptoms must be present for a significant period of time, typically for a month or more: delusions; hallucinations; disorganized speech; grossly disorganized or catatonic behavior; and negative symptoms, i.e., affective flattening, alogia, or avolition. At times, the first four of these symptoms appeared, although, again, Hitler obtained so much agreement from others as to be consensually validated, whereas the schizophrenic individual cannot really persuade others but is isolated in his idiosyncracy.

The fifth, the negative symptom category, may be the closest fit. For much of his youth and at later times episodically, Hitler was passive, emotionally flat, alogical, and lacking in will. As Victor (1998) explains, Hitler escaped this extreme passive nonfunctioning apathy by taking on an identity as divorced as possible from his real self, which he regarded as "rotten to the marrow" (page 18).

A particular form of a major disturbance in thinking is traditionally regarded as the core inability or deficit in schizophrenic disorders. Schizophrenic thinking has been defined as thinking that is severely and simultaneously illogical, impaired, and unwitting (Whitaker, 1992). Hitler showed illogicality in that he often contradicted himself both in word and action, although he most often thought logically, even if on utterly false premises. For example, he claimed that "the Jews" had caused wars and wanted wars (a false premise) and therefore (logically), they should be exterminated for safety's sake. And although he became even more severely impaired in his functioning and thinking ability as his regime spiraled downward, Hitler had often thought quite effectively, though with destructive aims. Was he unwitting? Certainly, in that he came to believe in his own lies and, therefore, was self-deluded.

Again, however, a hallmark of schizophrenic disorders is individual idiosyncrasy and lack of ideational and emotional communion with others resulting in lack of acceptability. Hitler was a master of persuasive communication.

What about Hitler as a psychopath, another diagnostic speculation made by Langer and his associates (1973)? While Hitler's mentality and behavior are suggestive but not protoypically schizophrenic, he clearly meets the criteria for psychopathic personality. For example, although Hitler's multitude of biographers often disagree with one another, all of the many accounts the present writer has read meet the applicable criteria on the Hare Psychopathy Checklist — Revised (PCL-R) as cited in Gacono and Meloy (1994, page 253), the first 10 being glibness/superficial charm, grandiose sense of self-worth, proneness to boredom/need for stimulation, pathological lying, conning/manipulative, lack of remorse, shallow affect, lack of empathy, parasitic life style, and poor behavior controls. It may be argued that Hitler did empathize with others, but he did so essentially only to con or manipulate them. He also fits virtually all of the 10 remaining criteria such as impulsivity, irresponsibility, failure to accept responsibility for his own actions, and criminal versatility, while two criteria (promiscuous sexual behavior and many marital relationships) appear inapplicable because of his avoidance of such intimacies.

Hitler was the predatory type of psychopath, calculating in the commission of violent acts, finding them enjoyable and useful for intimidating and controlling others and maintaining his grandiose self-image. Consistent with this depiction, Hitler clearly fits Victor's (1998) definition of evil: "passionate destructiveness justified by righteousness and expressed with little inhibition and with ruthless disregard for consequences" (page 85).

Langer's (1973) impression of Hitler as two personalities makes sense in terms of psychopathic personality psychodynamics. As Gacono and Meloy (1994) remark, "…the psychopath simultaneously contains highly unrealistic overvalued (grandiosity) and undervalued (worthlessness) representations of himself" (page 316). His grandiosity includes pride in criminal acts, perfectionism, uniqueness, and pretentiousness. Meanwhile, he believes he is totally worthless, a nothing who is all bad, that others share this belief about him, and that his condition will last forever, i.e., that it is hopeless.

We have here a solution to the controversy over whether the common blatant bragging and bravado of violent offenders shows a deficiency in self-esteem:

> Gacono discovered that conduct-disordered adolescents could readily verbalize their experiences of extreme envy and grandiosity coupled with inner boredom and emptiness. In response to the question of what they would be like without the part of them that was "superhuman" or better than anyone else, they replied, "Worthless, helpless"; " I would be like a guy in a three piece suit who goes to work everyday, nine to five"; "I would be helpless, vulnerable"; "It would be like death" (Gacona and Meloy, 1994, page 316).

Grandiosity, a desperate reaction to the suppressed sense of gross inferiority, is clearly manifest in attitudes of "ownership" and "entitlement" (Gacona and Meloy, 1994, page 85). It would be hard to exaggerate these attitudes in Hitler's case:

> …if I can send the flower of the German nation into the hell of war, without the smallest pity for the spilling of precious German blood, then surely I have a right to remove millions of an inferior race that breeds like vermin!
>
> Some day, when I order war, I shall not be in a position to hesitate because of the ten million young men I shall be sending to their death (Victor, 1998, page 84).

Unlike many psychopathic personalities, Hitler never killed anyone himself, but insisted on keeping his distance. He preached brutality and proudly extolled his own "manly" brutality, but few, if any, accounts in the literature depict him directly brutalizing except when he whipped his dog, as he did to impress a young woman. By all accounts, *Hitler was the ultimate "para-lethal,"* an insatiable perpetrator who always positioned himself at least at arm's length when it came to killing. In this way he incriminated others, much like but massively more so that his current counterparts who preach violence to others but stay out of reach themselves.

For those who wish a "capsule diagnosis," the most apt is probably severe borderline personality and psychopathic personality. The latter is defined as not merely an Antisocial Personality Disorder (American Psychiatric Association, 1994), i.e., harmfully deviant in terms of social norms, but severely destructively aggressive (Gacono and Meloy, 1994). Hitler was never far from a frankly psychotic state. But he "acted out" his own internal morbid condition, projecting it onto and persecuting others for it in ways that gained fanatically dedicated support and, until the end, gave him some semblance of functioning ability. His acting out, or externalizing of his personal demons, so aided and abetted by millions, made what would have been just his private psychosis into a massive group psychosis manifest in shared delusions.

The modern term "borderline personality disorder," which has much the same meaning as the "schizophrenic character" designation used by Schafer (1948) as noted above, helps to convey Hitler's schizophrenic-like mental status.

But while borderline personalities can be effectively manipulative and destructive, most such persons are not nearly so malignant in their narcissism as was Hitler. As DSM-IV puts it, "Although *antisocial personality disorder* and borderline personality disorder are both characterized by manipulative behavior, individuals with antisocial personality disorder are manipulative to gain profit, power, or some other material gratification, whereas the goal in borderline personality disorder is directed more toward gaining the concern of caregivers" (American Psychiatric Association, 1994, page 653).

Genesis of Hitler's Destructive Mentality

What part did Hitler's childhood experiences play in his becoming both mad in the psychopathological sense and bad in the sense of evil? What happened early on to make him a madman bent on destroying as many people as possible? Although earlier biographers lacked information about Hitler's childhood, more recent research has established its formative role. Early speculations about Hitler's father, Alois, made him appear benign instead of relentlessly brutal. But George Victor (1998) has provided a particularly clear interpretive account.

> Adolph became very stubborn with his father and, according to his sister Paula, provocative.... Paula said he beat Adolph daily and severely. Then, at ten, Adolph ... decided to run away. On discovering this, Alois beat him so severely that he went into a coma. For days the family did not know whether he would live.

Frequent or severe punishment conveys to children that they are evil. Being nearly killed by parents conveys that they are unworthy to live. Adolph began to experience himself as evil and worthless — feelings he would describe in middle age and be troubled by until death (page 29).

Hitler's mother, Klara, probably a direct victim of her husband's brutality, witnessed the beatings of her son and plied him with indulgences. Thus, Hitler's personality embodied both extreme rage and an extreme sense of entitlement. The combination meant that he was entitled to vent his rage on others, at least those who would tolerate it, including his teachers who also tended to be indulgent.

Ironically, as Hitler began to displace his anger into scapegoating others, he became like the father he hated, identifying with him in many particulars as well as generally. Like his father who carried a whip in the house (Victor, page 28), Hitler carried a whip. And like father, who always wore his uniform as a civil service tax collector, Hitler seldom appeared out of uniform, a symbol in both cases of their brandishing authority. Alois, the father, became his son's fateful masculine ideal of brutality which Hitler pursued insatiably.

Anna Freud, who together with her father, Sigmund, directly contended with the Nazi barbarity, formulated how fear and hatred of an aggressor can turn a victim into an aggressor who is even more aggressive than his mentor: "By impersonating the aggressor, assuming his attributes or imitating his aggression, the child transforms himself from the person threatened into the person who makes the threat" (Freud, 1957, page 121). Observing this defense mechanism in children, she remarked, "In passing from the passivity of experience to the activity of play the child applies to his playfellow the unpleasant occurrence that befell himself and so avenges himself on the person of this proxy" (Freud, 1957, page 122). Hitler's proxies, or stand-ins, became legion.

Lessons Tyrants Have Taught Us

The major lessons to be learned from Hitler and his Nazi regime as well as other tyrants include:

1. *Aggression begets aggression.*
2. *Entitlement begets entitlement.*
3. *Societal aiding and abetting of aggression and entitlement are essential to collective violence.*
4. *Pursuit of "racial purity" weakens rather than strengthens a population.*

A tyrant must be trained and assisted in mass destructiveness. In this case, the record efficiency of killing 20 million people could not have occurred without a madman of Hitler's conditioning and cleverness, nor could it have happened without the active and passive support of millions of people. But madmen and supporters of madmen are plentiful.

Granted that Hitler and his Nazi regime *may* remain the singularly most efficient perpetrators of atrocity in human history, the lessons apply to many other well-documented murderous regimes. Stalin, like Hitler (a maniacal psychopath), took more time than Hitler had available, but led a regime that killed 40 million Russians compared to Hitler's 20 million murders.

Even Nazi efficiency and cruelty may not have been as extreme over a very short time as Iris Chang has documented in *The Rape of Nanking* (1997). Between 260,000 and 350,000 Chinese citizens, noncombatants, were not only murdered in a mere few weeks beginining in December 1937, but the forms of cruelty even horrified the Nazis who witnessed it:

> Chinese men were used for bayonet practice and in decapitation contests. An estimated 20,000 to 80,000 Chinese women were raped. Many soldiers went beyond rape to disembowel women, slice off their breasts, nail them alive to walls. Fathers were forced to rape their daughters, and sons their mothers, as other family members watched. Not only did live burials, castration, the carving of organs, and the roasting of people become routine, but more diabolical tortures were practiced, such as hanging people by their tongues on iron hooks or burying people to their waist and watching them get torn apart by German shepherds. So sickening was the spectacle that even the Nazis in the city were horrified, one proclaiming the massacre to be the work of "bestial machinery" (Chang, 1997, page 6).

The genesis of these atrocities fits the same pattern as fits the Nazi and Stalinist regimes. The immediate or most proximate perpetrators of the atrocities were thoroughly conditioned by paralethal training conducted in cultural isolation. The regimented and robotic Japanese educational system of the 1930s set the stage with sadistic treatment of children. Viscious hazing was turned on its head ideationally as it was euphemized as love and caring. The schoolboy who decided on the culturally esteemed career of soldier was subjected to far more "love."

> According to the author Iritani Toshio, officers often justified unauthorized punishment by saying, "I do not beat you because I hate you. I beat you because I care for you. Do you think I perform these acts with hands swollen and bloody in a state of madness?" Some youths died under such brutal physical conditions; others committed suicide; the majority became tempered vessels into which the military could pour a new set of life goals (Chang, 1997, page 32).

Further conditioning included systematic desentization to killing others, ultimately in the most massively destructive and gruesome ways possible, all in the name of courage and loyalty to the emperor. Individual self-esteem was made nil; only one's "courage" and unquestioning readiness to die for the emperor made one worthwhile, just as dying for Hitler would be a Nazi soldier's greatest and probably only honor. All individual life per se, including the Japanese soldier's own, was worthless; hence murder and suicide became banal as the conditioning curriculum progressed. As a Japanese soldier recalled many decades later, "Everyone became a demon in three months" (as cited in Chang, 1997, page 58). Like their Nazi counterparts, the Japanese of this era were taught that they were the master race and entitled to destroy the other "inferior races."

The heritage of barbarity and dehumanization is continuing into the 21st century as daily life displays its myriad paralethal forms. All 60 Japanese animation videos for purchase or rent at the "most tasteful" video shop in our area are focused on extreme acts of violence, an offshoot of the Samurai tradition from which Japanese atrocity was fashioned. Video games in the lobbies of movie theaters in the U.S. remain exclusively violent. Gross driver discourtesy and even "road rage" is common. A Norwegian colleague tells me that she and her husband are relieved to go abroad on vacation to escape the "Aryan pride" arrogance of youths in their once peaceful neighborhood. Meanwhile, the U.S. still is the leading exporter of violent films and, together with France, of weaponry. And nuclear weaponry is nearly ready, if not already so, in a growing number of countries.

Clearly, we are not beyond atrocities; it is just that they can be perpetrated much more massively given the misuse of our technological talents. The heritage of brutality masquerading as courage, righteousness, manliness, and entertainment is potentially more destructive than ever before.

The lessons are clear: cultural exclusivity and isolation, authoritarian rule and disallowance of dissent, and training in brutality fostering identification with the aggressor are the conjoint causes of the madness of mass destruction, with the means increasingly amplified by technological advances.

Summary

Massive collective violence is most likely to be generated by authoritarian governments, not only toward other nations but even more toward people within their own nations. R. J. Rummel has called the latter form democide, which includes genocide and politicide. But as Barbara Tuchman has documented, even democracies can lapse into the folly and destructiveness of suppressing dissent as illustrated by the protraction of the Vietnam War by the U.S. Arrogating power into the hands of the few tends to produce a hostile exclusivity, for example, in ethnic or religious mania or in authoritarian governments, that eventuates in evil — cruelty performed with a sense of righteousness.

Developing and maintaining democracy, clearly the safest hedge against governmental violence, requires resisting the lure of domination and passivity which relinquishes responsibility for one's own life and fails to appreciate others. Adolph Hitler and the Nazi regime are discussed to delineate and illustrate how authoritarian personalities and regimes evolve, including through the use of propaganda. A table of euphemisms peculiar to the Nazi regime shows its gross dependence on the lying characteristic of tyrranical governments.

The actual Hitler was intelligent in the standard sense of the term but in most ways he was the opposite of the supposedly virile, manly model of Aryan superiority he and others claimed. His own personal evolution into the most efficiently destructive, and arguably the most evil, person in history resulted from the combination of his intelligence, an extremely brutalized but entitled upbringing, and the support of the many millions who supported him actively or passively.

The major lessons to be learned from Hitler and his Nazi regime as well as other tyrants include: aggression begets aggression; entitlement begets entitlement; societal aiding and abetting of aggression and entitlement are essential to collective violence; and pursuit of "racial purity" weakens rather than strengthens a population. Like other totalitarian leaders and their regimes, Hitler and the Nazi movement had within them the seeds of their own destruction.

Hostile exclusivity, authoritarian rule and disallowance of dissent, and training in brutality fostering identification with the aggressor become the conjoint causes of the evil and madness of mass destruction, the possibilities for which are increasingly amplified by technological advances. Atrocities can be perpetrated even more massively now given misuse of our technological talents and the heritage of brutality masquerading as courage, manliness, and entertainment.

Bibliography

Langer, W. C., *The Mind of Adolph Hitler: The Secret Wartime Report*, New York: Basic Books, then Mentor Books, 1972 (hardcover); 1973 (paperback), 286 pages.

Asked in 1943 to do a study of Nazi Germany's leader for the Office of Strategic Services (OSS), psychoanalyst Walter Langer, aided by colleagues, provided compelling insights and predictions. The whip-carrying fiery orator was revealed as ever on the edge of overt insanity. He used his hypnotic ability to persuade others to help him symbolically kill the demons in himself by insatiable actual killing of "inferior" people onto whom he projected his own shame. Hitler's hypermasculine image, equated with brutality, was used to conceal his sexual and social developmental inferiority; "…in all his history there is no record of a really intimate or lasting friendship" (page 157).

Rosenbaum, R., *Explaining Hitler*, New York: Random House, 1998, 445 pages.

Journalist Ron Rosenbaum's account of his interviews and archival research into various estimates and explanations of Hitler's role, with a focus on the Holocaust. Well written in the style of a mystery story, it keeps the reader going through a series of promising but often partially debunked theories. The reader gains considerable factual knowledge of Hitler as well as how interpreters' personal reactions play importantly into their views of the explanatory process.

Rummel, R. J., *Death by Government*, New Brunswick, NJ: Transaction Publishers, 1994 and 1997, 496 pages.

The author's fourth book on genocide and government mass murder ("democide") is an excellent statistically based exposition of facts, figures, and references together with narratives describing the depravity of mass human destructiveness. Rummel firmly establishes that lethal violence is directly associated with authoritarian (at the extreme, totalitarian) governments and that democracies rarely commit mass lethal violence.

Tuchman, B. W., *The March of Folly: From Troy to Vietnam*, New York: Knopf, 1984, 447 pages.

Historian Barbara Tuchman's superb, highly readable account of the mentality of individual and group folly. She includes the Renaissance Popes' provocation of the Protestant secession and the British provocation of the American Revolution. The reader learns the ominous signs of folly, defined as self-inflicted injury to self-interest mediated by self-deception and recognized as such by contemporaries. This is a history book that successfully focuses on the central role of errant irrationality in human destructiveness rather than imparting rational motivation and avoiding the challenge of deeper analysis.

Victor, G., *Hitler: The Pathology of Evil*, Dulles, VA: Brassey Publishers.

Integrating knowledge of social science and historical research, psychotherapist George Victor, Ph.D. gives a deeply insightful account of Hitler's development into a self-contradictory character and what he calls "The Twisted Road to Auschwitz." His book defines evil as "passionate destructiveness, justified by righteousness" (page 85). He notes that the first large group of people Hitler ordered killed were not only Aryan but Nazis" (page 80), that Hitler's real goal became, inexorably, destroying everyone, including Germany and himself. The deadly righteousness is exemplified by Hitler's 1933 claim of justification: "…if I can send the flower of the German nation into the hell of war, without the smallest pity for the spilling of precious blood, then surely I have a right to remove millions of an inferior race that breeds like vermin" (page 84).

References

American Psychiatric Association, *Diagnostic and Statistical Manual of Mental Disorders*, 4th ed., Washington, D.C., 1994.

Asimov, I., *Isaac Asimov's Book of Facts*, New York: Bell Publishing, 1981.

Chang, I., *The Rape of Nanking: The Forgotten Holocaust of World War II*, New York: Penguin Books, 1997.

Cohen, R., Why? New Eichmann tries to explain, *New York Times*, August 16, 1999, pp. A1, A3.

Eddington, A. (Ed.), *Essential Einstein*, Rohnert Park, CA: Pomegranate Art books.

Eisler, R., *Sacred Pleasure: Sex, Myth, and the Politics of the Body — New Paths to Power and Love*, New York: HarperCollins, 1996 (originally published in 1995).

Flanders, S. A. and Flanders, C. A., Eds., *Dictionary of American Foreign Affairs*, New York: Macmillan, 1993.

Freud, A., *The Ego and the Mechanisms of Defense*, New York: International Universities Press, 1957 (originally published in 1946).

Fromm, E., *Escape from Freedom*, New York: Avon Books, 1969.

Fromm, E., *The Anatomy of Human Destructiveness*, New York: Holt, Reinhart, & Winston, 1973.

Gacono, C. B. and Meloy, J. R., *The Rorschach Assessment of Aggressive and Psychopathic Personalities*, Hillsdale, NJ: Lawrence Erlbaum Associates, 1994.

Humes, J., *The Wit and Wisdom of Winston Churchill*, New York: Harper Collins, 1994.

Langer, W. C., *The Mind of Adolph Hitler: The Secret Wartime Report*, New York: Signet, 1973 (originally published 1972 by Basic Books of New York).

Robinson, F. G., *Love's Story Told: A Life of Henry A. Murray*, Cambridge, MA: Harvard University Press, 1992.

Rosenbaum, R., *Explaining Hitler*, New York: Random House, 1998.

Rummel, R. J., *Death by Government*, New Brunswick, NJ: Transaction Publishers, 1997 (originally published in 1994).

Schafer, R., *The Clinical Application of Psychological Tests*, New York: International Universities Press, 1948.

Thomas, J., New face of terror crimes: "lone wolf" weaned on hate, *New York Times*, August 16, 1999, pp. A1, A16.

Tuchman, B., *The March of Folly*, New York: Knopf, 1984.

Victor, G., *Hitler: The Pathology of Evil*, Dulles, VA: Brassey Publishers, 1998.

Waite, R., *The Psychopathic God*, New York: Basic Books, 1977.

Whitaker, L. C., *Schizophrenic Disorders: Sense and Nonsense in Conceptualization, Assessment, and Treatment*, New York: Plenum Press, 1992.

Whitaker, L. C., Treating students with personality disorders: a costly dilemma, *J. Coll. Stud. Psychother.*, 10(3), 29-44, 1996.

Transcendence: Constructive vs. Destructive Mentality

6

Where there is great love,
There are always miracles
— Willa Sibert Cather

In this chapter the contrast between constructive and destructive mentality is exemplified by how people have prevented imminent killing of fellow humans at the risk of their own lives, and how individuals have managed to keep their own spirits alive. Based on principles developed throughout this book, recommendations are made for replacing destructive with constructive behavior and creating a saner, more caring society.

Courage and Kindness of Rescue Conspiracies

As Ernest Becker (1975) concluded, "Life seeks to expand in unknown directions for unknown reasons.... The urge to cosmic heroism, then, is sacred and mysterious and not to be neatly ordered and rationalized by science and secularism" (page 284). Extraordinary human kindness in the face of peril and in service of others as well as oneself exemplifies the genuine courage of real heroism.

Constructive mentality is put to the test and shows itself best in the midst of adversity. Throughout the Nazi regime countless individuals and groups not only resisted the Nazis but dedicated their lives to saving fellow human beings. Their courage and transcendent spirits saved great numbers of Jewish people from the Holocaust. In that process they actualized the essence of the constructive mentality and gave the world hope for the future of the human race. Their deeds, some only lately revealed, tell us how to be and what to do to assert the best.

William R. Perl and the Sealifts

As a young lawyer in Vienna, Perl organized 62 clandestine voyages on cattle boats, run-down freighters, and sailboats to Palestine from Romania, Greece,

Yugoslavia, and other countries, saving 40,000 Jews (Goldstein, 1998). His subterfuges included forging documents to obviate British blocking of large-scale Jewish immigration to Palestine, which the British did to preserve their influence in the Arab world. At one point he outfoxed Adolph Eichmann of the German SS who confronted him with a pistol in his back. Three years into his rescuing missions (1940) he was arrested in Greece and put on a train for Berlin, at the behest of the British he believed. He escaped and managed to carry out a few more missions until 1944. He went on to a distinguised career in U.S. military intelligence and became, after the war, the chief interrogator of German SS staff involved in the massacre of American prisoners of war.

Perl then added a doctorate in clinical psychology to his doctorate in law. He taught, practiced psychotherapy, and became, ultimately, an official of the militant Jewish Defense League, and was placed on 3 years probation for a firearms conviction related to protesting treatment of Soviet Jews. He died in 1998 at age 92, survived by his wife who had coverted to Judaism shortly before their marriage in 1938 and was imprisoned in a concentration camp from 1942 to 1944 for trying to hide a Jewish neighbor. The Perls leave a spiritual legacy, having risked their lives in a high cause and serving all humanity in the process.

Corrie ten Boom and the Dutch

In contrast to the bombast and braggadocio of Hitler and the Nazis, Corrie ten Boom and her family were unassuming. Corrie grew up with her watch-maker father, mother, sister, and brother, an intensely Christian family that gave no credence to narrow religiosity. Their home, called the Beje, became *The Hiding Place* (ten Boom, 1971) for Jewish people trying to escape the Nazi extermination program.

Altogether, 80 non-Jewish Dutch people — adolescent, middle-aged, and elderly — formed a conspiracy of kindness and courage with the Beje as headquarters. Their heroism placed their own lives in danger not only from the Nazis but from the Dutch version of the Norwegian "quislings" or puppets of the Nazi invaders. Eventually, Casper, the father, and Corrie's sister and brother would lose their lives in the cause while Corrie would barely survive concentration camps. But they and their fellow conspirators saved a long succession of people while living up to the personal meaning they found in their Dutch Reformed Church.

The father, a skilled watchmaker still working in his 80s, imparted his own deep faith which showed itself not in exclusivity but in having the honor to serve his fellow humans in need. When a pastor presented a Jewish mother and her newborn for hiding, knowing that the baby's crying would compromise careful concealment: "Father held the baby close, his white beard brushing its cheek, looking into the little face with eyes as blue and innocent as the baby's own. At last he looked up at the pastor, 'You say we could lose our lives for this child. I would consider that the greatest honor that could come to my family'" (ten Boom, 1984, page 95). At another point, confronted by the Gestapo chief in The Hague, the father said, "I will open my door to anyone in need…" (ten Boom, 1984, p.210). This kind of courage and spirituality, transcending the bigotry at the core of Nazi tyranny, pervaded the family's life. Even prior to the Nazi invasion of Holland, at the father's instigation they had already taken in and nurtured 11 homeless children.

But their insistence on straightforward honesty met a difficult challenge in the Nazi quest for people to victimize. They chose not to counter Nazi violence with violence but did choose to fight fire with fire when it came to the Nazi's disguise of atrocity by use of euphemism. Watches took on other meanings: "I have a watch here with a face that's causing difficulty. One of the numbers has worked loose and it's holding back the hand. Do you know anyone who does this kind of repair work? (We have a Jew here whose features are especially Semitic. Do you know anyone would be willing to take an extra risk?)" To this kind of request for watch repair, Corrie replied, "Send the watch over and I'll see what we can do in our own shop" (ten Boom, 1984, page 96).

The family wrestled with the dishonesty of their own deceptive practices of communicating and structuring their house misleadingly through clever carpentry work. They did so to save lives rather than — like the Nazis — destroy lives. As ethically defensible as that is, it raises the question of how far one should proceed along the continuum of deceit, stretching from the Dutch kindness conspiracy at one extreme end to the Nazi atrocity program at the other. Exemplifying a position somewhere in-between is the U.S. Central Intelligence Agency (CIA), discussed in Chapter 4, which for more than 50 years conducted spying and espionage as means to attain "good ends."

Must any effective resistance to deceptively programmed brutality require using some of the the perpetrators' own measures? Typically, such fighting of fire with fire does happen and it usually goes far beyond harmless deception. Democracies, which are much more peace-minded than authoritarian nations, attempt to negotiate but also commonly respond to violent force with violent force and often kill people in the process. Must peaceful people be sullied by their own tactics in resisting tyranny? Let us return to the question after noting an only recently told story of a massively successful rescue of would-be Holocaust victims.

Bulgaria's Protective Coalition

Michael Bar-Zohar (1998), whose mother lived in the era of Nazi occupation of Bulgaria, was surprised that the story of her country's rescue of Jews had not been added to the well-documented rescues by the Danish and Italians and by the Swedish Raoul Wallenberg and the German Oscar Schindler.

The nation of Bulgaria, caught both ideologically and geographically between Nazi Germany to the Northwest and the Communism of Soviet Russia to the East, had to choose what it hoped might be the lesser evil. Born and reared in Germany and of German and French ancestry, Bulgaria's King Boris III made a choice deserving of Hitler's name for him: "The Fox."

An autocrat by upbringing, "…Boris III was a democrat at heart and an enlightened ruler. He had nothing in common with people like Mussolini and Hitler… He was a simple and modest man, devoted to his people" (Bar-Zohar, 1998, page 17). He had supported the League of Nations after World War I and as World War II approached he tried to assure Bulgaria's neutrality. But the emotional bond between the Bulgarians and their Russian "brothers," coupled with the growing power of the Bulgarian Communist party, posed an imminent danger of invasion and "Bolshevization" that Boris wished to avert. Hitler then won over Boris by supporting his territorial claims to Dobrudja, then a part of Romania. In exchange for this bribery and German "protection," Bulgaria paid a price in anti-Semitic legislation directed at its 45,558 Jews, 0.7% of the population in its 1934 census.

The characteristic Nazi penchant for euphemistically concealing atrocity showed itself in the new "Law for the Defense of the Nation," abbreviated as ZZN. The ZZN had staunch Bulgarian supporters in the extreme political right. Despite that support and Bulgaria's moves toward alliance with Nazi Germany, great numbers of non-Jewish Bulgarian citizens in all walks of life instantly and insistently asserted their objections to this oppression of Bulgaria's Jewish minority. Hastily passed and meekly signed by King Boris III, it soon became obvious that, instead of "protecting" Bulgarians from their constructive Jewish minority, the law would deprive Bulgaria of valued and highly regarded fellow citizens. In the process, all citizens would lose their cherished Bulgarian ideal of really protecting those in need. The law's regulations were published in February 1941, and Bulgaria became an official ally of Germany on March 1.

Bulgarians, sullied and dissatisfied, were more than appeased just a few months later when Hitler's armies quickly collapsed Greece and Yugoslavia and asked Bulgaria to occupy Thrace in Yugoslavia and Macedonia in Greece, seemingly returning them to Bulgarian rule. Huge demonstrations of popular rejoicing broke out throughout the country. "King Boris, yesterday so dejected about the German alliance, was this day at the peak of his glory. First Dobrudja, now Thrace and Macedonia. In a few months Boris had achieved Bulgaria's territorial dreams without firing a single bullet" (Bar-Zohar, 1998, page 43).

Caught between two devils, Bulgaria had made a pact with one of them, but gave itself room to curry favor with the other, so that each could be played off against the other. Bulgaria never declared war on the Soviet Union which continued to have an embassy in the Bulgarian capitol of Sofia throughout the war.

Protesters against the ZZN continued to object vociferously while Jewish citizens lost rights and possessions on a path to deportation and death. But King Boris and other Bulgarian government leaders saw to it that Jewish men, who were not allowed to serve in the army, were saved by dint of forcing them to build ostensibly much needed roads. The living conditions of the Jewish laborers deteriorated but they worked with "patriotic fervor" under Bulgarian officers, many of whom were cruel. Ultimately, not a single Bulgarian Jew was deported or exterminated despite years of tremendous systematic effort by the Nazis and their Bulgarian "quisling" types.

The Bulgarians' rescue of their nation's Jews was effected by both blatantly oppositional behavior and conspiracy. Dimitev Peshev, the Parliament Deputy Speaker, was a member of the pro-fascist majority but acted openly to prevent the deportation, ruining his political career in the process. Metropolitan Stefan, the titular head of the Church of Bulgaria's capital, Sofia, took one risk after another, including lying in the path of a deportation train to prevent its moving, and the entire Bulgarian Church denounced the ZZN. Bar-Zohar has concluded, "There is no doubt that in the entire history of the Holocaust, the Bulgarian church stood high above any other Pravoslav, Protestant, or Catholic church, in her bold and unyielding struggle to rescue the Jews" (page 210).

Other rescuers took more devious roles, including King Boris who stonewalled Hitler's extermination efforts throughout the entire Nazi regime. Some practiced the most extreme deceit. Lilliana Panitza was a young secretary in love with her boss, Alexander Belev, the Commissariat for Jewish Questions. Belev was not only pro-German and rabidly anti-Jewish but had all the resources needed to do his job including ample money from the "Jewish communities fund," by which Jews were paying for their own forced removal, and the cooperation of the army, police, and railroad authority. He planned deportation missions to the last detail, overcoming setbacks and obstacles along the way. But Panitza quietly and repeatedly informed people in a position to foil Belev's plans.

In great contrast to Adolph Hitler's distinctly non-Aryan appearance, Lilliana Panitza was blond, blue-eyed, oval faced, and lovely. She was also highly intelligent and worked diligently at her job, ironically enabling her to provide the precise details of the plans to influential Jewish leaders. Thus, together with co-conspirators as well as many groups openly in opposition to the ZZN, Panitza managed to separate her love for Belev from his cruelty.

She projected an outward image of cruelty on her job in that she was ostensibly aiding the persecution of Jews while, underneath, she was a crucial part of a massive conspiracy of kindness.

So it was by dint of ceaseless courage and effort that a sizable minority of non-Jewish Bulgarians, together with Jewish Bulgarians, saved all of the Jews in their country. Furthermore, unlike Jews in any other Nazi-dominated country, the Bulgarian Jews actually increased their numbers during the Nazi occupation to over 50,000 by the end of the war. The non-Jewish rescuers were not merely tolerant of Jews; they appreciated them to the point of repeatedly risking their lives to save them.

Jews from "liberated" Thrace and Macedonia were not so fortunate; they were deported to death camps despite heroic efforts to save them also. Bulgaria's celebration of acquiring these territories compromised the Jews there as Bulgaria was eager to please Hitler as its "benefactor."

Nor were all the rescuers treated well after the Soviet invasion of Bulgaria after which Bulgaria fought on the Soviet side against Germany. Lilliana Panitza was imprisoned for more than 6 months and was interrogated, beaten, and tortured to reveal Belev's whereabouts, which she did not know. King Boris, openly defying Hitler in a personal meeting with him, died mysteriously shortly afterwards and was thought to have been poisoned. Dimitev Peshev was ousted as Parliament Deputy Speaker by his own fellow Parliamentarians for his outspokeness against the ZZN and was later arrested by the Soviets. But nearly all of Bulgaria's Jews emigrated to Israel, a nation that has honored their heroic rescuers, as has Bar-Zohar's stirring book.

Returning to the question of the ethics of deception, clearly neither the Dutch nor Bulgarian kindness conspiracies were intended to hurt anyone nor did they unless we consider that Belev, for example, by having his deportation plans foiled, fell out of favor with his superiors. But no one was killed due to the conspiracy. On the other hand, we cannot always predict the consequences of deception. Probably, the key considerations are the intent and the intelligence involved in "plotting" good deeds without the use of violence. In these instances, and in others such as Oscar Schindler's surreptitiously saving his Jewish slave laborers, the rescue acts combined intelligence, courage, and spiritual transcendence. Thanks to historians of these rescues, the rescuers have achieved a kind of immortality in a world they have physically departed.

We can also ask whether people should simply be martyrs to oppressors. Shouldn't they simply submit to the authorities and the laws? If they simply submit, they aid and abet violence and atrocity; they become passive supporters of evil without whom tyrants cannot prevail. Lack of opposition to violence means paralethal support. People who do not object to tyranny and violence by word or deed become part of the evil.

By practicing absolute nonviolence, the great reformers, Jesus, Ghandi, and Martin Luther King, communicated most clearly their objections to violence in both word and deed. "Turning the other cheek," so often misinterpreted as mere submission, is in their ethos an extreme act of defiance, a radical subversion of authoritarian dominance. In this light, the subversive tactics of rescue become part of personal and societal transcendence. In contrast to bombastic belief in "racial and ethnic superiority" and in religious exclusivity, spiritual people reach out across the lines of bigotry in recognition of the wholeness of humankind.

Transcendence in Concentration Camps

The sampling of heroic rescues related so far illustrates but does not wholly explain the courage and strength of their progenitors. We do know that they brought to the task character formed earlier in their lives, enough apparently to transcend circumstances. In yet many other cases, even people confined to concentration camps found ways to be outside themselves, saving themselves as well as others in the process.

Pepi Deutsch and her daughter, Clara Knopfler, managed to stay together and survive through four Nazi slave camps although they lost 37 relatives (Berger, 1999). The mother nurtured her daughter, even celebrating her 17th bithday with a birthday cake of bread and marmalade, and later saved her from being raped by a drunken Russian soldier when "liberation" came. And the daughter repaid her, including as her companion for the next 5 decades until the mother died at age 101 in 1999. Their devotion and survival appeared related to the mother's faith, expressed in love as well as refusing rations of lard and fasting on Yom Kippur. They evidently lived for each other and something spiritual beyond them both.

We have seen how a transcending religious faith, whether the Christian Dutch Reformed Church or the Bulgarian Church or the Jewish faith helped rescuers and survivors alike to be more than themselves. The crucial ingredient is not religion per se but spirituality which can be found in ostensibly nonreligious people and absent in the ostensibly religious.

In Viktor Frankl's *Man's Search for Meaning* (1984), originally published in 1959, both the often paralyzing challenges and hard-won victories of spiritual development are registered in this classic account. Psychiatrist Frankl traces the typical human reactions to the traumas of concentration camps from the vantage point of his own incarceration. Following the initial shock, prisoners took on a protective apathy, a necessary defense that, if sustained, leads to emotional death. In this dangerous course, analogous to the transition from an acute to a chronic schizophrenic disorder (Whitaker,

1992), the retreat from emotions makes desire itself a pain to be avoided. If this immediately necessary psychological brain-mediated "stimulus barrier" response to overwhelming stress persists, hopelessness reigns, and even physical death becomes more likely.

Frankl had lost his wife but had a "conversation" with her while experiencing a slow dying of his spirit himself in a concentration camp. "In a last violent protest against the hopelessness of imminent death, I sensed my spirit piercing through the enveloping gloom. I felt it transcend that hopeless, meaningless world, and from somewhere I heard a victorious "Yes" in answer to my question of the existence of an ultimate purpose" (Frankl, 1984, page 51).

The intensification of his inner life made him more aware and appreciative of beauty and humor which served as ways of lifting himself and others up rather than giving in to apathy. Frankl found that he could retain his human dignity even in a concentration camp. Instead of giving in to insidious withdrawal, he devoted himself to helping his fellow prisoners and, together, they found better ways to survive and even to enjoy moments together. They also had to find meaning in their omnipresent suffering. New perspectives emerged. A young woman said, "I am grateful that fate has hit me so hard. In my former life I was spoiled and did not take spiritual accomplishments seriously" (as quoted by Frankl, page 78). "Right action and right conduct" became the answer and spiritual growth resulted. Serving one another became the means. Sometimes the serving meant sharing an otherwise scarce sense of humor. Frankl's emphasis on the necessity of hope correctly points the way to survival physically as well as spiritually.

The present writer remembers an older cousin, a U.S. Air Force navigator reported "missing in action" for 2 years. As we learned later, his plane was shot down over Austria, and he parachuted to Earth but sprained his ankle on landing and was captured by the Nazis. For 2 years he was in a camp very like the concentration camps. When finally released at the end of the war, the former star football and baseball player weighed no more than 140 pounds and had lost all his hair.

One Christmas some years after his imprisonment, he told me a little about his otherwise untold experiences. He recalled that during a Christmas day in the prison all he had to eat was a rotten cabbage from the gutter. To stave off psychological and physical death, he developed a career plan. He would become the head of a large U.S. corporation by the time he was 40 years old.

After being decorated and honorably discharged, he built himself up physically including by working as a street laborer, his hair grew back, and he played semiprofessional football to earn money for college, which he attended at night. By age 40 he was president and CEO of a large U.S. corporation, and he then went on to become head of a giant multinational corporation. He lived his life with an intensity seemingly born not only of his narrow escape but his "fantasy work" in the camp. I remember him for his drive but also his abundant generosity and good humor.

Viktor Frankl also used career planning. While imprisoned, he imagined himself in the future lecturing on what he had learned in the concentration camp, thus rising above the sufferings of the moment. Frankl's search for meaning to his existence led to an important insight at the core of his work as a psychiatrist:

> A man's concern, even his despair, over the worthwhileness of life is an *existential distress* but by no means a *mental disease*. It may well be that interpreting the first in terms of the latter motivates a doctor to bury his patient's existential despair under a heap of tranquilizing drugs. It is his task, rather, to pilot the patient through the existential crises of growth and development (Frankl, 1984, page 108).

Developing Constructive Mentality

As discussed in Chapter 1, the word "mentality" refers to both intelligence in the traditional sense *and* to mental set or disposition and, therefore, to both kinds of "intelligence." Whether called character, emotional intelligence, or moral intelligence, clearly a person can be highly intelligent in the traditional sense of the term and yet be, as some would say, "a moral imbecile." The 20th century has had more than a century's share of emotional or moral retardation judging by the numbers of killings and other atrocities, but not because of lack of intelligence in the traditional sense.

Violence prevention will be most effective when society succeeds at developing constructive mentality, balancing intellectual with character development. The rescue and survival stories related earlier in this chapter featured heroic levels of character development. How do people get that way?

Child psychiatrist and pediatrician Robert Coles has done much to illuminate the need for and the development of what he has called *The Moral Intelligence of Children* (1997). Citing Emerson's adage that "character is higher than intellect," he has emphasized the disparity between character and intellect that is so common in education and, for that matter, in our "civilization" generally.

By being treated with love, empathy, and respect for oneself and others, children tend to grow up treating others the same way because children readily imitate and model themselves after adults. Conversely, as discussed previously, children given a gross sense of entitlement do not mature beyond what Coles calls "unreflecting egoism. Generally speaking, what characterizes a not-so-good person is a heightened, destructive self-absorption..."

(page 22). If, as Hitler was, they are also treated abusively, they will assume, to various degrees, a "right" to scapegoat and, if allowed, they will draw like-minded followers if they are clever enough.

Many influences beyond those of parents pervasively affect children's development. In the U.S. and, increasingly worldwide, television is used as a baby sitter. Its messages, while often positive, are more often negative and destructive in the service of holding attention and selling products. Parents do well to minimize reliance on television and to give their chidren more personal attention.

Schools that favor the development of character as well as intellectual learning help to avoid the skewing of education toward the strictly academic. Teaching respect for oneself and others does not violate the separation of church and state nor does it proclaim or denigrate religion. Administrators and faculties of schools and colleges are often fearful of insisting on standards of conduct, however, partly because parents may object and blame school personnel for students' misconduct to the point of launching lawsuits.

Coles devotes a major portion of his book to his own experience with this dilemma: what to do when he realized how thoroughly entrenched a prep school crowd was in destructive use of alcohol and other drugs. He ended up telling the students his concerns and even telling the headmaster, but there was no further action. The adults continued being passive conspirators in this situation, like the vast majority of adults throughout our educational systems. Parents, at least, can speak up about their own children without fear of loss of job or a lawsuit although they may suffer unpopularity with their children, the children's peers, and other parents. But what is courage for if not to counter destructiveness?

Solving this dilemma does not require intelligence so much as awareness and a modicum of courage. We have seen how the gradualism of destructive behavior makes it acceptable, so that people actively or passively contribute to destructiveness. In contrast, we have also seen how courage can be contagious, uniting otherwise quite disparate people as happened in Nazi-occupied Bulgaria. Even if one is not successful in turning things around, being courageous for a good cause promotes self-respect in the knowledge that one has not entirely failed oneself or one's fellow human beings. Courage of this sort is in one's self-interest in terms of self-development.

A man looking back on his youth related a few stories about his personal developmental dilemma. In the first, he is 7 years old and makes friends at school with a Black classmate. The friendship grows and the first boy invites the second to his neighborhood where they enjoy trying out the first boy's new bow and arrow in a nearby field. They then approach the first boy's house and are intercepted by his mother who tells him he cannot bring the "colored" boy into their neighborhood. The first boy is confused and upset, largely because he has heard a local white priest preach against bigotry, and has observed his public school principal's daily warm and respectful behavior toward all students. It occurs to the first boy that both he and his friend are being denied freedom to choose their friends.

In the second story, the boy is now a young man working his way through college as a pipefitter in the summer on the night shift on the docks of an oil refinery. His boss, Binder, is outstandingly skilled at this work which he has done for several years and he turns out to be a good teacher. A second pipefitter, Stan, who is part of the three-man "gang," was an all-state football player in high school. Both are in their mid-20s. The work is demanding and occasionally dangerous.

Two pipefitters in another gang had their backs broken that summer when winches dropped heavy piping on them. The young man began as a replacement for the first and, later, while working in that gang, observed that gang's boss doing a deliberate drop on the second man, who pays with a broken back, as it were, for his religious beliefs.

But sometimes life on the docks gets boring as hours become idle as a gang waits for an oil tanker to come in. One night Binder says the next ship won't be in for a few hours. The college student has heard that another college student on a dock nearby is majoring in English literature and thinks it would be interesting to talk with him for a while. He is told that the docks are segregated and not to go there, but also learns there is no other reason for not going. He tells Binder and Stan he'll be back in an hour. Sure enough, the "colored" college student-dock worker turns out to be interesting and they enjoy their conversation.

On returning to the "white" dock, he finds Binder and Stan waiting for him, standing together, their oversize wrenches in hand though no ship is in. He walks right up to them and stands closer than he would ordinarily and looks into their eyes and says "I'm back." They do nothing except put their wrenches down.

Weeks later Binder, Stan, and the college guy they now call "Slim" finish hooking up a supertanker and, as is the custom, are invited by the captain to have coffee and doughnuts on board his ship. Now that all four men are in the ship's galley, the captain has a seemingly captive audience upon whom he vents his hatred of "niggers," blamimg them for the world's ills and standing there vituperatively while the gang sits. Slim looks Binder and Stan in the eyes and gets up from the table and exits without a word, while they follow him. No discussion follows. But, at the end of the summer, Binder and Stan say they hope Slim, after he finishes college, will return and become their boss.

His third story takes place in 1956 when he is in Florida for a baseball tryout. The "color barrier" in major league baseball had been broken by Jackie Robinson in 1947 and so, naively, he does not expect segregation off the field either. On the first day in Tampa he is given a ticket to watch the New York Yankees play the Cincinnati Reds in an exhibition game. Boarding a bus to go to the stadium he discovers that "whites" are sitting in the front and "colored" in the back. Quietly, he takes a seat in the back, but is told both by a gentleman in the back as well as the White bus driver that he must sit in the front. He concedes to both enough to sit in the White-only row immediately in front of the colored section and stikes up a conversation continuing into the stadium where he sits in the "colored" section, this time without interference, and enjoys more conversation with the men there. He feels that to do otherwise would have been to cast a vote for segregation, not unlike the hundreds of millions of people who were passive in the face of persecution of Jews.

He explained: "I was very aware of *my* need to protect *myself* against violation of *my freedom* of choice in companions as much as it was to vouch for the freedom and dignity of my fellow baseball fans. As on many other occasions before and afterward, I was aware that unfairly restricting others not only threatened me but restricted me, too."

That day, he and fellow fans watched Yankee manager Casey Stengel introduce the famous women athlete Babe Didrickson Zaharias to Mickey Mantle and other Yankees. And the great pitcher Joe Black, then with Cincinnati, who had pitched a no-hitter for the Brooklyn Dodgers, was also on the field. She and he had overcome bigotry and contributed greatly to fairness in sports in terms of gender and ethnicity and, by their example, invited others to follow. The least we can do is to emulate such people, even if only to promote a constructive gradualism.

Parents want and need specific advice on how to bring up their children, particularly considering what has happened to children and youth over the latter decades of the 20th century. In his Foreword to the excellent book *Emotionally Intelligent Parenting* (Elias et al., 1999), Daniel Goleman, who coined the expression "emotional intelligence," noted a study first done in the mid-1970s that was repeated with a similar cohort of children in the late 1980s. The children declined on 42 indicators of emotional intelligence and improved on none. Not coincidentally, teen violence, suicide, rape, and weapons carrying showed abrupt jumps during those intervening years.

Conclusion

A courageous scientific imagination was needed to realize fully that not the behavior of bodies, but the behavior of something between them, that is, the field, may be essential for ordering and understanding events. (Albert Einstein and Leopold Infeld, *The Evolution of Physics*, 1938, page 296.)

What exists between and among people, the psychosocial atmosphere and its changes over time, must be understood and accounted for to create a saner, less violent society. Neither violent nor constructive acts can or do occur in isolation.

Our systems of justice, however, at best strive for but never completely achieve an understanding adequate to prevent destructive behavior. Popular sentiment, as we have seen, forces a focus on mostly proximate causes, for example, who pulled the trigger, rather than on the pattern of causation, the temporal-spatial field of forces as it is called in physics.

Justice systems have to be practical, which means (1) designating who can be held accountable in the here and now, (2) representing the public interest, and (3) responding to lawyerly skills. As has been discussed, death penalties, imprisonments, and other "practical" reactions tend to win the day. Preventive measures are left largely to legislatures which are also limited by public opinion. We cannot, in fairness, simply blame justice and legislative systems; they have to be supported by current public sentiment as well as by established law. What is needed is a wide-awake public to change the pattern of forces that determine constructive vs. destructive behavior.

The causal explanation challenge, featuring the typical overemphasis on the immediate, is illustrated by the classic debate over whether juvenile criminals from extremely disadvantaged backgrounds ought to be held fully accountable for their crimes. In these cases, both the prosecutor's argument for proximate cause, focusing intently on the alleged criminal's act, and the defender's argument to take into account the "deeper causes" present only part explanations which, by themselves, are easily parried. In defense of the criminal, it may be said truthfully that he (like everyone else) was strongly influenced by his past, a past he was not in a position to fully determine. The prosecutor can argue truthfully that the criminal, and not his past, committed the crime. But, given the adversarial system, neither the prosecutor nor the defender can be counted on to provide the whole truth.

The only adequate explanation is to take into account both arguments as partial but insufficient truths, which may but seldom does happen in a court of law. Judicial decisions tend to be based as much as possible on clear evidentiary grounds — the substantially clear "facts of the case" — not on what tends to be regarded as speculation about the more remote, albeit often more profound, causes. The farther afield and the more remote in time are the causes, the less likely they can be substantiated convincingly by means of hard evidence. Nor are courts empowered to hand out verdicts and punishments to all possible contributors to violence even if they could establish cause.

Even legal suits and legislation against more remote causal agents such as gun manufacturers or violence entertainers are difficult to mount and are likely to be extremely expensive, time-consuming, and politically antagonistic against powerful vested interests able to buy the best lawyers. Political expediencies, including the short terms of legislators and their need to please quickly and to obey opinion polls, the ever-present lobbying pressure by powerful industry and business groups that must be attended to, and a myriad other pressures tend to forestall looking deeply into the merits of socially constructive legislation. Consideration of the complexity and depth of violence causality, the ease of deniability, and the limitations of judicial and legislative answers helps make understandable how difficult it is to prevent violence through government and law enforcement means alone. Finally, the old saw that morality cannot be legislated has some truth.

By now, we can be clear about many specific contributing influences which interact synergistically to maintain or change the interpersonal atmosphere. And, if we are not in denial, we can readily spot the obvious dangers. For example, guns in the hands of angry, alienated, or disaffected persons pose extreme danger. Markedly reducing gun availability is extremely likely to reduce the homicide rate. Similarly, reducing television, movie, videogame, and computer-communicated violence will lessen programming for violence and make room for constructive influences.

The enormous amounts of time and money that now go into commercial paralethal businesses are enough to forge a society virtually free of poverty, illiteracy, crime, and the chronic anxiety, anger, and depression that are otherwise inevitable in a hostile environment.

We also know, however, that contributors to violence deny their contributions in the interest of continuing and expanding the market for their products. For them, contributing to violence means profits. Their powerful lobbies show interest only in blocking restrictive measures. Democracy is weakened by their money-backed persuasiveness in legislatures, as well as by advertising and public relations campaigns. The paralethal merchandisers of guns, violence "entertainment," tobacco, alcohol, and other drugs can never be counted on to admit their own destructiveness. In true democratic fashion, therefore, the public must be awake to their influence and must use its own influence and free speech rights to protect themselves and their fellow humans.

Nonviolent dissent is crucial to strengthening our democracy and preventing exploitative violence. Legislative initiatives against paraviolence industries are steps in the right direction. We can also engage in boycotts, people acting together in abstaining from using, buying, or dealing with these industries, to express disapproval of them and reduce their economic foundation. We could then stop worrying about the supply of paralethal products because, without the demand, the supplies will stop coming in and the paralethal industries will collapse. Our power to not buy can be more effective than any legislation or law enforcement and it can be implemented immediately, including by you, the reader.

We can also foster constructive change every day by treating ourselves and others with kindness and respect. Neutrality is impossible, a mere myth. We are always influencing the interpersonal atmosphere, using our considerable power to respect or disrespect and making a difference thereby.

Any acts of courtesy and kindness will help. Being a courteous driver will impress and hearten many another driver or pedestrian, and such behavior will begin to replace the relatively new epidemic called "road rage" with better feelings about one another. Holding a door for someone, stopping a minute to help someone with directions, helping to clean up a neighborhood, thanking people for their courtesy; these are just a few of dozens of positive contributions almost anyone can make in a given day or week.

And instead of just "tolerating" differences in gender, ethnicity, religion, sexual preference, and the endless other ways people provide the richness of diversity, we are wise to appreciate diversity for genetic, psychological, economic, and spiritual reasons. Hitler and his like were dead wrong. Diversity is infinitely superior to a limiting conformity that would strive for a "master race." There is only one race of humans: the human race. Appreciating the diversity of life is vital to the survival and prosperity of the human race. So, let us forget about "political correctness" because the issue is far more profound.

Hitler mentalities are a dime a dozen, but not every madman can gain the massive popular support, the hundreds of millions of passive and active collaborators who gave him the power to destroy. If more people had risen up to confront and condemn his behavior, Hitler would have been powerless. In the U.S. alone we have a huge supply of Hitler mentalities. The Columbine High School killers, like Hitler, sought "immortality" in mortality, predicting people would adore them for their brutality — the bogus masculinity that fills our large and small screens every day, serving as an all-pervasive training program for persuading people, especially young and immature people, to be violent. When all is said and done, there is nothing truly unique or outstanding about the behavior of Hitler or any of his followers. Like the Columbine killers who took their lessons from the game called "Doom," they are monotonously focused on death as a cop-out from life.

In contrast, acts of kindness contribute to constructive behavior in its never-ending variety. But kindness takes real courage, which means facing rather than anxiously short-circuiting our own and others' lives, extending ourselves rather than retreating from life into destructiveness. The challenge is to appreciate the preciousness of life in the face of the inevitability of our own and others' deaths. It demands from us that we construct meaningful lives instead of lapsing into the deadly sameness of destructiveness.

As discussed in Chapters 1 and 5, language clearly conveys mentality. Constructive people prefer to say what they mean and mean what they say. People conniving to damage and destroy commonly prefer euphemism in the service of deception, often excused by remarks such as, "I didn't mean what I said," or, "It's only words," or, "It's only semantics." Becoming alert to and opposing language degradation helps to limit destructiveness. The old adage, "sticks and stones may hurt us but words never will," has little basis in fact. Hate language both reflects and furthers destruction of human rights. Too often, the right to freedom of speech is co-opted to abuse and is not used to oppose abuse. Speaking out against abusive language is necessary to preserve everyone's right to speak freely. This kind of give and take, of course, is anathema to tyrants; they are intolerant of criticism and others' rights, including the right to free speech.

The playright Wole Soyinka, who won the Nobel Prize in Literature in 1986, has spoken eloquently to the crucial importance of human rights, including the right to free speech and dissent, as in "Every Dictator's Nightmare" (1999). He remarks that the main occupation of dictatorships is the suppression of these rights, whether the dictatorship is secular or theocratic, on the right or the left, military or civilian. He says it is also their nightmare that:

> ... they cannot exorcise, not even through the most unconscionable pograms, scorched Earth campaigns and crimes against humanity... Its gospel of universalism is anchored in the most affective impulse that cynics attribute to the choices made by humanity, self-love, but one that now translates humanity as one's own self (Soyinka, 1999, page 92).

Our needed alertness to paralethal influences must extend even to subtleties in language degradation, prejudice, and the ways in which power imbalances result in destructive dominator rather than constructive partner relationships. Riane Eisler's superb book, *Sacred Pleasure* (1996) shows that partnership, with all its challenges, is not only preferrable to traditional dominator relationships but is the necessary answer to our civilization's rush to adjust people to the banality of everyday violence. She exposes the ubiquitous antisexuality of evil in its infinite number of readily overlooked forms. Recognizing the sacredness of sexuality and the truly erotic, she contrasts the constructiveness of the basic life force with the eroticization of violence at the core of the destructive mentality. Merging sexuality and violence damages sexuality, as exemplified by rape and pornography which admix sexuality and violence. Eisler (1996) clarifies:

> On the one side are all those who still try to "adjust" to an inherently painful system because they think it is inevitable — be it through abusive and

violent scapegoating and fantasies of a better hereafter, nihilism and cynicism, the excessive use of alcohol and drugs (including mood elevators and tranquilizers sold by the buckets in the U.S.), or the mind-numbing and empathy-deadening "entertaining" abuse and violence today marketed by our media. On the other side are those who have the courage to question the false myths of dominator inevitability, to face ourselves and our world, and most important, to try to change it (page 393).

To develop constructive mentality, we have to tolerate — or better, appreciate — ambiguity and uncertainty just as we need to appreciate diversity. Only death is certain and, if we cannot tolerate uncertainty and diversity, we will choose to short-circuit life and hasten death. As far as we know, the universe is infinite and it is infinitely mysterious so there is much to be uncertain about and fascinated with. All tyrants are notoriously intolerant of uncertainty and diversity. "Demons" like Hitler or Stalin always need a supportive psychotemporal field of forces, a predisposing interpersonal atmosphere to gain the willing cooperation of millions of active contributors and, just as importantly, the passive compliance of hundreds of millions of passive contributors who are content with the demon's dogma.

Being constructive means undoing denial even when perpetrators of violence are unwitting. Perpetrators usually act and may genuinely feel as if their contributions are negligible or irrelevant. Whether among definitely legal institutions — like the gun, tobacco, or violent entertainment industries — or in institutions with aims to subvert the law — like the Aryan Nations, Aum, or the CIA — or in legally constituted governments where the law itself is destructive of human lives — like Nazi Germany, the Soviet Union, and Communist China — we find denial in the face of accusation. The rampant denial of the 20th century, expressed so esoterically and yet so clearly, when seen as the century's plethora of euphemisms for violence, has itself been a huge contributor to the century's megaviolence. Deniers and their cultivation of "plausible deniability" contribute greatly to an atmosphere conducive to violence. Thus, countering and undoing denial is a major way to prevent violence.

Denial is made easy by the fact that there really is no *one* cause for violence. Because violence can be seen to have virtually innumerable contributors when viewed broadly and over time, any contributor can claim correctly that his or her contribution is not *the* cause. Thus, the gun manufacturer or dealer or purchaser or gun advocate can claim, "I didn't do it." So can the producer, director, actor, film distributor, or film patron of any violent entertainment movie deny being *the* cause. And if one is not *the* cause, it is feasible to deny and get away with contributing to the causation. When this naive concept of causation is allowed to persist, so does denial and so does violence. Although no one "cause" is adequate to explain violence, it does not follow that its contribution to violence, whether contemporaneous or historical, should be excused.

A simple, initial way of depicting the multicausation of violence is to envision a container, say a bucket that can accept, at any given time, a certain amount of input without overflowing, bursting, exploding, or leaking. It can incorporate and tolerate a variety and quantity of negative influences before exploding or, perhaps, even appearing on the verge of exploding. But then something, a kind of trigger event, puts its contents "over the top" and the violence is committed. The tolerance varies from person to person and from group to group but every person and every group has its limit.

When the container bursts or overflows, naturally enough the first guess at causation points to the immediately precipitating input or event, particularly the most negative input, or a lessening of inhibition. On reflection, people may say, "we could see it coming" or even that "it was inevitable." But, all too commonly, the tendency is to settle on one or a couple of causes and for the contributing individuals or groups to downplay or deny the causative forces to which they are linked. Rarely do such contributors step forward and admit their contribution, apologize, and make amends. Imagine how astonishing it would be if, for example, the gun or violence entertainment industries stepped forward after a lethal event related to them and promised the immediate victims and the public at large to change their practices to help prevent further violence (Figure 6.1).

But the contents of the violence mix are not simply additive. They have effects on one another, activating one another synergistically, so that the resulting quantity or pressure is greater than one would surmise just from adding up the list. This mutually activating characteristic suggests the kind of causative process delineated in Chapter 2 in terms of the first and second laws of cybernetics. In summary, the first law, exemplified by how a thermostat maintains a constant atmosphere, say, the same room temperature, helps to explain how either constructive or negative forces are maintained, and how stability is made possible. The second law of cybernetics shows how deviations from a given condition are amplified progressively, again whether for constructive or destructive results. Both laws help to explain not only how violence is caused but also what interventions can be made to prevent violence.

The mutually activating nature of destructive influences results in a "vicious cycle" that produces violence more rapidly than one might think when assuming that the ingredients are merely additive. This concept helps explain why just "adding a little" (Figure 6.2) to the mix can have unforeseen disastrous results. In common parlance, we use explanatory expressions like "the straw that broke the camel's back," i.e., produced the violence, but the brew is more dynamic than that. Thus, adding a seemingly nonappreciable amount of an ingredient may put the brew close to or over the edge. The

Welcome to Violence Entertainment

Figure 6.1 Inducements to violence emanating from television, movie, video-game, and computer screens.

result may be a sudden explosive interaction that sets off such vast, far-reaching violence as to appear incomprehensible. For example, World War I is said to have been set off by "the shot heard around the world." (The assassination of Archduke Francis Ferdinand and his wife in Sarajevo, Yugoslavia on June 28, 1914 triggered the outbreak of World War I.)

Since violence causation is not merely additive but synergistic, a matter of progressive deviation amplification, contributors can facilely deny their contributions and others can easily acquiesce in the denial. Most people do not understand the synergistically interactive nature of violence causation. Nor do they understand how even small contributions to constructive behavior can become powerful.

In conclusion, destructive mentality and behavior are the results of a complex psychotemporal field of forces, not single causes and not even several causes simply added up. The forces interact synergistically over time and may

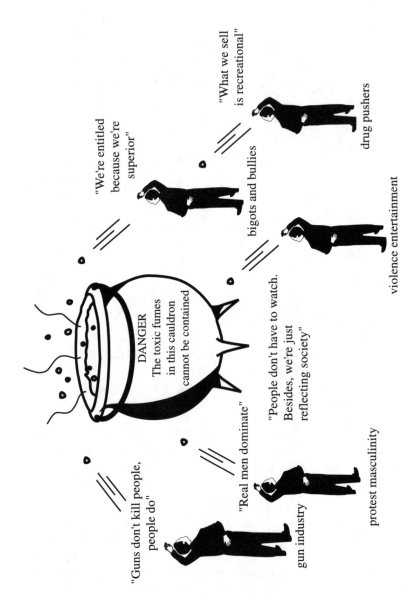

FIGURE 6.2 Contributors to the violence cauldron speak.

be "long in the simmering" stages. The forces potentiate one another to produce amplification deviation in the form of vicious cycles, in keeping with the second law of cybernetics. Consequently, what may appear as mild and quite tolerable contributions to violence may result in shockingly great destructiveness given time and other contributions.

Examined over time, destructive mentality and behavior represent developmental failure for individual persons and for society; maturity and the genuine courage to face life in its uncertainty and variety have not been achieved. Such failure of development is the major problem of contemporary civilization. It needs far more attention than we give it because, as we have seen, humans' capacity for evil is limited only by the means and victims at their disposal. It is our alertness and active attention that is needed. In contrast, as psychologist Mihaly Csikszentmihaly claims, people who rely on being passive consumers, whether of ideas, products, or mind-altering drugs, will probably be disappointed. He suggests that one try to see through clever and convincing materialist propaganda, though that is not easy, especially for young people who need to discriminate short-term from long-term consequences.

> This is why John Locke cautioned people not to mistake imaginary happiness for real happiness and why 25 centuries ago Plato wrote that the most urgent task for educators is to teach young people to find pleasure in the right things (Csikszentmihalyi, 1999, page 827).

Humans are also capable of such extreme goodness as to achieve the truly spiritual. Whereas the destructive mentality wastes others' lives and its own, the constructive mentality creates and enhances life for others and itself. Instead of promoting deadly conformity, constructive mentality nurtures the richness and vitality of variety. Humble in recognition of its limitations but proud to do what it can, it nevertheless achieves a kind of transcendence by contributing to life for itself and beyond itself.

Summary

The contrast between constructive and destructive mentalities is highlighted by examples of the courage and kindness of rescue conspiracies in the face of Nazi persecution of Jews. William R. Perl and his sealifts, Corrie ten Boom and the Dutch hiding place, and Bulgaria's protective coalition illustrate the spiritual transcendence of such extremely caring individuals and groups in contrast to the narrowness and destructiveness of tyrants.

Transcendence over circumstances and oppression is illustrated also by the relentlessly constructive behavior of people in concentration and prisoner of war camps. The question of how such constructive mentality is developed is addressed both in these accounts and then in a further section of the chapter on this topic. The constructive person recognizes that really serving the self means serving others as well, whereas destructive mentality, having failed to develop beyond unreflecting egoism and to develop broader awareness short-circuits life's possibilities both for the self and others.

The concluding section discusses the limitations of governmental judicial and legislative systems to prevent violence. All persons have the power to make a practical difference every day by not supporting destructive enterprises and by engaging in acts of kindness and positive appreciation of the richness and diversity of peoples and their cultures. The enormous amounts of time and money that now go into commercial paralethal businesses are enough to forge a society virtually free of poverty, illiteracy, crime, and the chronic anxiety, anger, and depression that are otherwise inevitable in a hostile environment. Whereas humans are clearly capable of engaging in ever more destructiveness, further potentiated by technology, they are also capable of extreme goodness.

Bibliography

Bar-Zohar, Michael, *Beyond Hitler's Grasp: The Heroic Rescue of Bulgaria's Jews,* Holbrook, MA: Adams Media, 1988, 298 pages.

As a child, historian Bar-Zohar escaped Bulgaria and emigrated to Israel as did 90% of Bulgaria's Jews. An unlikely coalition of intellectuals, professionals, religious leaders, communists, King Boris III, and the secretary-lover of the Nazi official in charge of deportation to death camps risked their lives and successfully conspired to save all of the the nation's 50,000 Jews. Their courageous attitude was exemplified by: "The Pravoslav Bulgarian Church ... cannot accept ideas like the racist idea, by which people can be inspired with hatred..." (page 172).

Coles, Robert, *The Moral Intelligence of Children,* London: Bloomsbury, 1997, 218 pages.

Pediatrician, psychiatrist, and psychoanalyst Coles traces and documents moral development and its vicissitudes from infancy through the college and university years, drawing on his considerable education and experiences of a lifetime. His book is a powerful argument for filling in the moral and spiritual gap in education that has grown large in recent decades. He withholds judgment in the moralistic sense while reflecting assiduously on how children and adolescents learn to respect themselves and others, and how they can be helped in this vital aspect of their development.

Eisler, Riane, *Sacred Pleasure: Sex, Myth, and the Politics of the Body,* New York: HarperCollins, 1996, 405 pages.

At once a powerful condemnation of violence in all its ubiquity and iniquity, and a correspondingly powerful appreciation of love and nurture, this book is astonishingly sane. For that reason, the reader is made acutely aware that much of what we blithely accept as normal turns out to be the insanity of everyday life, all the more destructive for its banality. Eisler's highly readable text brims with sophisticated scholarly analyses that have immediate practical applications in every sphere of life. She shows that

> "...if we are to construct a society where sex will be linked not with violence and domination but with the truly erotic — with the life-and-pleasure-giving powers within us and around us in the world — we need to fully extricate ourselves from all that has for so long unconsciously bound us to painful and unhealthy myths and realities" (page 200).

Frankl, Viktor E., *Man's Search for Meaning*, Simon & Schuster, 1984 (originally published 1959), 189 pages.

A classic work that takes the reader from concentration camp to powerful insights about the challenge to all humans to find meaning for their lives. Psychiatrist Frankl ranges all the way from the deepest existential despair to the transcendence of discovery. Along the way he humanizes not only life in concentration camps but the often otherwise desolate landscapes of ordinary existence. Today, his book is an antidote to the "brave new world" of quelling the search with psychiatric drugs.

ten Boom, Corrie, *The Hiding Place*, Grand Rapids, MI: Chosen Books, 1984 (originally published 1971), 221 pages.

A Dutch woman's story of her family using their home to hide Jewish people from the Nazis in World War II. The only member of her deeply Christian family to survive their rescue operations, she expresses throughout the story not only the intricacies and drama of the operations but the sustaining spirit of her family and community that inspired them. Her elderly watchmaker father epitomized their reverence for Jewish people as loved brothers and sisters. Seeing German soldiers who had just forced men, women, and children, all wearing the yellow star, into a truck, the father said, "I pity the poor Germans, Corrie. They have touched the apple of God's eye" (page 68).

References

Bar-Zohar, M., *Beyond Hitler's Grasp: The Heroic Rescue of Bulgaria's Jews*, Holbrook, MA: Adams Media, 1998.

Berger, J., Pepi Deutsch, 101, Holocaust survivor with remarkable tale, *New York Times*, November 8, 1999, p. B11.

Coles, R., *The Moral Intelligence of Children*, London: Bloomsbury, 1997.

Csikszentmihalyi, M., If we are so rich, why aren't we happy?, *Am. Psychol.*, 54(10), 821-827, 1999.

Eisler, R., *Sacred Pleasure: Sex, Myth, and the Politics of the Body — New Paths to Power and Love*, San Francisco: HarperCollins, 1996.

Elias, M. J., Tobias, S. E., and Friedlander, B. S., *Emotionally Intelligent Parenting*, New York: Harmony Books, 1999.

Frankl, V. E., *Man's Search for Meaning*, New York: Simon & Schuster, 1984 (originally published 1959).

Goldstein, R., Willam R. Perl is dead at 92; built sealift rescue of Jews, *New York Times*, December 29, 1998.

Soyinka, W., Every dictator's nightmare, *New York Times Magazine*, April 18, 1999, pp. 90-92.

ten Boom, C., *The Hiding Place*, Grand Rapids, MI: Chosen Books, 1996 (originally published 1971).

Whitaker, L.C., *Schizophrenic Disorders: Sense and Nonsense in Conceptualization, Assessment, and Treatment*, New York: Plenum Press, 1992.

Index